917

W9-DBE-789

KIDS

LOVE

MICHIGAN

Your Family Travel Guide to Exploring Kid-Tested Michigan. 600 Fun Stops & Unique Spots

Michele Darrall Zavatsky

Hamburg Township Library
10411 Merrill Rd. Box 247
Hamburg, MI 48139
810.231.1771

Dedicated to the Families
of Michigan

☒ Copyright 2013, Kids Love Publications

For the latest major updates corresponding to the pages in this book visit our website:

www.KidsLoveTravel.com

All rights reserved. No part of this book may be reproduced or transmitted in any form or by any means, electronic or mechanical, including photocopying, recording or by any information storage and retrieval system without the written permission from the authors, except for the inclusion of brief quotations in a review.

Although the authors have exhaustively researched all sources to ensure accuracy and completeness of the information contained in this book, we assume no responsibility for errors, inaccuracies, omissions or any other inconsistency herein. Any slights against any entries or organizations are unintentional.

REMEMBER: *Museum exhibits change frequently. Check the site's website before you visit to note any changes. Also, HOURS and ADMISSIONS are subject to change at the owner's discretion. If you are tight on time or money, check the attraction's website or call before you visit.*

INTERNET PRECAUTION: *All websites mentioned in KIDS LOVE MICHIGAN have been checked for appropriate content. However, due to the fast-changing nature of the Internet, we strongly urge parents to preview any recommended sites and to always supervise their children when on-line.*

EDUCATORS: *There are suggestions for finding FREE lessons plans embedded in many listings as helpful notes for educators.*

ISBN-13: 978-0-6156776-4-4

KIDS LOVE Michigan ☒   Kids Love Publications, LLC

TABLE OF CONTENTS

(Amusements, Animals & Farms, Museums, Outdoors, State History, Tours, etc.)

State Detail Map

(With Major Routes and Cities Marked)

Chapter Area Map

(Chapters arranged alphabetically by chapter name)

HOW TO USE THIS BOOK

(a few hints to make your adventures run smoothly:)

BEFORE YOU LEAVE:

- Each chapter represents a two hour radius area of the state or a Day Trip. The chapter begins with an introduction and Quick Tour of favorites within the chapter. The listings are by City and then alphabetical by name, numeric by zip code. Each listing has tons of important details (pricing, hours, website, etc.) and a review noting the most engaging aspects of the place. Our popular Activity Index in back is helpful if you want to focus on a particular type of attraction (i.e. History, Tours, Outdoor Exploring, Animals & Farms, etc.).

- Begin by assigning each family member a different colored highlighter (for example: Daniel gets blue, Jenny gets pink, Mommy gets yellow and Daddy gets green). At your leisure, begin to read each review and put a highlighter "check" mark next to the sites that most interest each family member or highlight the features you most want to see. Now, when you go to plan a quick trip - or a long van ride - you can easily choose different stops in one day to please everyone.

- Know directions and parking. Use a GPS system or print off directions from websites.

- Most attractions are closed major holidays unless noted.

- When children are in tow, it is better to make your lodging reservations ahead of time. Every time we've tried to "wing it", we've always ended up at a place that was overpriced, in a unsafe area, or not super clean. We've never been satisfied when we didn't make a reservation ahead of time.

- If you have a large family, or are traveling with extended family or friends, most places offer group discounts. Check out the company's website for details.

- For the latest critical updates corresponding to the pages in this book, visit our website: www.kidslovetravel.com. Click on Updates.

ON THE ROAD:

- Consider the child's age before you stop at an exit. Some attractions and restaurants, even hotels, are too formal for young ones or not enough of an adventure for teens. Read our trusted reviews first.

- Estimate the duration of the trip and how many stops you can afford to make. From our experience, it is best to stop every two hours to stretch your legs or eat/snack or maybe visit an inexpensive attraction.

- Bring along travel books and games for "quiet time" in the van. (see tested travel products on www.kidslovetravel.com) As an added bonus, these "enriching" games also stimulate conversation - you may get to know your family better and create memorable life lessons.

- In between meals, we offer the family snacks like: pretzels, whole grain chips, nuts, water bottles, bite-size (dark) chocolates, grapes and apples. None of these are messy and all are healthy.
- Plan picnics along the way. Many Historical sites and State Parks are scattered along the highway. Allow time for a rest stop or a scenic byway to take advantage of these free picnic facilities.

WHEN YOU GET HOME:

- Make a family "treasure chest". Decorate a big box or use an old popcorn tin. Store memorabilia from a fun outing, journals, pictures, brochures and souvenirs. Once a year, look through the "treasure chest" and reminisce.

WAYS TO SAVE MONEY:

- Memberships - many children's museums, science centers, zoos and aquariums are members of associations that provide FREE or Discounted reciprocity to other such museums across the country. AAA Auto Club cards offer discounts to many of the activities and hotels in this book. If grandparents are along for the ride, they can use their AARP card and get discounts. Be sure to carry your member cards with you as proof to receive the discounts.
- Supermarket Customer Cards - national and local supermarkets often offer good discounted tickets to major attractions in the area.
- Internet Hotel Reservations - if you're traveling with kids, don't take the risk of being spontaneous with lodging. Make reservations ahead of time. We don't use non-refundable, deep discount hotel "scouting" websites (ex. Hotwire) unless we're traveling on business - just adults. You can't cancel your reservation, or change them, and you can't be guaranteed the type of room you want (ex. non-smoking, two beds). Instead, stick with a national hotel chain you trust and join their rewards program (ex. Choice Privileges) to accumulate points towards FREE night stays.
- State Travel Centers - as you enter a new state, their welcome centers offer many current promotions.
- Hotel Lobbies - often have a display of discount coupons to area shops and restaurants. When you check in, ask the clerk for discount pizza coupons they may have at the front desk.
- Attraction Online Coupons - check the websites listed with each review for possible printable coupons or discounted online tickets good towards the attraction.

General State Agency & Recreational Information

Call *(or visit websites)* for the services of interest. Request to be added to their mailing lists.

☐ **DNR PARKS & RECREATION** - (517) 373-9900 or (800) 44-PARKS or www.michigan. gov/dnr

☐ **STATE PARK EXPLORER PROGRAMS:** www.michigan.gov/dnr/. Each summer, state park explorer programs are offered to campers and day visitors at 41 of Michigan's 97 state parks. Armed with field guides, animal skins, bug boxes and other hands-on materials, state park explorer guides lead informal programs and hikes that feature each location's unique natural, cultural and historic resources.

☐ **FISHING IN THE PARK PROGRAMS**: www.michigan.gov/dnr/ The instruction and fishing is FREE! Persons under age 17 don't need to have a license. Plus, you're welcome to bring your own equipment, but if you don't have a rod and reel, don't worry. The Fishing in the Parks program supplies everything you need to get started.

☐ Fisheries Division - (517) 373-1280

☐ Fishing Hotline - (800) 275-3474

☐ Skiing - www.ultimateskiguide.com

☐ Snowmobiling, Skiing and Cross-Country Skiing - (888) 78-GREAT, www.michigan.org

☐ Michigan Festivals and Events Association - www.mfea.org.

☐ Michigan Association of Recreational Vehicles and Campgrounds, MARVAC - (800) 422-6478, www.MARVAC.org

☐ Michigan Association of Private Campground Owners (MAPCO) - www.michcampgrounds.com

☐ Oakland County Parks - (248) 858-0306

☐ West Michigan Tourist Association Grand Rapids (800) 442-2084 or www.wmta.org

☐ Travel Michigan - (888) 784-7328 or http://travel.michigan.org

☐ MSU Sports (517) 355-1610

☐ U of M Sports (734) 647-2583 or www. umich.edu

☐ **CE** - Blue Water Area – Port Huron along Rte. 25 on the St. Clair River. CVB info: www.bluewater.org or (800) 852-4242.

☐ **NE** - Mackinaw Area Visitors Bureau (800) 666-0160 or www.mackinawcity.com

☐ **SE** - Detroit CVB (800) Detroit or www. visitdetroit.com

☐ **SE** - Greater Lansing CVB (888) 2-LANSING or www.lansing.org

☐ **SE** - Huron-Clinton Metroparks (800) 47-PARKS or www.metroparks.com

MISSION STATEMENT

At first glance, you may think that this is a book that just lists hundreds of places to travel. While it is true that we've invested thousands of hours of exhaustive research (*and drove over 3000 miles in Michigan*) to prepare this travel resource...just listing places to travel is not the mission statement of these projects.

When I was young, my family was able to travel extensively throughout the United States. I consider these family times some of the greatest memories I cherish today. I, quite frankly, felt that most children had this opportunity to travel with their family as we did. However, as I became an adult and started my own family, I found that this wasn't necessarily the case. We continually heard friends express several concerns when deciding how to spend "quality" and "quantity" family time. 1) What to do? 2) Where to do it? 3) How much will it cost? 4) How do I know that my kids will enjoy it?

Interestingly enough, as I reflect on our travels, many of our fondest memories were not made at an expensive attraction, but rather when it was least expected.

It is my belief and mission statement that if you as a family will study and use the contained information to create family memories, these memories will develop a love and a passion for quality family experiences that your children can pass to another generation of family travelers.

I thank you for purchasing this book, and hope to see you on the road (*and hear your travel stories!*) God bless your journeys and Happy Exploring!

EXTRA SPECIAL THANKS TO:

I also want to express our thanks to the many Convention & Visitor Bureaus' staff for providing the attention to detail that helps to complete a project. We felt very welcome during our travels in Florida and would be proud to call it home!

My kids, Jenny and Daniel, were delightful and fun children during our trips across the state...we couldn't do it without them as our "kid-testers"!

We think Michigan is a wonderful, friendly area of the country with more activities than you could imagine. Our sincere wish is that this book will help everyone "fall in love" with more of the unique spots of Michigan.

AIRPORTS - All children love to visit the airport! Why not take a tour and understand all the jobs it takes to run an airport? Tour the terminal, baggage claim, gates and security / currency exchange. Maybe you'll even get to board a plane.

ANIMAL SHELTERS - Great for the would-be pet owner. Not only will you see many cats and dogs available for adoption, but a guide will show you the clinic and explain the needs of a pet. Be prepared to have the children "fall in love" with one of the animals while they are there!

BANKS - Take a "behind the scenes" look at automated teller machines, bank vaults and drive-thru window chutes. You may want to take this tour and then open a savings account for your child.

CITY HALLS - Halls of Fame, City Council Chambers & Meeting Room, Mayor's Office and famous statues.

ELECTRIC COMPANY / POWER PLANTS - Modern science has created many ways to generate electricity today, but what really goes on with the "flip of a switch". Because coal can be dirty, wear old, comfortable clothes. Coal furnaces heat water, which produces steam, that propels turbines, that drives generators, that make electricity.

FIRE STATIONS - Many Open Houses in October, Fire Prevention Month. Take a look into the life of the firefighters servicing your area and try on their gear. See where they hang out, sleep and eat. Hop aboard a real-life fire engine truck and learn fire safety too.

HOSPITALS - Some Children's Hospitals offer pre-surgery and general tours.

NEWSPAPERS - You'll be amazed at all the new technology. See monster printers and robotics. See samples in the layout department and maybe try to put together your own page. After seeing a newspaper made, most companies give you a free copy (dated that day) as your souvenir. National Newspaper Week is in October.

PETCO - Various stores. Contact each store manager to see if they participate. The Fur, Feathers & Fins ™ program allows children to learn about the characteristics and habitats of fish, reptiles, birds, and small animals. At your local Petco, lessons in science, math and geography come to life through this hands-on field trip. As students develop a respect for animals, they will also develop a greater sense of responsibility.

PIZZA HUT & PAPA JOHN'S - Participating locations. Telephone the store manager. Best days are Monday, Tuesday and Wednesday mid-afternoon. Minimum of 10 people. Small charge per person. All children love pizza – especially when they can create their own! As the children tour the kitchen, they learn how to make a pizza, bake it, and then eat it. The admission charge generally includes lots of creatively made pizzas, beverage and coloring book.

KRISPY KREME DONUTS - Participating locations. Get an "inside look" and learn the techniques that make these donuts some of our favorites! Watch the dough being made in "giant" mixers, being formed into donuts and taking a "trip" through the fryer. Seeing them being iced and topped with colorful sprinkles is always a favorite with the kids. Contact your local store manager. They prefer Monday or Tuesday. Free.

SUPERMARKETS - Kids are fascinated to go behind the scenes of the same store where Mom and Dad shop. Usually you will see them grind meat, walk into large freezer rooms, watch cakes and bread bake and receive free samples along the way. Maybe you'll even get to pet a live lobster!

TV / RADIO STATIONS - Studios, newsrooms, Fox kids clubs. Why do weathermen never wear blue/green clothes on TV? What makes a "DJ's" voice sound so deep and smooth?

WATER TREATMENT PLANTS - A giant science experiment! You can watch seven stages of water treatment. The favorite is usually the wall of bright buttons flashing as workers monitor the different processes.

U.S. MAIN POST OFFICES - Did you know Ben Franklin was the first Postmaster General (over 200 years ago)? Most interesting is the high-speed automated mail processing equipment. Learn how to address envelopes so they will be sent quicker (there are secrets). To make your tour more interesting, have your children write a letter to themselves and address it with colorful markers. Mail it earlier that day and they will stay interested trying to locate their letter in all the high-speed machinery.

GEOCACHING AND LETTERBOXING

Geocaching and Letterboxing are the ultimate treasure hunt and can add excitement and fun to your driving, camping and hiking experiences. Geocaching employs the use of a GPS device (global positioning device) to find the cache.

Letterboxing uses clues from one location to the next to find the letterbox; sometimes a compass is needed. Both methods use the Internet advertising the cache, providing basic maps and creating a forum for cache hunters.

GEOCACHING

The object of Geocaching is to find the hidden container filled with a logbook, pencil and sometimes prizes! Where are Caches? Everywhere! But to be safe, be sure you're treading on Public Property. When you find the cache, write your name and the date you found it in the logbook. Larger caches might contain maps, books, toys, even money! When you take something from the cache you are honor-bound to leave something else in its place. Usually cache hunters will report their individual cache experiences on the Internet. (www.geocaching.com)

- ### GPS RECEIVER

   You'll need a GPS receiver that will determine your position on the planet in relation to the cache's "waypoint," its longitude/latitude coordinates. You can buy a decent GPS receiver for around $100. More expensive ones have built-in electronic compasses and topographical maps, but you don't need all the extras to have fun geocaching.

LETTERBOXING

The object is similar to geocaching — find the Letterbox — but instead of just signing and dating the logbook, use a personalized rubber stamp. Most letterboxes include another rubber stamp for your own logbook. The creator of the letterbox provides clues to its location. Finding solutions to clues might require a compass, map and solving puzzles and riddles! This activity is great fun for the entire family! (www.letterboxing.org)

Chapter 1
Central East

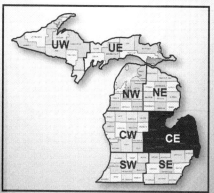

A Quick Tour of our Hand-Picked Favorites Around...

Central East Michigan

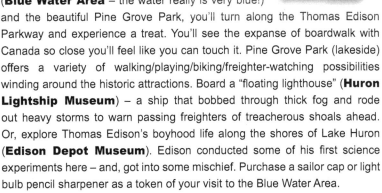

If Michigan is a mitten, you're in the thumb, folks. Let's start on the far east portion on I-94 north at I-69 east in Port Huron. The drive from Detroit is best done along the "shores" paralleling US 25. As you approach Port Huron's stunning waterway (**Blue Water Area** – the water really is very blue!) and the beautiful Pine Grove Park, you'll turn along the Thomas Edison Parkway and experience a treat. You'll see the expanse of boardwalk with Canada so close you'll feel like you can touch it. Pine Grove Park (lakeside) offers a variety of walking/playing/biking/freighter-watching possibilities winding around the historic attractions. Board a "floating lighthouse" (**Huron Lightship Museum**) – a ship that bobbed through thick fog and rode out heavy storms to warn passing freighters of treacherous shoals ahead. Or, explore Thomas Edison's boyhood life along the shores of Lake Huron (**Edison Depot Museum**). Edison conducted some of his first science experiments here – and, got into some mischief. Purchase a sailor cap or light bulb pencil sharpener as a token of your visit to the Blue Water Area.

Continue north on US 25 and make a quick stop near Bay City in Bad Axe at **Sanilac Petroglyphs** (ancient Indian etchings). At the tip of the Thumb is Port Austin, a great little town for fishing, boating and summer shopping. The sandy beach is perfect for family swimming and paddleboat rentals. Follow M-25 to Caseville for a popular port for camping, fishing and watersports.

Want to meet another famous Michigan inventor? Take US 10 west to Midland and the **Herbert H. Dow Historical Museum**. Most kids absolutely love exploring a famous person's home BEFORE they were discovered. This is where young Dow pioneered experiments producing chemicals and cleaners found in most every household. The surrounding Heritage Park offers a variety of walking/playing possibilities on a gravel path winding around the historic area.

Now, head south on I-75/US 23. The Arts and animals are great finds in Saginaw. The town of Frankenmuth offers up old world charm and its famous family style chicken dinners…and now, two different **Indoor Waterparks**. When you're waterlogged or stuffed full of chicken dinner, try walking off some calories on South Main Street. We've all seen freshly shaven sheep and probably own wool clothing – but how is it processed? At the **Frankenmuth Woolen Mill**, you'll watch them wash, air dry (it gets really fluffy that way) and card fresh wool. You can watch first from the observation windows, and then handle some wool yourself. Across the street is the **Frankenmuth Cheese Haus**. Ever tried "chocolate" or "strawberry" CHEESE? Watch a video of the cheesemaking process, or, if you time it right, actually see the ladies make it from scratch. There are plenty of other shops, amusements and a historical museum to peek in, too. Be sure to catch the night lights at **Bronners** every evening – it's Christmas year-round there.

Finally, we'll travel a little further south to the town of Flint, the birthplace of General Motors. Probably our favorite special events attraction in the region is **Crossroads Village**. The 1860's era living village is a collection of 30 authentic buildings that form a town bigger than Walnut Grove (Little House on the Prairie)! Dad could get a shave while the kids shop for toys in the General Store (no batteries required toys!) and Mom tries on bonnets. When your feet get tired, hop on a riverboat or the Huckleberry Railroad train.

Sites and attractions are listed in order by City, Zip Code, and Name. Symbols indicated represent:

 Festivals    Restaurants   Lodging

Alma

ALMA HIGHLAND FESTIVAL AND GAMES

Alma - Alma College, downtown. (989) 463-8979. www.almahighlandfestival.com. More than 600 costumed bagpipers and drummers march onto the athletic field for performances and competitions. Dancers perform the sailor's hornpipe and Highland fling. Highland shortbread and briddies (pastries stuffed with ground meat). Competitions include border collie sheep-herding and tossing capers. Admission age 6+. (Memorial Day weekend)

☒

CHAPTER AT A GLANCE

Bad Axe * Samilac Petroglyphs

Bay City

* Bay City St Rec Area

* Bay Cty Hist Museum

* Delta College Planetarium

* River of Time Encampment

Birch Run * Wilderness Trails

Bridgeport * Junction Valley RR

Caseville * Sleeper St Pk

Corunna * Country Corn Maze

Durnad * Durand Union Station

Flint

* Flint Cultural Ctr

* Sloan Museum

* Longway Planetarium

* Flint Symphony

* Flint Children's Museum

* Crossroads Village

* Genessee Rec Area

* For-Mar Nature Preserve

Frankenmuth

* Bavarian Belle

* Bavarian Inn

* Frankenmuth Cheese Haus

* Bronners

* Frankenmuth Historical

* Frankenmuth Woolen Mill

* Grandpa Tiny's Farm

* Riverplace

* Zehnders

Freeland * Apple Mtn Ski Area

Lakeport * Lakeport St PK

Metamora

* Metamora-Hadley St Rec Area

Midland

* Dow Museum of Science & Art

* Chippiwa Nature Ctr

* Dow Gardens

* Great Lakes Loons

* HH Dow Historical Museum

* Riverdays Festival

* Balloon Fest

Pinconning * Deer Acres

Port Austin * Port Crescent St Pk

Port Huron

* Blue Water Trolley

* Edison Depot

* Fort Gratiot LIghthouse

* Huron LIghtship

* Huron Lady Scenic Cruises

* Feast of the Sainte Claire

Port Sanilac * Sanilac Cty Historical

Saginaw

* Saginaw Childrens Museum

* Shiawassee Natl Wildlife Refuge

* Saginaw Art Museum

* Marshall Fredericks Sculpture

Sebewain

* Michigan Sugar Fest

St Johns

* Uncle Johns Cider Mill

* Andy Ts Farms

Bad Axe

SANILAC PETROGLYPHS HISTORIC STATE PARK

Bad Axe - 8251 Germania Road, Cass City 48726. (M-53 to Bay City - Forestville Road Exit - East to Germania Road South) 48413. www.michigan.gov/ sanilacpetroglyphs. Phone: (517) 373-3559. Hours: Petroglyphs: Wednesday-Sunday 10am-5pm (Memorial Day-Labor Day). The one-mile hiking trail is open from 8:00am to 10:00pm year-round. Admission: FREE.

Take a 1-mile, self-guided walking trail through the forest along the Cass River. Stop at the 19th Century logging camp or 100+ year old white pine tree. The main reason you probably came though is the petroglyphs. The petroglyphs include depictions of swirls, lines, handprints, flying birds and bow-wielding men, created by an unknown Native American tribe on a 1000 square foot sandstone rock in Sanilac County, Michigan between 400 and 1,000 years ago. The petroglyphs are the only known such carvings in the state of Michigan. In the late 1800's, forest fires revealed chiseled sandstone etchings by Native Americans of an ancient woodland people. Look for figures like a hunter / archer or animals and birds. Because of weathering and abuse, the etchings are fading and efforts are being made to preserve the slab.

Bay City

BAY CITY STATE RECREATION AREA

Bay City - 3582 State Park Drive (I-75 exit 168 east to Euclid Avenue) 48706. Phone: (989) 684-3020. www.michigandnr.com/parksandtrails/. Admission: $6.00-$8.00 per vehicle.

Lots of camping (tent and cabins) plus a swimming beach free from sharp zebra mussels found in the area, make this an attraction. Also find boating, fishing, trails, winter sports. Another highlight is the Saginaw Bay Visitors Center which focuses on the importance of wetlands to the bay. It's open Tuesday - Sunday, Noon - 5:00pm. A great spot for birding, you'll also learn from the 15 minute video presentation, boardwalks and observation trails. More than seven miles of trails help visitors explore the wetlands close-up. Includes over three miles of paved accessible pathways, three observation towers, boardwalks, viewing platforms and shoreline spotting scopes. Bicycles and rollerblades are welcome.

BAY COUNTY HISTORICAL MUSEUM

Bay City - 321 Washington Avenue (I-75, take exit 162A to Downtown) 48708. Phone: (989) 893-5733. www.bchsmuseum.org. Hours: Monday-Friday 10:00am-5:00pm, Saturday & Sunday Noon-4:00pm. Admission: FREE. Note: Every Saturday at 2:00pm, a trolley leaves from the Museum for a 75-minute tour.

Visitors will experience maritime history from the geological formation of the Great Lakes and the Saginaw River to the completion of the area's first lighthouse. Exhibits focus on the shipbuilding and lumbering industries. Visitors will enter a re-creation of the tug wheelhouse, experience what the docks were like, and view an interactive shipwreck exhibit. A series of seven period rooms compares and contrasts life in the 1880s to the early 1930s. Visitors will see recreated rooms of the era and also see how consumerism helped to develop the "modern" home. You can also learn about Native Americans and the fur trade and early Bay County settlers. Many industries such as agriculture, lumbering and manufacturing will highlight the recent history section of the gallery.

DELTA COLLEGE PLANETARIUM & LEARNING CENTER

Bay City - 100 Center Avenue 48708. www.delta.edu/planet/. Phone: (989) 667-2260. Hours: Call or visit website for schedule. Note: Show lengths vary. Allow a one hour block of time. Pre- and post-visit materials are available for selected shows. Admission: $4-$6 per person.

A wonderful place to teach children the fun of star-gazing. The planetarium is state-of-the-art and the rooftop observatory seats over 100 people. The audience actually gets to choose what to see in the solar system. Look for programs about sky pirates or cowboys or Garfield.

DELTA PLANETARIUM HOLIDAY SHOWS

Bay City. Delta College Planetarium. www.delta.edu/planet/. The Christmas Star (Grades 4 - Adult): The most popular planetarium topic during the holidays. Was there really a "Star of Bethlehem?" Can it be explained by a natural occurrence like a comet or exploding star, or do we still not know the truth 2000 years later? HOLIDAY STORIES (Grades 3 - Adult): This show unwraps the origins of many holiday traditions such as candles, gift-giving and Christmas trees. Plus, come along with us as we enjoy a dark winter night sky and explore possible explanations for the Star of Bethlehem. Admission. (weekends beginning Thanksgiving – before New Years)

RIVER OF TIME LIVING HISTORY ENCAMPMENT

Bay City - South end of Veterans Memorial Park. Started in 1990, the River of Time Living History Encampment is a free educational event for people of all ages. The encampment draws re-enactors from around the Midwest, who come to dress and live the roles of folks from a more simplistic and sometimes more difficult time. Visit Historical Camps; See Live Reenactments; Taste Kettle Korn & Old-Time Root Beer; Witness Skirmishes; and Shop Sutlers' Row. FEATURING: Native Americans, Colonial, French and Indian, Civil War, Mexican War, The Wild West, World War I & World War II & Vietnam time period. Donations accepted. (last full weekend in September)

⊠

Birch Run

WILDERNESS TRAILS ANIMAL PARK

Birch Run - 11721 Gera Road - M-83 (I-75 to Birch Run Exit) 48415. Phone: (989) 624-6177.   www.wildernesstrailszoo.org.   Hours: Monday-Saturday 10:00am-6:00pm, Sunday 11:00am-5:00pm (May-October). Admission: $9.75 adult, $8.00 senior (60+), $6.50 child (3-15). Note: Picnic area. Playground.

One of the most popular privately owned animal exhibits in the state, Wilderness Trails offers over 50 acres and 60 different types of animals. See lions, a Siberian tiger and bear, bison, elk, black bears, and deer just to name a few. Two gravel walking trails wind through park or a horse drawn covered wagon is available for a small charge. Kids can have fun touching the alpaca, watching the flirting butterflies, and feeding the baby animals in the petting area.

Bridgeport

JUNCTION VALLEY RAILROAD

Bridgeport - 7065 Dixie Highway (I-75, exit 144 south - Just before you turn to head into Frankenmuth) 48722. Phone: (989) 777-3480.   www.jvrailroad.com. Hours: Monday-Saturday 10:00am-4:00pm, Sunday 1:00-5:00pm. (Memorial Day Weekend-Labor Day Weekend). Weekends Only (September & October & Special events). Admission: $5.25-$6.50 per person (age 2+). Note: Picnic area/ playground. You'll pull into a business parking lot.

See and ride the world's largest ¼ scale railroad. Voyage on rides through the woods, past miniature buildings, through a 100 foot long tunnel, and over 865 feet of trestles (one has diamonds underneath). Look for the roundhouse with a turntable and the 5-track switch yard.

GRANDPARENT'S DAY TRAIN

Bridgeport, Junction Valley Railroad. (989) 777-3480. www.jvrailroad.com. Grandparents Day (Sunday) in September. When accompanied by paying grandchildren, grandparents are given a discount rate. Bring young and old to ride on the largest quarter size railroad in the world. (September)

Caseville

SLEEPER STATE PARK

Caseville - 6573 State Park Road (5 miles east of town on SR 25) 48725. Phone: (989) 856-4411. www.michigan.gov/sleeper. Admission: $8.00-$10.00 per vehicle for recreation passport.

Hundreds of acres of woods and beachfront with camping make this a fun park. Nearby hiking trails provide miles of multi-use recreational opportunities. Lake Huron is a ½ mile away and may be reached by hiking trail or a short drive. Also featured are hiking trails, winter sports, mini-cabins, fishing, & boating.

DEPNER FARMS CORN MAZE

Caseville - (989) 856-4688 or www.DepnerFarms.com. The Depner Farms have their corn maze opened each fall on 6 acres. They also have a mini maze for the youngsters. Admission. (Labor Day weekend thru the first weekend in November)

Corunna

COUNTRY CORN MAZE

Corunna - 450 N. Vernon Road. (989) 743-6899. www.cornmazefun.net. Three professionally designed and cut mazes to challenge all skill levels. Seasonal produce and pumpkin patch. Admission. (Thursday-Sunday, end of August thru early November)

Durand

DURAND UNION STATION (MICHIGAN RAILROAD HISTORY MUSEUM)

Durand - 200 Railroad Street 48429. Phone: (989) 288-3561. Hours: Tuesday, Saturday, and Sunday 1:00pm-5:00pm. Wednesday, Thursday, and Friday 10:00am-5:00pm. Closed Mondays and Major Holidays.

Visitors stop at the Durand Depot to study area history or maybe catch an Amtrak train roundtrip from Chesaning-to-Owosso. Learn about the Great Wallace Brothers Circus Wreck of 1903 or the Knights Templar Wreck of 1923. Do you know which presidents have made "whistle stops" here?

Flint

FLINT CULTURAL CENTER

Flint - 1221 East Kearsley Street (I-475, exit 8A) 48503. Phone: (810) 237-7330 or (888) 8CENTER. www.flintculturalcenter.com. Hours: Museum: Monday-Friday 10:00am-5:00pm, Saturday & Sunday Noon-5:00pm. Admission: $9.00 adult, $8.00 senior, $6.00 child (4-11). $2.00 off coupon online. Combo prices. Note: Museum Store. Café.

Institutions on the Flint Cultural Center campus include Sloan Museum, Buick Gallery & Research Center, Longway Planetarium, The Whiting, Flint Youth Theatre, Flint Institute of Arts and Flint Institute of Music.

The **SLOAN MUSEUM** (810-237-3450 or www.sloanlongway.org) highlights include: "FLINT AND THE AMERICAN DREAM" - 20th Century Flint beginning with the birth of General Motors, United Auto Workers, and then neon colorful advertising. Also 1950's - 70's typical household furnishings. Check out the 1950's station wagon (a Buick Super) that was available before today's vans and sport utility vehicles. "HOMETOWN GALLERY" - the area's early history with displays on fur trading, pioneer life, lumbering, and carriage making. Look for the 10,000 year old mastodon and Woodland Indian wigwam. Weekend hands-on history activities. "SCIENCE DISCOVERY CENTER" - hands-on science, weekends only.

Also in the same complex (recommended for grade school and up):

- ❑ **FLINT INSTITUTE OF ARTS** - 1120 East Kearsley. (810) 234-1695. FREE.

- ❑ **LONGWAY PLANETARIUM** - 1310 East Kearsley. (810) 237-3400 or www.longway.org. Monday - Friday 9:00 am-4:00pm, Saturday & Sunday 1:00-4:30pm. Free displays. $4.00-5.00 for light & astronomy shows. The largest planetarium in Michigan and in the north-central U.S.!! 282 seats under a 60 foot dome. Check out the planetarium shows--the Sky Theater has been completely renovated with a new Digistar 2 projector, seats, sound system, and video projection system. Enjoy laser light shows featuring both rock music and family oriented fare. Popular hands-on science activities provide families with opportunities to have fun while learning about science.

❑ **SHOWCASE SERIES, (THE)** - Whiting Auditorium. Broadway, dance, classic theater & holiday shows. www.flintyouththeatre.com

LONGWAY PLANETARIUM HOLIDAY SHOWS

Flint - (810) 237-3400 or www.longway.org. Friday evenings at 7:30pm, Saturday afternoon and evening, Sunday afternoon throughout December. Night sky shows with traditional and contemporary themes. Admission. (December)

FLINT SYMPHONY ORCHESTRA

Flint - 1244 East Kearsley Street (Whiting Auditorium) 48503. Phone: (810) 237-7333 or (888) 8CENTER. www.thefim.com.

Led by world-renowned music director and conductor, Enrique Diemecke, this orchestra showcases exciting and moving renditions of music by the world's greatest composers. The orchestra performs six classical concerts each season, as well as family concerts, summer parks concerts.

FLINT CHILDREN'S MUSEUM

Flint - 1602 West 3rd Avenue, Kettering University Campus (I-75 exit 118 - Corunna Rd. east. Left on Ballenger Hwy., right on Sunset Drive, turns into 3rd) 48504. Phone: (810) 767-5437. www.flintchildrensmuseum.org. Hours: Tuesday-Friday 9:00am-5:00pm, Saturday 10:00am-5:00pm. Sunday Noon-5pm. Closed major holidays. Admission: $6.00 general (age 1+). Note: Recommended for ages 2-10. Gift shop.

Over 40 exhibits focused on science, technology, and the arts. Kids' favorites are the Crazy Mirrors and the Lego table. Be sure to check out the different theme rooms: Mr. Bones, showing how our skeletons work as you take a bicycle ride together. Our Town, where they can shop for groceries at the Smart Mart or visit Frac-tions Pizza Parlor; a picnic lunch in Sproutside; and Center Stage, where young performers can act out anything they imagine with puppets and costumes. The parent-friendly exhibit signs helps adult chaperones guide children's understanding of each concept from simple machines to math to health and safety.

CROSSROADS VILLAGE & HUCKLEBERRY RAILROAD

Flint - 6140 Bray Road (I-475, exit 13 - follow signs) 48505. Phone: (810) 736-7100 or (800) 648-PARK. www.geneseecountyparks.org/pages/crossroads. Hours: Wednesday-Sunday, Holidays 10:00am-5:00pm (mid-May to early September). Weekends in October and December for seasonal events. Admission: $10.00 adult, $9.00 senior (60+), $8.00 child (2-12) - Village only. Train/Boat combination tickets available at small additional cost. Note: Mill Street Warehouse, Cross Roads Café, Concessions, Carousel, Venetian Swing, Ferris Wheel and Wagon Rides (pulled by mechanical ponies) - rides additional charge. Seasonal events keep the village open throughout the year.

The 1860's era CROSSROADS living village is a collection of 30 authentic buildings that were relocated here to form a village. Friendly, costumed villagers fill you in on the events of the day and answer questions. For example, the barber shop (still operational) staff will share their charges for a cut, shave or bath.  We learned that they let a dental patient (yes, they were the town dentist then) take a swig of vanilla extract (full tilt variety!) before they extracted a tooth. The fellas at the cider and sawmill will remind you of characters from "Little House on the Prairie" as they demonstrate their craft. Be sure to buy a cup of cider there - all natural with no added sugar. You'll also meet the town blacksmith, printer (try your hand printing a souvenir off the "kissing" press), doctor, storekeeper at the General Store (with cute, old-fashioned novelties for sale), and toymaker (try your hand walking on stilts).

Before you leave, take a relaxing slow ride on the **HUCKLEBERRY RAILROAD**. The original line went so slow that passengers claimed they could get off - pick huckleberries along the tracks (still growing plentifully today) and catch the caboose a few minutes later. Watch out for the playful train robber skit - (don't worry…even pre-schoolers won't be scared!).

GENESSEE BELLE: a paddle-wheel riverboat, offers scenic cruises on unspoiled Mott Lake. The Genesee Belle has an open-air upper deck for unobstructed sightseeing and the lower deck is climate-controlled in summer and fall. Although the Genesee Belle is a replica of the steamboats that traveled during the era of Mark Twain, it is very safe and especially designed for sightseeing and relaxation. 45 minute cruises on the lake.

CHRISTMAS AT CROSSROADS

Flint - Crossroads Village. (800) 648-7275. Over 400,000 lights light up Crossroads Village and trackside displays. (Drive-thru viewing Monday nights in December). Craft demos, train rides, live entertainment in the Opera House, and festive traditional buffets (Sundays). www.geneseecountyparks.org/crossroadsvillage.htm. Discounted admission. (Tuesday-Sunday evenings beginning Friday after Thanksgiving)

GENESEE RECREATION AREA

Flint - (I-475 exit 13) 48506. www.geneseecountyparks.org. Phone: (800) 648-7275.

This area includes Stepping Stone Falls on Mott Lake on Branch Road which are lit with color evenings between Memorial Day and Labor Day. Genesee County's first Splash Pad Spray Ground shoots water in a timed sequence from the ground and from various play structures on the Splash Pad. There is no charge to use the Splash Pad Spray Ground. You can also find camping, hiking, boating, fishing, beach swimming, bicycle trails, and winter sports. Hours vary by activity (mostly dawn to dusk). (Memorial Day-October).

FOR-MAR NATURE PRESERVE & ARBORETUM

Flint (Burton) - 2142 North Genesee Road 48509. Phone: (810) 789-8567 or (800) 648-7275. www.geneseecountyparks.org/pages/formar. Hours: Wednesday-Sunday 8:00am-5:00pm. Trails 8:00am -Sunset. Special programs on Saturdays.

A 380 acre preserve with 7 miles of trails. There are hundreds of wonderful things to see and learn at For-Mar Nature Preserve and Arboretum. To help you experience everything nature has to offer, For-Mar now loans Discovery Backpacks. There are three types of Discovery Backpacks : Michigan Naturalist, Basic Birding and Insect Investigator. Each backpack offers different tools and materials that will help you and your family enrich your outdoor experience. These backpacks may be borrowed for up to two hours with a valid driver's license from an adult, 18 years of age or older. Visitor Center with Gift Shop. Cross-country skiing in winter. Guided programs charge admission.

Frankenmuth

BAVARIAN BELLE RIVERBOAT TOURS

Frankenmuth - 925 South Main Street (RiverPlace) 48734. Phone: (866) 808-BOAT. www.bavarianbelle.com Hours: Departures 11:00am until dusk (May thru mid-October). Admission: $10.00 adult, $4.00 child (10 and under).

One hour sightseeing cruises narrated about the Cass River folklore and history. Learn about the local covered bridge, the beginnings of the shops and Bavarian Inn and a brief background on the boat itself. Open air canopied upper deck and enclosed lower salon (air-conditioned and heated). Snack bar and restrooms on board.

BAVARIAN INN

Frankenmuth - 713 South Main Street 48734. www.bavarianinn.com. Phone: (800) BAVARIA.

A famous Frankenmuth restaurant (established in 1888) offering family style dinners. An authentically dressed server (aren't their hats cute?) will help introduce your kids to all the menu offerings they will like such as potato pancakes, veal cutlets, baked chicken, etc. (except maybe the sauerkraut). None of the food is over-seasoned...all kid friendly...but the adults may want to use extra all purpose seasonings available at each table. Also see the Glockenspiel Clock Tower (with performances telling the Pied Piper of Hamelin story in music) and the Doll and Toy Factory (see dolls created before your eyes).

THE LODGE has five pools and overnight accommodations. Inside the Lodge you'll find: an **indoor waterpark** (including one courtyard pool and whirlpool especially for adults, a water cannon & lazy river pool, waterfall pool & whirlpool, fun center pool & whirlpool, plus a wading pool for little ones), 100+ video and redemption games, 18-hole indoor miniature golf, Children's Play Village, exercise room, and plenty of sitting areas for you to relax in comfort with your family. Hours: Daily Lunch, Dinner or Overnight.

BRONNER'S CHRISTMAS WONDERLAND

Frankenmuth - 25 Christmas Lane (I-75, northbound to exit 136, southbound to exit 144 - follow signs off Main Street M-83) 48734. Phone: (989) 652-9931 or (800) ALL-YEAR. www.bronners.com. Hours: Monday-Saturday 9:00am-5:30pm,

Sunday Noon-5:30pm, Open Friday until 9:00pm (January-May). Monday-Saturday 9:00am-9:00pm, Sunday Noon-7:00pm (June-December). Closed Winter holidays including Easter and Good Friday. Admission: FREE. Note: "Season's Eatings" snack area. A visit to Michigan wouldn't be complete without seeing the "World's Largest Christmas Store" that hosts over 2,000,000 visitors each year! View nativity scenes, 260 decorated trees, and 200 styles of nutcrackers. As dusk approaches

Holding Gigantic ornaments...!

drive through "Christmas Lane" that sparkles with

Geocaching?

Bronner's joined the world of Geocaching on May 15, 2007, with the placement of a cache on the Bronner property.

over 40,000+ lights. While you're there be sure to check out the "World of Bronners" (an 18 minute multi-image slide show) that highlights the design and production of their selection of trains. Visit "Bronner's Silent Night Memorial Chapel" - named after the famous song (the chapel was originally made in Austria). Kids seem to be most fascinated with the "It Feels Like Christmas" drive around the vast parking lot and the animated displays of seasonal bears, elves, and children playing around the upper perimeter of each theme room. Be sure to get at least one ornament to keep - but "oh" - how to decide!

FRANKENMUTH CHEESE HAUS

Frankenmuth - 561 South Main St 48734. www. frankenmuthcheesehaus.com. Phone: (989) 652-6727. Hours: Daily 9:30am-6:00pm. Open until 9:30pm (summer). Admission: FREE

Lots of tasting going on here! Ever tried "Chocolate" or "Strawberry" cheese? Not only will you sample some... you can also try cheese spreads (smooth, creamy and fresh tasting) or over 140 different kinds of cheese.

Watch a video of the cheesemaking process, or if you time it right, actually see the ladies make it from scratch. They have giant photographs of each step of the process, so if the kids can't see it all they can still understand the process from the pictures. Yummy samples of cheese spreads in varieties from Garden Vegetable to Jalapeno! You will want some to take home (although this souvenir will soon be eaten with a box of crackers!)

FRANKENMUTH HISTORICAL MUSEUM

Frankenmuth - 613 South Main Street (I-75 to Frankenmuth Exit - Next to the Visitor's Center, Fischer Hall) 48734. Phone: (989) 652-9701. www.frankenmuthmuseum. org. Hours: Monday-Thursday 10:00am-5:00pm, Friday & Saturday 10:00am-8:00pm, Sunday Noon-6:00pm. (April-December). Shorter hours (January-March). Closed winter holidays. Admission: $1.00-$2.00 per person. Note: Museum Gift Shop with folk art and toy objects.

Frankenmuth Historical Museum is a small, easily navigated exhibits geared specifically toward the history of Frankenmuth. Exhibits depict the area's German history from Indian mission days to a town called "Michigan's Little Bavaria". Begin onboard the immigrants' ship traveling from Bavaria to the Saginaw Valley. There are a number of hands on exhibits for kids. Test your strength by lifting two water buckets on a yoke. Feel the different pelts of native animals. All the exhibits have extensive placarding, and there is also an audio narrative as you walk through the different rooms. Perhaps the most interesting of the exhibits for school students are the actual letters that these early settlers wrote to their families and friends back in Germany. You can find them in the "Outgoing Mail" section of the Post Office exhibit. The museum is small, and you can easily go through it in about half an hour, more if you read all the letters.

FRANKENMUTH WOOLEN MILL

Frankenmuth - 570 South Main Street (I-75 to Frankenmuth Exit - Follow signs to downtown) 48734. Phone: (989) 652-8121. www.frankenmuthwoolenmill.com. Hours: Daily 10:00am-9:00pm (Summer). Daily 10:00am-6:00m (Winter). Admission: FREE.

We've all seen freshly shaven sheep and probably own wool clothing. But how is it processed? Here's your unique chance to see how it all happens. They began here in 1894 and the mill has produced over 250,000 hand-made, wool-filled comforters since then. See the mill in action where you can begin by looking through a window of the wash basins (great viewing for smaller children) where they clean wool brought in from farmers. Washed fleece is then air dried (it gets really fluffy that way) and then put through a "carding machine". The wool passes through wire-spiked rollers until it is untangled and meshed together to form a sheet. Comforters are assembled according to Bavarian tradition (hand-tied). Throughout the tour, your guide will let you handle samples of wool at different stages of the process. The kids will find "raw" wool disgusting, but love the way that it turns out. This "hands-on" activity keeps their interest throughout the demonstration.

GRANDPA TINY'S FARM

Frankenmuth - 7775 Weiss Street (across from Bronners) 48734. Phone: (989) 652-KIDS (5437). www.grandpatinysfarm.com. Hours: Daily 10:00am -5:00pm. (April-October) Admission: $5.00 (age 3+). Maximum Family Price $20.00 (Price includes horse drawn wagon ride.)

Step back in time at this working Historical Farm and Petting Farm. Hold cuddly baby bunnies and chicks. Watch playful lambs and goats. Feed and play with the farm animals, gather your own eggs and take a horse-drawn wagon ride! Enjoy seasonal demonstrations of draft horses plowing, planting and harvesting. Special activities are scheduled, weather permitting.

RIVERPLACE

Frankenmuth - 925 South Main Street 48734. www.frankenmuthriverplace.com. Phone: (800) 600-0105. Hours: Sunday-Thursday 10:00am-7:00pm, Friday-Saturday 10:00am-9:00pm (September-December, May). Slightly more limited hours (January-April). Daily 10:00am-9:00pm (June-August). Admission: Varies with activity. Gameroom, toy stores and treats shops, too.

A-MAZE-N-MIRRORS - life size maze of mirrors and glass. MOONWALK MAN'S HOUSE - bounce inflatable playplace. BAVARIAN BELLE - see separate listing. LIGHTS FANTASTIC - nightly laser-light shows in amphitheater. FREE.

ZEHNDER'S SPLASH VILLAGE HOTEL & WATERPARK

Frankenmuth - 1365 S. Main Street (next to Bronner's Christmas Wonderland) 48734. Phone: (800) 863-7999. www.zehnders.com. Admission: Room packages are most appealing. Seasonal room and waterpark inclusive rates range: $109.00-$409.00 per night. Note: Zehnder's offers a full-service menu that features all-you-can-eat family-style chicken dinners, seafood, steaks, fresh baked goods and European desserts. Dinners range from $15.25 to $21.50, with children's portions and special event menus available. Luncheon menu is available Monday through Saturday from 11:00am-2:00pm. Zehnder's is open seven days a week.

The Zehnder family transformed its Bavarian Haus Motel into the Splash Village Hotel and Waterpark. Zehnder's Splash Village offers 152 deluxe accommodations including 63 new suites. Enjoy over 30,000 sq. ft. of indoor aquatic fun with Splash landing play area, dumping bucket, giggling gorge and Perilous plunge-a four story tube slides. Relax in the whimsical whirl hot tub or just float along the Crooked Brook Creek lazy river. For the landlubber have fun at the arcade or lunch at Elf hollow café. A towering 26-foot tree is a prominent feature in the hotel lobby with a large gas fireplace built into the trunk. Zehnder's Splash Village includes elves and fairies as part of the waterpark and hotel's overall theme. Complimentary shuttle service is available to Zehnder's Restaurant and the Fortress golf course.

ZEHNDER'S SNOWFEST

Frankenmuth. www.zehnders.com. Zehnder's Snowfest will dazzle and excite you with snow and ices sculptures created by professional ice and snow carvers from around the world. Host to the National Collegiate Ice Carving Championship and the High School Snow Sculpting Competition. In addition, entertainment for the entire family in the warming tent, a fireworks display, petting zoo and children's activities. (6 days end of January)

Freeland

APPLE MOUNTAIN SKI AREA

Freeland - 4519 North River Road 48623. Phone: (989) 781-6789 or (888) 781-6789. www.applemountain.com. Hours: Daily 10:00am-10:00pm (mid-December to mid-March).

Guests arriving at Apple Mountain will find their experience to be a memorable one - whether it's a round of golf, a day of skiing, or dinner at Kathleen's Restaurant and the Mountain View. Night skiing, snow boarding, equipment rental, and instructions are available. Specials online.

Lakeport

LAKEPORT STATE PARK

Lakeport - 7605 Lakeshore Road SR 25 north 48059. Phone: (810) 327-6224. www.michigan.gov/lakeport. Admission: $8.00-$10.00 per vehicle for recreation passport.

Located along the shore of Lake Huron, the park has two distinct units separated by the village of Lakeport. Camping/cabins, hiking trails, boating, and fishing. Beach access to Lake Huron. Camping is king here.

Metamora

METAMORA-HADLEY STATE RECREATION AREA

Metamora - 3871 Hurd Road (off SR 24 south) 48455. Phone: (810) 797-4439. www.michigan.gov/metamorahadley.   Admission: $8.00-$10.00 per vehicle for recreation passport.

The park consists of 723 acres with 80-acre Lake Minnewanna in the center. Camping, hiking trails, boating, fishing and swimming. Row boats, paddle boats and canoes can be rented at the concession between from May 28 to September 5. The hiker will find more than six miles of marked hiking trails that meander through the woods and fields of the park.

Midland

DOW MUSEUM OF SCIENCE AND ART

Midland - 1801 West Saint Andrews Rd 48640. www.mcfta.org. Phone: (989) 631-5930.   Hours: Tuesday-Saturday 10:00am-5:00pm, Sunday 1:00-5:00pm, except Holidays. Admission: $8.00 adult, $5.00 child (ages 4-14). Hall of Ideas alone: $3.00 per person. Note: Art Gallery, Peanut Gallery (Theatre Guild's family division).

What's 10 feet tall, 10,000 years old, hairy and wears size 80 sneakers? See, touch, hear, explore the world's natural wonders of science, history, and art. "Captain" a Great Lakes fishing boat or set off a mine blast! Ride a John Deere combine (cab of one with panoramic view of field in front of you). Create computer music, visit an old-time theater and say "hi" to an American mastodon skeleton with size 80 feet! Light, sound, lasers and motion abound.

CHIPPEWA NATURE CENTER

Midland - 400 South Badour Road   48640. www.chippewanaturecenter.com. Phone: (989) 631-0830. Hours: Monday-Friday 8:00am-5:00pm, Saturday 9:00am-5:00pm. Sunday and most Holidays 1:00-5:00pm. Admission: Donation.

Chippewa Nature Center contains an 1000-acre network of interpretive trails that meander through wetlands, lowland forest, and upland meadows at the confluence of the Pine and Chippewa Rivers. Learn about the wildlife and history of the area at the extensive visitor center and exhibit gallery. Be sure to stop at the viewing window that overlooks the river. Outdoors, there's a wildlife viewing area, wildflower walkway, scenic river overlook, 1870 Homestead Farm (cabin, schoolhouse, heirloom/herb garden, farm animals) and The Arboretum of Michigan Trees and Shrubs. The Archeological District is the site of a territorial Indian battle.

DOW GARDENS

Midland - 1018 West Main Street (corner of Eastman Ave. and West St. Andrews Street, next to the Midland Center for the Arts) 48640. Phone: (800) 362-4874. www.dowgardens.org. Hours: 9:00am - just before sunset, daily except Winter holidays. Admission: $5.00 adult, $1.00 student (6-17). Note: Picnic areas. No pets allowed.

These gardens were started in 1899 as landscaping around Dow's home. Now there are 100 acres of gardens featuring flowers, trees, rocks and water. Seasonal tulips and wildflowers are pretty to look at. The Barnyard Garden is home to the hog sculpture, ponytail grass, lambs ears and an array of other plants with farm animal names. The Children's Garden has a treehouse and fountains. Other favorite areas for kids are the ABC Garden, Rainbow Garden and Weather Station. Grab a scavenger hunt, catch a jumping jewel, crawl through tunnels, and water some plants along the way.They also have seasonal, weekly storytimes with stories and "work" (ex. Harvesting).

GREAT LAKES LOONS

Midland - 825 E. Main Street (Dow Diamond) 48640. Reservations: (989) 837-2255. Phone: (989) 837-2255. www.loons.com.

The Great Lakes Loons, based in Midland, is a Class A minor league baseball team, affiliated with the Los Angeles Dodgers. The team plays in the Midwest League and their home park is Dow Diamond. Dow Diamond features a 17 ft. by 36 ft. video board, up to 24 concession facilities, an indoor fireplace, two outdoor fire pits, the two-story Loon Loft team retail store, 12 luxury suites, and a group picnic area. Kids can go to the Lou E. Loon playground and Kids Club.

H.H. DOW HISTORICAL MUSEUM/ MIDLAND HISTORICAL

Midland - 3100 Cook Road, Heritage Park (US Business 10 into town. Head NW on Main Street from downtown to Cook Road south) 48640. Phone: (989) 832-5319. www.mcfta.org/A_MCHS.html. Hours: Thursday-Saturday 11:00am-4:00pm. Admission: $5.00 adult, $3.00 child (under 14). Admits patron to both museums.

H.H. DOW MUSEUM: First of all, please purchase the Children's Guidebook and use it as you go through the museum. It's sure to keep the kids attention because each page has an activity for them to do. You'll want to start at the replica of Evens Flour Mill Complex - the original Midland Chemical Company. This is where young Dow pioneered experiments of separation of bromine from brine using electrolysis. See a prototype of his first lab. Wood scraps were used to build electrolysis boxes that feed onto "spread beds" that feed into a wood tower full of scrap metal. The metal catches the bromine liquid vapor. The museum has many clever interactive

See the early Chemistry Lab where a world-wide business was born...

(holograms, manual, conversation) displays conveying why Midland, Michigan was an ideal spot to experiment, how Dow's parents felt about his work (proud Dad, worried Mom), and his supportive wife. See a scene where Herbert is running his business yet trying not to be a workaholic. We feel the exhibits will inspire cleverness, tenacity, association with other great wise minds, hard work, and, in some, a zest for making money with science.

MIDLAND HISTORY CENTER: The Gateway to Heritage Park offers hands-on interactive exhibits where you can "talk" to Midland's founders, be "privy" to some of its secrets, and visit Main Street of long ago.

RIVERDAYS FESTIVAL

Midland - Chippewassee Park and area surrounding the Tridge. (989) 839-9661 or www.midlandfoundation.com. 17th and 18th century voyageurs reenactment, Valley Fife & Drum Corps music and pageantry. Paddlewheel cruises aboard the Princess Laura or get "hands-on" experience paddling the 32 foot canoe. Milk Jug Raft Race, Pancake Breakfast, Dinners, children's activities and concerts. (third weekend in July for 4 days)

BALLOON FEST

Midland - Midland County Fairgrounds. www.remax-midland-mi.com/balloonfest.cfm. (989) 832-0090 or Third weekend in September, Friday - Sunday. "Lift-off" to the United Way campaign with daily morning launches of 50 or so balloons. "After Glows" both Friday and Saturday nights. Skydiver shows. FREE admission. (mid-September)

Pinconning

DEER ACRES

Pinconning - 2346 North Huron Rd (I-75 to exit 164, go north on M-13) 48650. Phone: (989) 879-2849. www.deeracresfunpark.com. reopening in 2013.

Watching your children's eyes light up as they see a deer eating out of their hand is something that you'll never forget. At Deer Acres, the deer are so tame that they even know to come toward you when they hear the food dispensers clicking! Additional fun attractions (small additional fee) include several amusement rides (antique cars, Ferris wheel, carousel, moonwalk) and a narrated safari trip (don't miss the monkeys). Story Book Village brings all of your child's fantasy characters to life like "The Three Little Pigs", "Old Woman In a Shoe", "Old Mother Hubbard" and many others.

Port Austin

PORT CRESCENT STATE PARK

Port Austin - 1775 Port Austin Road (along M-25, 5 miles southwest of town) 48467. Phone: (989) 738-8663. www.michigan.gov/portcrescent. Admission: $8.00-$10.00 per vehicle for recreation passport.

Port Crescent State Park is located at the tip of Michigan's "thumb" along three miles of sandy shoreline of the Saginaw Bay. Some of the modern campsites offer a waterfront view, either of Lake Huron or the Pinnebog River. A 900-foot boardwalk and five picnic decks offer scenic vistas from the top of sand dunes in the day-use area. A unique feature is their undeveloped beaches and sand dunes contrasted with many forest hiking trails. Camping and mini-cabins plus these activities are available: fishing, swimming, winter sports.

Port Huron

BLUE WATER TROLLEY

Port Huron - (Off I-94, I-69 to Military to the Black River) 48060. Phone: (810) 987-8687. www.bwbus.com. Daily 10am-2 or 4 pm (Summertime). Saturdays in Sept.

Admission: 10 cents. The one hour tour, which includes a swing by various local points of interest, takes you through the heart of Port Huron and along the river front for a panoramic glimpse of the Blue Water Bridges, the Thomas Edison Statue and Depot.

EDISON DEPOT MUSEUM

Port Huron - Thomas Edison Parkway (under the Blue Water Bridge) 48060. Phone: (810) 982-0891. www.phmuseum.org. Hours: Friday-Monday 11:00am-5:00pm (Sept/Oct/May). Summer hours: Daily 11:00am-5:00pm. Wkends only (Nov - April) Admission: $7.00 adult, $5.00 senior (60+) and student (7-17). Discount combo pricing with Lightship & Port Huron Museum.

The Museum is housed inside the historic Fort Gratiot depot. Exhibits portray Edison's boyhood story of creativity, family support, adversity, perseverance, and ultimate triumph as the greatest inventor of our times. While living in his boyhood home along the shores of Lake Huron (age 7-16), Tom Edison conducted some of his first science experiments here (see demos of them) and also sold candy and hand-printed newspapers to train passengers. The story traces young Tom's boyhood and school experiences, his avid curiosity and scientific study fostered by his mother, adolescent entrepreneurial efforts and his work on trains - and in this very depot. Outside the depot, a restored baggage car rests on a spur of railroad track. Inside this baggage car, visitors discover a re-creation of young Edison's mobile chemistry lab and printing shop. See actual artifacts from Tom's lab (glass bottles) and lead type from his printing press. The movie played in the simulated Black Maria (Tom's name for the first movie theatre) is very well done and easy to follow. The museum flows thru his life at a very nice pace. The dioramas and multitude of hands-on opportunities here qualify this Edison Museum as a new favorite.

FORT GRATIOT LIGHTHOUSE

Port Huron - 2802 Omar Street (Lake Huron near the mouth of the St. Clair River) 48060. Phone: (810) 982-3659. www.phmuseum.org/lighthouse.html. Grounds are FREE. TOUR AND TOWER CLIMB IS $5.00 (No open toe shoes in tower). Summers open daily 11am-5pm. Wkends only Sept-mid Dec.

This lighthouse, the oldest in Michigan, was constructed north of the fort in 1829. Originally sixty-five feet high, the white painted brick tower was extended to its present height of eighty-six feet. The green flashing light that was automated in 1933 may be seen for seventeen miles. Today, Coast Guardsmen are stationed at this point and occupy the keeper's house. The lighthouse watches over one of the busiest waterways in the world.

HURON LADY II SCENIC CRUISES

Port Huron - 207 Water Street (On Black River behind LaSalle Bank) 48060. Phone: (810) 984-1500 or (888) 873-6726. www.huronlady.com. Hours: Seasonal (early summer thru early October). See website for schedule. Most 1.5 hour sightseeing tours depart at 1pm. Admission: $16.00 adult, $15.00 senior (Age 60+), $8.00 child (Age 5-12).

For extra fun, have the kids bring along a sticker book, coloring book or small toys to play with as you sail.

This well-narrated boat tour passing giant oil refineries, limestone factories and many passing freighters. When passing the freighters (closely), the captain will tell you about their cargo and capacity (did you know it costs less than a Big Mac and Fries to move each item across the Great Lakes by freighter – very efficient). Maybe catch a freighter in the "repair shop" or wave to the Coast Guard by the Fort Gratiot lighthouse or a Captain aboard the Lightship or Edison depot...even pass the Canada coastline. Very clean, comfortable all-weather boat with a modest snack bar.

Daniel keeping a careful watch....

HURON LIGHTSHIP MUSEUM

Port Huron - (End of I-94 east - Moored at Pine Grove Park along the St. Clair River) 48060. Phone: (810) 982-0891. www.phmuseum.org. Hours: Daily 11:00am -5:00pm (Summer). Friday-Monday only (fall and spring). Closed January-March.

Nearby is the PORT HURON MUSEUM - 1115 Sixth Street, that traces 300 years of local history, especially American Indian and marine history (step into a real ship's pilot house).

Admission: $7.00 adult, $5.00 senior (60+) & student (7+). Discount combo pricing with 2 other Port Huron museums.

Your entire family will really enjoy the brief tour of this unique lighthouse. It is the last "floating lighthouse" to sail the Great Lakes (decommissioned in 1970) called the "Huron". Used where it wasn't practical to build a lighthouse, it was built in 1920 and was operated by a crew of 11 who took 3 week turns (16 days out, 5 days in). Board the boat that bobbed through thick fog and rode out heavy storms to warn passing freighters of treacherous shoals ahead in the channel. Listen to the fog horn's "heeeee....ooohhhh" deep sound that bellows the sound of the ship's heart. What has replaced the Huron? Find out with self-guided tours of the interior hull, mess hall, captain's quarters, and then experience a panoramic view of the Blue Water Bridge from the pilothouse on top of the boat. It was most interesting to hear

A "lighthouse" ship...very innovative...

stories of freighters like the famous "Edmund Fitzgerald" and to know the dangers of being in a smaller boat that is calling giant ships right to you!

FEAST OF THE SAINTE CLAIRE

Port Huron - Pine Grove Park. www.phmuseum.org. (810) 982-0891. I-94/I-64 Business Loop into downtown. This feast recreates and demonstrates the four periods of early Michigan history in the Blue Water area. Staying in their historic, time period camps, these re-enactors provide an example of the daily life style of the 18th and 19th century. Lots to look at as you observe the ongoing demos of early American living, cooking, crafts

and activities like: Tomahawk Throw, Fife & Drum Show, Colonial Wrestling, Frying Pan toss, Battles, Celtic Dancers, Dulcimer concerts and Highland Games. Feast on authentic colonial style foods like: black pot bean soup in a bread bowl, celtic turkey legs, bread pudding, old-time root beer and corn on the cob. Admission. (Memorial Day Weekend)

QUALITY INN HOTEL & SUITES

Port Huron - 1720 Hancock Street (under the bridge to Canada), just off Pine Grove Avenue North. (810) 987-5999 OR *www.qualityinn.com/hotel-port_huron-michigan-MI370*. They offer an indoor heated swimming pool, jacuzzi, children's playland, fitness center and a complimentary Breakfast Bar served each morning with a big smile and welcome. There are clean, open eating and playing areas. A gameroom too. The staff here are the friendliest you'll ever find!

PORT HURON TO MACKINAC RACE

Port Huron to Mackinac - (800) 852-4242 or www.byc.com. Parades, street vendors and the largest fresh water sailing event in the world. Race week starts officially with the International Day Parade on Wednesday. Family activities at the waterfront. (second or third week of July)

Port Sanilac

SANILAC COUNTY HISTORICAL MUSEUM & VILLAGE

Port Sanilac - 228 South Ridge Road - (SR25) 48469. Phone: (810) 622-9946. www. sanilacmuseum.org. Hours: Wednesday-Friday 11:00am-4:30pm, Weekends Noon-4:00pm (early June-late August). Admission: $3.00-$5.00.

Start at the 1875 Victorian Home with original home furnishings, period medical instruments, original post office cancellation stamps, and an "American" sewing machine (later they changed their name to "Singer"). The Dairy Museum features cheesemaking equipment and you can wander through the Log Cabin where they used some charred logs from the tragic Thumb Area fire of 1881. See an old schoolhouse and stop at the General Store (really cute - try a bottle of old-fashioned "body splash" or some penny candy - lots of licorice!)

Saginaw

SAGINAW CHILDREN'S ZOO

Saginaw - 1730 South Washington (I-675 to 5th/6th Exit to Celebration Square) 48601. Phone: (989) 759-1408. www.saginawzoo.com. Hours: Monday-Sunday 10:00am-5:00pm (April-Labor Day). Daily Noon-5pm (Sept/October). Admission: $5-$7.00 per person (age 1+). Carousel $2.00 extra.

This "kid-sized" zoo features all the fun animals including: monkeys, bald eagles, alligators, and farm animals. The zoo's Awareness Amphitheater holds regular shows, each highlighting 3 animals such as pygmy goats, river otters or kangaroos. Take a miniature train or pony ride and then see and ride a unique, locally built carousel. After choosing your mount (from horses, rabbits, ponies or sea horses), enjoy the views of hand-painted panels depicting scenes of Saginaw's history.

HOLIDAYS AT THE ZOO

Saginaw - Children's Zoo and Celebration Square. www.saginawzoo.com. (989) 752-6338. See Santa and his reindeer along with wolves, bobcat and eagles. Ride the carousel. Lights. Refreshments. Admission. (select Friday & Saturday evenings beginning day after Thanksgiving until day after Christmas)

SHIAWASSEE NATIONAL WILDLIFE REFUGE

Saginaw - Green Point Environmental Learning Center is at 3010 Maple Street in town. (Refuge is 6 miles south of town, west of SR13) 48601. Phone: (989) 777-5930 or (989) 759-1669 (Learning Center). www.midwest.fws.gov/Shiawassee/. Hours: Dawn to Dusk.

The 9000 acre Refuge provides food and rest for a variety of birds and other wildlife. This includes 250 species of birds, 10 miles of observation trails to walk, two observation decks with scopes, and The Green Point Environmental Learning Center. The Center offers 2.5 miles of hiking trails, indoor exhibits and many displays. For Shiawassee Flats "Michigan Everglades" Boat Trips, call Johnny Panther Quests (listed on previous page).

SAGINAW ART MUSEUM

Saginaw - 1126 North Michigan Avenue 48602. www.saginawartmuseum.org. Phone: (989) 754-2491. Hours: Tuesday-Saturday 10:00am-5:00pm, Sunday 1:00-5:00pm. Closed holidays. Admission: $5.00 adults (age 17+).

Housed in an early 1900's mansion, you'll mostly find 19th and 20th century American art. The Visionarea Hands-On Room is the best place to spend time with kids (see kids making easy art jewelry, prints or art science - uninstructed play).

SAGINAW SPIRIT HOCKEY

Saginaw - Dow Event Center 48607. www.saginawspirit.com. Phone: (989) 497-7747.

Experience the excitement of OHL hockey and the Saginaw Spirit when they play at home. Meet with the mascot Sammy Spirit and join the Kids Club. The Spirit have one of the highest attendance rates in the Ontario Hockey League. Season tickets are available. Individual tickets range from $8.50-15.50. Season: September-March.

MARSHALL M. FREDERICKS SCULPTURE GALLERY

Saginaw (University Center) - 7400 Bay Road (SR84) (Arbury Fine Arts Center on Saginaw Valley State University) 48710. www.svsu.edu/mfsm/. Phone: (989) 790-5667. Hours: Monday-Friday 11am-5pm. Saturday Noon-5:00pm. Closed university holidays. Admission: FREE. K-12 tours are free. $2.00 per student hands on activity fee. Adult tours are $3.00 per person, $2.00 per senior.

Home to more than 200 sculptures by the same artist. He is known nationally and internationally for his impressive monumental figurative sculpture, public memorials and fountains, portraits, medals, and animal sculptures. Free-standing sculptures, drawings and portraits, and photos of bronze pieces are displayed. Plaster models used to cast the sculptor's work in bronze constitute the bulk of the collection indoors. There's a sculpture garden and fountain, too.

Sebewaing

MICHIGAN SUGAR FESTIVAL

Sebewaing - http://main.sebewaingchamber.com. (800) 35-THUMB. How sweet it is... visit the sugar beet capital of the state for a parade, fireworks, sweet foods and the crowning of the sugar queen. (mid-June)

St. Johns

UNCLE JOHN'S CIDER MILL

St. Johns - 8614 North US-27. www.ujcidermill.com. (989) 224-3686. Apples in September, pumpkins in October. Walk along the nature trail, take a tractor ride tour through the orchards, play in the fun house or check out the petting zoo and train rides. Corn Maze, Fruit Fling, Inflatables, and Horse-Drawn Wagon Rides, too. Small admission per activity. Farm store open daily 9:00am-dark, May-December. (Weekends in September and October)

ANDY T'S FARMS

St. Johns - 3131 South US-27. (989) 224-7674. www.andyts.com. Open, daily 9:00am - 8:00pm (April-December). Family fun farm with fresh veggies and fruit (esp. apples and pumpkins), U-pick tours, hayrides, a petting barn, holiday decorations and bakery. (October)

CW CHAPTER AT A GLANCE

Baldwin * Shrine of the Pines

Cannonsburg * **Ski area**

Cedar Springs * Red Flannel Fest

Coopersville & Marne Railway

Fremont * Natl Baby Food Fest

Grand Haven

* Grand Haven St Pk

* Musical Fountain

* Great Lakes Sport Kite Fest

* Coast Guard Fest

Grand Rapids

* Fish Ladder Sculpture

* Grand Rapids Children's Museum

* Grand Rapids Civic Theatre

* Griffins Hockey

* Grand Rapids Symphony

* Bland Ford Nature Ctr

* Gerald Ford Museum

* John Ball Park Zoo

* Public Museum of Grand Rapids

* Meijer Gardens

* Robinettes Apple Haus

* Whitecaps Baseball

* Jersey Junction * Riverfront Hotel

* Nite Lltes * One Trick Pony

Jenison * Grand Lady

Greenville * Klackle Orchards

Harrison * Wilson St Pk

Holland

* Holland Museum * Windmill Island

* Deklomp Wooden Shoes

* Dutch Village * Holland St Park

* Saugatuck Dunes St Park

* Tuliptime * Dutch Winterfest

Ionia * Ionia St Rec Area

Ludington

* Ludington City Beach * State Park

* Big Sable Point Lighthouse

* SS Badger * White Pine Village

Mears

* Hart-Montague Trail St Park

* Mac Woods Dune Rides

* Silver Lake St Park

* Little Sable Point Lighthouse

* West MI Sand Dragway

* Sierra SAnds at the Dunes

Muskegon

* Lakeshore Museum Ctr

* Lumberjacks Hockey

* Port City Princess Cruises

* Milwaukee Clipper

* Hoffmaster St Pk/Gillete Dune Ctr

* USS Silversides

* Michigan Adventure & Wildwater

New Era * Country Dairy

Newaygo * Newaygo St Park

North Muskegon

* Duck Lake St Pk * Muskegon StPk

* Muskegon Winter Sports Complex

Pentwater * Mears St Pk

Rothbury * Double JJ Resort

Shelby * Gemstones

Whitehall * White River Lt Station

Chapter 2
Central West

A Quick Tour of our Hand-Picked Favorites Around...

Central West Michigan

Most of this region is pretty near the water. Visit and stay in the grand city of Grand Rapids and play on the nearby sugar-sand beaches of Lake Michigan. The towns of Muskegon, Grand Haven and Holland offer pristine beaches, cozy lodging, gorgeous sunsets, amazing natural beauty, lighthouses and much more. All within a 60-minute drive, you get a spectacular city, beautiful beaches and quaint lakeshore towns. Easily follow I-96, US 31 or US 131 to get to favorite points.

Start in the quaint town of Holland and the land of **Windmill Islands, Dutch Villages** and **Wooden Shoes**. Watch local craftsmen carve "Klompen" shoes using machines from the Netherlands and then see the shoes put to use in a dance as those wooden shoes "klomp" to the beat.

Grand Rapids Museums, downtown, offer the city experience—along with the finest in culture, restaurants and hotels. The Children's Museum, the Gerald Ford Museum, and the Grand Rapids Museum are bursting at the seams with interesting, changing exhibits. Along the East Beltline is the **Frederik Meijer Gardens**. Inside, children seem to find the most unusual shapes of cacti that look like spaghetti or fingers. Outside, the nature trails pass sculptures that resemble animals. The Farm Garden replica farm is clean and playful while the Children's Garden (one of the largest in the nation) is for the senses. Water, rocks, a log cabin, a climbing tree house and butterfly maze make for an adventure day. Cap off your summer day by driving a short distance to the nightly showing of the **Grand Haven Musical Fountain** – the world's largest synchronized light, water and music show.

Got Dunes? Well, ride on or from the **Dunes** of Lake Michigan as you spend some lazy days along US 31. Personal or group **Dune Buggies** take you on smooth, perfect sand dunes with easy dips and more than one gorgeous view of Lake Michigan. Maybe even drive through the Lake (or, part of its tributary)! Take a dune-climbing stairway to the top overlook (it's a workout) at **Hoffmaster State Park**. The Gillette Dune Center has live dune animal exhibits and a display of a giant crystal of sand and samples of different types of sand found around America.

Ready for a giant cruise on water vs. sand? You have to experience a cruise on a ship like the **S.S. Badger** at least once in your lifetime. With the excitement and romance of a sea voyage, plus uninterrupted time with family and friends...the journey is as much fun as the destination. Family amenities like bingo, on board movies, reading rooms, decks to capture some brilliant sun, navigation tracking and on board food service make the long trips across Lake Michigan fast.

Sites and attractions are listed in order by City, Zip Code, and Name. Symbols indicated represent:

 Festivals   Restaurants   Lodging

Baldwin

SHRINE OF THE PINES

Baldwin - 8962 South M-37 (along the Pere Marquette Riverbanks) 49304. Phone: (231) 745-7892. Hours: Monday-Saturday 10:00am-6:00pm, Sunday 1:30-6:00pm (May 15-October 15). Admission: $1.00-$3.75 (age 6+).

It was Raymond W. Overholzer's (a hunting and fishing guide) vision to create a shrine to the white pine trees that once covered Michigan. He began hand-carving and hand-polishing stumps, roots, and trunks (using the simplest of tools). Over 30 years of "works of art" are shown here including candlesticks,

Cannonsburg

CANNONSBURG SKI AREA

Cannonsburg (Belmont) - 6800 Cannonsburg Road NE (10 miles east of US-131 on West River Dr) 49306. Phone: (616) 874-6711.   www.cannonsburg.com.

Day and night skiing with 10 runs. Lessons and equipment rental are available. Cannonsburg offers the highest vertical in Southwest Michigan.

Cedar Springs

RED FLANNEL FESTIVAL

Cedar Springs - Main Street and Morley Park, downtown, (US-131 exit 104). (616) 696-2662 or (800) 763-3273 Shoppe. http://redflannelfestival.org. Lumberjacks and clowns wore them - the original trapdoor red flannels made in this town since the early

1900's. They're still made here (purchase some at Cedar Specialties Store). An historical museum in Morley Park is usually open and features the history of red flannels (ex. Why the trapdoor?). A warning to visitors: be sure to wear red flannel (pajamas, long johns, shirts) as you walk the downtown streets or else the Keystone Cops might arrest you! Lumberjack food served. Parade. There's plenty of red flannel (many still with trapdoors) for yourself or your teddy bear to purchase. They're so adorable on our teddy! (end of September or beginning of October)

☒

Clare

CLARE IRISH FESTIVAL

Clare -   (888)   AT-CLARE.   **www.facebook.com/pages/Clare-Irish-Festival/56626303014** Admission charged to some events. Everyone's Irish. Parade, leprechaun contest, Irish stew, music and dancing. (second weekend in March)

☒

Coopersville

COOPERSVILLE & MARNE RAILWAY

Coopersville - Train Departs from Downtown (I-96 to Exit 16 or 19) 49404. Phone: (616) 997-7000.   www.coopersvilleandmarne.org.   Admission: $10.50 adult, $9.50 senior, $8.50 child (2-12).   Tours: Wednesdays & SAturdays 11am & 1pm (May-October). Saturdays only in March, April, Nov & December. Added theme rides in spring and fall.

A great way to introduce your children to rail travel at a relaxed pace. The summer rides offer a 5 mile tour though rural Michigan to the town of Marne and then returns on the same line. During the trip, the Conductor describes points of interest while train music from the 1800s plays. Look for deer, hawks, eagles and farm animals. You'll cross over an open deck girder bridge and four creeks. There are special theme rides that include The Great Train Robbery with Chuck Wagon Barbecue, The Pumpkin Train (in October), and The Santa Train (in December).

PUMPKIN TRAIN

Coopersville - Coopersville & Marne Railway. www.coopersvilleandmarne.org. Twice a day in the afternoon. Take a train with the Great Pumpkin. On board entertainment and refreshments. Pick your own pumpkin from the giant pile. Admission. (Weekends in October)

Fremont

NATIONAL BABY FOOD FESTIVAL

Fremont - Downtown. (800) 592-BABY or http://babyfoodfest.com/. Five days of baby contests and people acting like baby contests. Try entering a Gerber (headquartered here) baby food eating contest (1st one to down 5 jars wins) or enter a baby in the baby crawl race (imagine what parents hold as prizes to get their babies to move towards the finish line!). A baby food cook-off, top live entertainment, a midway, and 2 downtown parades. (third long weekend in July)

Grand Haven

GRAND HAVEN STATE PARK

Grand Haven - 1001 Harbor Avenue (Take US-31 into Grand Haven and follow the "waterfront" signs. Go south at the waterfront to the park entrance) 49417. Phone: (616) 847-1309.   www.michigan.gov/grandhaven. Admission: $8.00-$10.00 per vehicle for recreation passport.

48 acre park with the beautiful sandy shore of Lake Michigan along the west side of the park and the Grand River along the north side of the park. The park consists entirely of beach sand and provides scenic views of Lake Michigan and the Grand Haven pier and lighthouse (you can't miss the lighthouse - it's bright red). There's also boating, fishing and swimming.

MUSICAL FOUNTAIN

Grand Haven - (Downtown Riverfront. Viewing best at Grandstand at Harbor and Washington Streets) 49417. www.grandhaven.org/recreation/musical-fountain-schedule/. Phone: (616) 842-2550. Hours: Summer Fridays & Saturdays at dusk-approximately 9:30pm. Admission: Donations.

> Tri-Cities Museum is in front of the grandstand and is open most evenings until the concert begins. It contains displays on railroading, shipping, pioneers, the lumber industry, Coast Guard and Maritime vessels in a former railroad depot.

The world's largest synchronized light, water and music show. For 30 years now, jets of water up to 125 feet high go through a series of pipes to create displays that change color to the beat of music. We thought some looked like angel wings and sunrises. The Musical, lighted fountains show takes (32) 600 watt subwoofers; (12) High-frequency horns; and (14) Power amplifiers. The show lasts approximately 20 minutes.

MUSICAL FOUNTAIN NATIVITY

Grand Haven - Grandstand at Harbor and Washington Streets on the riverfront. (800) 303-4096. A 40 foot nativity scene on Dewey Hill offers evening performances focused on the "spirit" of the holiday. There are dancing bears, Santa in a boat, candles, spiral Christmas trees and lots of snowflakes. It also features a Nativity scene, a Kwanzaa candle and a menorah. Visitors can watch the shows from their cars and listen to the short-wave broadcast on 88.1 FM. Donations. (Evening performances in December, parade is first Saturday)

_____

GREAT LAKES SPORT KITE FESTIVAL

Grand Haven - Grand Haven State Park Beach. www.mackite.com/glskc.htm. (800) 303-4097. Sponsored by the Mackinaw Kite Company, this event fills the air with brightly colored, high-flying kites everywhere. One of the largest kite festivals in the Nation, you'll find up to 40,000 spectators, pilots flying kites (some craft up to 40 foot long), kite ballet events and lessons for beginners. (third long weekend in May)

_____

COAST GUARD FESTIVAL

Grand Haven - (888) 207-2434 or www.ghcgfest.org. A Coast Guard tradition filled with family entertainment day and night leading up to the final Saturday. Saturday starts with the biggest and best parade in all of West Michigan, a carnival on Main Street, all leading up to the musical fountains & fantastic fireworks late at night. (begins last weekend in July for 10 days)

Grand Ledge

YANKEE DOODLE DAYS

Grand Ledge - www.charlemontfairgrounds.org/YankeeDoodleDays.htm. Festivities will include children's carnival rides, boat cruises on the Princess Laura Riverboat, pig roast, entertainment tent, canoe races, dunk tank, tug of rope contest, duck race, fishing contest, garden club tour, fashion show and battle of the bands. The Yankee Doodle Days parade will be Friday night, Saturday morning and night. Mudge's Follies will be performing the best music of the last 25 years, plus favorite patriotic music and a freedom finale. Admission. (last full long weekend in June)

Grand Rapids

FISH LADDER SCULPTURE

Grand Rapids - (US131 East to exit 87 - turn right onto Front Street - On Grand River at junction of 4th and Front Streets) 49503. Phone: (800) 678-9859.   Hours: Daily, daylight hours. Admission: FREE

A concrete, 5 step ladder (actually a series of steps) was built by a local artist to assist salmon in jumping up a 6 foot dam to reach their popular spawning grounds further upstream. Leaping fish can be seen anytime, but the best time is late September to late October. If you spend about 20 minutes there you will witness at least one fish make it up all five steps! We sure are glad that Grand Rapids decided to help these pretty "fishies" out!

GRAND RAPIDS CHILDREN'S MUSEUM

Grand Rapids - 22 Sheldon Avenue NE (Division to Library Street, downtown) 49503. Phone: (616) 235-4726.   www.grcm.org. Hours: Tuesday-Saturday 9:30am-5:00pm, Sunday Noon-5:00pm. Also Thursday from 5:00-8:00pm. Open summer Mondays. General Admission: $7.50(ages 1+). Family Night: $1.50 Note: Curriculum based handouts online: www.grcm.org/learn/educators/.

A well supported hands-on museum focuses on learning. Parents and kids truly learn the art of play here - and, new fun exhibits appear every season. Besides the great "light table" (with clear, colored Legos - you can never play enough with Legos!), they also have giant LIte Brite playstation and another play table with sand. The "dress up" area includes a dressing room and large stage w/ ticket booth to "role-play" perform. Dress up in all kinds of clothes, choose an array of backgrounds and watch as your image is transformed from

in front of a green screen to in front of a weather map or city scapes and more. Another permanent exhibit at the museum is the grocery store, where kids can play cashier, shop, weigh realistic-looking fruits and veggies, and even stock the shelves. Bubbles (play with lights and shapes in a world of bubbles) and Bees

Another day at the jobsite...

(watch as bees live their lives making honey, beeswax and taking care of the queen), too. The space is well proportioned and it's easy to keep an eye on everyone as they fan out.

NEW YEAR'S EARLY EVE

Grand Rapids - Children's Museum. www.grcm.org. Take fun pictures, do a craft, face painting, snacks and juice, dress up and play. Entertainment and a balloon drop at 7:30pm. Admission. (New Years Eve 6:00-8:00pm)

GRAND RAPIDS CIVIC THEATRE

Grand Rapids - 30 North Division Street, 49503. www.grct.org. Phone: (616) 222-6650. Admission: $6.00-$12.00.

Children's Theatre with productions like Frog and Toad or the Wizard of Oz. Storybooks come to life, as well as classic dramas like the Sound of Music. The second largest community theatre in the U.S. Season runs year round now.

GRAND RAPIDS GRIFFINS HOCKEY

Grand Rapids - 130 West Fulton (Van Andel Arena) 49503. Phone: (616) 774-4585. www.griffinshockey.com. Admission: $5.00-$25.00.

This AHL team plays October through April. Griff is their mascot. Look for family Open Skate Nights. Affiliate of Detroit Red Wings.

GRAND RAPIDS SYMPHONY/YOUTH SYMPHONY

Grand Rapids - 169 Louis Campau Promenade, Suite One (DeVos Hall) 49503. Phone: (616) 454-9451. www.grymphony.org.

Family and Lollipop Series available September-May. Great for families with young or elementary-aged children! These thematic chamber orchestra concerts offer a first exposure to a live symphony orchestra. Lollipop Concerts are approximately 45 minutes in length and are presented throughout the greater Grand Rapids area. Tickets are $5 per person, regardless of age, for general admission seats. The Family Series has pre-concert activities in the lobbies, featuring an Instrument Petting Zoo and much more! Single tickets range from $9.00 for children 12 and under and $15.00 for adults. Picnic Pops. Holiday Pops. Youth Symphony concerts feature the 100+ member ensemble (ages 12-21) performing classical favorites. Admission charged.

BLANDFORD NATURE CENTER

Grand Rapids - 1715 Hillburn Avenue NW (US 131 to Leonard Street exit west to Hillburn) 49504. Phone: (616) 453-6192. www.mixedgreens.org. Hours: Monday-Friday 9:00am-5:00pm. Weekends 1:00-5:00pm. Closed major holidays. Trails are open from dawn to dusk. Free general admission. $5 fee for events.

The visitor center is probably where you'll start. Learn about their wildlife care program and then go out on the grounds along self-guided trails to see wildlife. A total of 140 or so acres of fields, forests, ponds and streams can be leisurely explored. An observation deck overlooks a woodland stream in a ravine, and a tall observation tower gives a bird's eye view of a pond and wetlands. Blandford staff often offer guided walks to see owls, bats, frogs, toads, turtles, snakes, and animal tracks. The evening "Owl Prowls" are very popular in the fall. Forested portions of the preserve offer a chorus of frogs and spring peepers add charming background music. Blandford also has an active wildlife rehabilitation clinic, with many permanent wild residents on public display in outside enclosures, including owls, turkey vultures, a fox, and more. Other trails pass the Carriage Barn, Sugar House, Blacksmith, General

Store, Barn & Log Cabin (most open summertime). The trails turn into cross-country ski areas in the winter.

GERALD FORD MUSEUM

Grand Rapids - 303 Pearl Street NW (I-196 to US131 to Pearl Street Exit - East - on the West bank of the Grand River) 49504. www.ford.utexas.edu. Phone: (616) 451-9263. Hours: Daily, 9:00am-5:00pm. Closed New Year's Day, Thanksgiving Day, and Christmas Day. Admission: $7.00 adult, $6.00 senior (62+) or military, $5.00 college students with ID, $3.00 youth (6-18). Children FREE (under 7). Educators: Gerald & Betty Ford Biography info online.

This display of history through artifacts is outstanding to parents, but kids will gravitate to only a handful of displays. As you may have to race through some interesting exhibits, be sure to help your kids look for these (hey...tell them it's a scavenger hunt!): See Elvis' suit, James Dean's motorcycle, Bert and Ernie, A pole sitter, the first video game, Mr. Roger's sweater, and those "groovy" platform tennis shoes (since they are now back in style they may be wearing something similar!). The best areas for kids:

❏ OVAL OFFICE REPLICA - See the room that very few people ever see and listen as you eavesdrop on a typical day in the Ford Presidency.

❏ HOLOGRAPHIC WHITE HOUSE TOUR - Tour (using photographs taken by the Fords) up to 11 rooms usually off limits to the public. Attend a White House State Dinner or play in the Solarium.

❏ CABINET ROOM/CAMPAIGNS - Deliver a speech like the President using a teleprompter or sit at the cabinet table while videos highlight 3 major events discussed by the President and his Cabinet. We have a great video of this memory.

JOHN BALL PARK ZOO

Grand Rapids - 1300 West Fulton Street (Take I-196 to Lake Michigan Drive or Lane Street exit, follow signs) 49504. www.johnballzoosociety.org. Phone: (616) 336-4300. Hours: Daily 9:00am-6:00pm (mid-May to Labor Day). Daily 10:00am-4:00pm (rest of the year). Closed Christmas Day only. Admission: $8.50 adult (14-61), $7.50 (62+), $6.50 child (3-13) (mid-May to Labor Day). Admission discounted ~$2.00 rest of year. Note: Camel ride $4.00, Swan Boat ride $5.00. Touch or Feed Stingrays or Sharks $1.00.

See more than 1000 specimens (you know...animals, fish, amphibians, etc.) from around the world at the state's second largest zoo. In addition to the usual lions, tigers, and bears there is a special exhibit on Nocturnal Animals and an African Pygmy goat petting zoo with farm animals for the young kids. Newer additions include the Spider Monkeys, Bongo, Penguins, and a sassy Hornbill. Look for octopus and moon jellies (w/ their 3 life cycles). The monkeys antics are fun to watch. In Stingray Lagoon watch a school of Cownose Stingrays fly through water as they nose the perimeter exploring the petting hands of kids. Swimming alongside the stingrays are the Leopard sharks. Walk through the Budgie Aviary or Wallaby walk thru. At one spot, you can acutally share a rock with the lions! Check website for zipline and ropes course times and tickets. The camel rides are back, too.

PUBLIC MUSEUM OF GRAND RAPIDS

Grand Rapids - 272 Pearl Street NW (US131 to Pearl Street, exit 85B) 49504. Phone: (616) 456-3977. www.grmuseum.org. Hours: Monday-Saturday 9:00am-5:00pm, Sundays (seasonally) Noon-5:00pm. Admission: $8.00 adult, $7.00 senior (62+), $3.00 child (3-17). Note: Planetarium and laser shows (additional charge). Museum Café. Curiosity Shop. Carousel rides for small fee.

Exhibits that depict heritage and manufacturers of the region. Best picks for children might be:

❑   FURNITURE CITY - a partially operational reconstruction of an early 1900's furniture factory and displays of artistic and funky chairs.

❑   THE 1890's DOWNTOWN - a recreated street with a theater and shops plus the sights and sounds of transportation and people's conversations as you wait with them at the train station.

❑   AMERICAN INDIANS - Anishinabe people were the first inhabitants of the area. Why do they re-tell the stories of their ancestry so much? Great storytelling theme here.

❑   COLLECTING A THROUGH Z - This alphabet-linked exhibit provides a means to bring out artifacts from many of the museum's collections e.g. "D is for Dolls"

Be on the lookout for the 76-foot finback whale skeleton which greets you at the entrance in the main hallway. Many other smaller fossils are snuck in different exhibit spaces. Look for the coat made of buttons. Families should take advantage of interactive ops like I Spy cards or a download of the Mini Bite Tour. Also, you'll feel like you're in the movie "Back to the Future" when you see the Giant Clock taken from Old City Hall (it's transparent so you can see the mechanisms - and it's still keeping time).

MEIJER GARDENS, FREDERIK & SCULPTURE PARK

Grand Rapids - 1000 East Beltline NE (I-96 to East Beltline exit - go north) 49525. Phone: (616) 957-1580. www.meijergardens.org. Hours: Monday-Saturday 9:00am-5:00pm. (until 9:00 on Tuesday). Sunday Noon-5:00pm. Closed only Christmas and New Years. Admission: $12.00 adult, $9.00 senior (65+) and student, $6.00 child (5-13), $4.00 child (3-4). Small admission for preschoolers. Outdoor tram rides for about $1-$3.00 each - weekends only. Note: Gift shop and café. Current special events are available on their website.

A 125-acre complex featuring indoor (5 stories tall) and outdoor gardens that combine the visual art of man with the visual art of nature. Inside, children

seem to find the most unusual shapes in the Arid Climate Garden w/ cacti that look like spaghetti and skinny fingers. Outside, see tropical and various plants from five continents on nature trails. The sculpture park offers 25 works by renowned artists. The collection is subdivided into two categories: the Sculpture Park and Gallery Collection focuses on work from the era of Auguste Rodin to the present, while the Garden Trails and Conservatory Collection focuses primarily on representational, animal imagery displayed in natural surroundings (change color with the seasons). The Michigan Farm Garden is a replica farm like Mrs. Meijer grew up on. It's fairly "allergy-free" as farms go because all the animals are bronze sculptures. In the big barn they have games for kids like: Tool ID, posing as the famous farmer couple (complete with apron, pitchfork, and farmhouse backdrop), Chore Champions (try gathering eggs, churning butter), Farm Animal drawings, Paper Patchwork quilts and leather Braiding. The

Jenny becomes a GIANT butterfly...

Children's Garden is one of the largest in the nation with a: Kid Sense Garden,

Water Garden (Great Lakes shape), Wetland Tower (shows natural filtration process of storm water), Quarry (geologists & dino dig), Log Cabin, Tree House Village (rope bridges and boardwalks), Butterfly Maze and Overlook, Sculpture Walk and a Storytelling Garden. These new additions make this a complete family day trip. You'll be surprised how well kids respond to sculpture art.

ROBINETTES APPLE HAUS

Grand Rapids - 3142 Four Mile Road (off the East Beltline) 49525. Phone: (616) 361-5567. www.robinettes.com. Hours: Open daily until 6:00pm. Admission: FREE to shop. Cider mill restaurant. Fees for orchard tours and Extreme Mountain Bike Trails. Tours: include a tractor pulled wagon ride trip to the orchard to pick an apple, watch cider made, and then try some w/ a donut.

After visiting Meijer Gardens, head up the East Beltline for a light meal and see this historic restaurant/cider mill and gobs of apple & cherry trees. In the apple room, you can get a taste of many different apple varieties or watch cider making. Every batch is different because each

An apple a day keeps the doctor away...We LOVE apples!

has a different mix of apple varieties. Try a homemade sandwich or soup topped off with real apple cider or cherry juice and a fresh apple dessert with ice cream! Teens may want to check out the Extreme Mountain Bike Trails on the property - wild! - see the video online. Nicest folks and they give group tours of the orchards in large wagons along with a corn maze (by appointment, weekends in September and October).

WHITECAPS BASEBALL

Grand Rapids - US 131 & West River Drive (Fifth/Third Ballpark - Old Kent Park) 49544. Phone: (616) 784-4131 or (800) CAPS-WIN. www.whitecaps-baseball.com. Admission: $5.00-$10.00.

A baseball stadium with lawn seats? Bleacher and box seats are also available too. The Whitecaps are the Class "A" farm team for the Detroit Tigers and always offer a great family fun value. Meet Crash the River Rascal. Playland. (April - September).

NITE LITES

Grand Rapids - Fifth Third Ballpark. Grnow.com. Follow the light as you drive through the Whitecaps stadium parking lot. The Great Awakening has lighted trees, reindeer, nativity scene, decorated tunnels and trees. Admission. (week of Thanksgiving until early January for six weeks)

JERSEY JUNCTION ICE CREAM

Grand Rapids (East) - 652 Croswell Ave SE #1. 49506. www.jerseyjunction.com. A Sunday afternoon drive isn't complete without a sweet treat for the entire family. Originally opened in 1963 by Doris VanAllsburg, mother of author Chris VanAllsburg and his famous Christmas-classic, *The Polar Express*. Maintained as an old fashioned ice cream parlor, complete with a model train that runs the ceiling of the main parlor, the store owns bragging rights for the number one dip shop in Michigan. If you aren't in the mood for a sundae, peruse the packaged and bulk candy displays, try a hand-made frozen treat, or even just nibble on a homemade waffle cone. .

ONE TRICK PONY RESTAURANT

Grand Rapids - 136 East Fulton Street. www.onetrick.biz/. Just a block away from the Children's Museum is One Trick Pony Restaurant with a children's menu. This place is the oldest building in Grand Rapids used for businesses from dress makers to meat markets…every business has done one thing well…including the current specialty pizzas made here now. Parents may want to try the cherry or pecan chicken dish.

RIVERFRONT HOTEL GRAND RAPIDS

Grand Rapids - 270 Ann Street NW 49504. https://ontherivergr.com. When touring Grand Rapids w/kids, maybe stay close to most everything at this hotel off US 131 & 270 Ann Street. They have a large, recently remodeled indoor pool, whirlpool and game room and pizza delivery room service. Rates (including breakfast buffet) start at $129/night

For updates & travel games visit: **www.KidsLoveTravel.com**

Grandville

GRAND LADY RIVERBOAT CRUISES

Jenison - 775 Taylor St. 49428. Phone: (616) 457-4837. www.grandlady.info/. Admission: $15.00 adult (for sightseeing tours). Children 10 and under are FREE. Longer tours available.

Their 1½ hour sightseeing cruise tells the story of sites you view and riverboat landings you pass between Grand Rapids & Grand Haven. One of the main features of early riverboats was the giant paddlewheel. The Grand Lady has two identical sternwheels, which may be operated independently. This allows her to be easily maneuvered in the narrow channels and sandbars of the river. The paddle wheels also allow her to operate in very shallow water (as little as 2 ½ feet), where a modern vessel would be grounded. Call or visit website for seasonal schedule of events. Sightseeing tours Daily, subject to prior charters (May-October).

Greenville

KLACKLE ORCHARDS

Greenville - 11466 W. Carson City Road (M59). www.klackleorchards.com. (616) 754-8632 or Corn maze, labyrinth, wagon pumpkin rides, elephant rides, inflatable play, U-Pick apples/pumpkins, hayrides, pony rides, petting zoo, sand pile play area, pedal tractors & trikes, straw barn fort, kids crafts and music. (daily in October)

Harrison

WILSON STATE PARK

Harrison - 910 North First Street (BR-27 one mile north of Harrison) 48625. Phone: (989) 539-3021. www.michigandnr.com/parksandtrails/parkmap.aspx. Admission: $8.00-$10.00 per vehicle for recreation passport.

Situated on 36 beautifully wooded acres with a sandy beach, Wilson State Park is located on the north end of Budd Lake in Clare County. Budd Lake, a 175- acre lake, boasts great fishing. A large fish population of muskellunge, bass, panfish, perch and walleye inhabit the lake. Besides fishing, pleasure boating and water-skiing are also popular activities on Budd Lake. Camping/ cabins, boating and boat rental, and swimming.

Holland

HOLLAND MUSEUM

Holland - 1 Lincoln Avenue (I-196 at 10th St. & River Ave, downtown) 49423. Phone: (888) 200-9123. www.hollandmuseum.org. Hours: Monday, Wednesday-Saturday 10:00am-5:00pm, Sunday 12:00-5:00pm. Admission: $7.00 adult, $6.00 senior, $4.00 student.

As you enter, you'll be mesmerized by the collection of miniature glass churches built by Dutch immigrants for a World's Fair. Most all the displays are "no touch" but kids take an interest in the Dutch Fisherman's Cottage (kids sleep in bunks in the walls) and the carousel made by a Dutch sailor for his kids. They've also developed an interactive experience for children of all ages to learn about Holland and its history through hands-on activities. Watch a video, try on clothing, complete a craft, and have fun. Activities change regularly.

WINDMILL ISLAND

Holland - 7th Street and Lincoln Avenue (US 31 to 8th Street) 49423. Phone: (616) 355-1030. www.windmillisland.org. Hours: Daily 9:30am-6:00pm. Admission: $7.50 adult, $4.50 child (5-15). Holland residents free. Note: Candle, sweets, and gift shop. Every windmill product you could imagine is in there. Some activities are for summer only.

"DeZwann" (Dutch for the swan) is a 230+ year old, 12-story high, working, authentic Dutch windmill. It's the only one operating in the United States...they produce graham flour almost daily and sell it at the complex. Take a tour of all of the floors, learn how they change the direction of the windmill, see the mechanical wood gears turn (if there's at least a 15 MPH wind) and learn how the miller worked upstairs and sold product on the first floor at the same time. After your tour, Klompen (wooden shoe) dancers perform to organ music as those wooden shoes "klomp" to the beat. The Posthouse museum is an exact architectural replica of a 14th century wayside Inn and features a 12 minute slide presentation of Windmills, The Netherlands and our "De Zwaan". See a display of the Netherlands in miniature. The kids won't believe how water canals are used as streets.

DEKLOMP WOODEN SHOE AND DELFTWARE FACTORY

Holland - 12755 Quincy Street - US31 49424. www.veldheer.com. Phone: (616) 399-1900. Hours: Daily 9:00am-5:00pm. Extended weekday hours. Admission: FREE Note: Veldheer Tulip Gardens. Colorful tulips, peonies, daylilies, iris, Dutch lilies, daffodils. Admission charged for gardens (when in season). When you pull in to park, notice the herd of American buffalo.

The Dutch began making wooden shoes as a replacement for leather which was too expensive and deteriorated quickly because of all the exposure to water in the Netherlands. Watch local craftsmen carve "Klompen" (wooden shoes) on machines brought over from the Netherlands. Sizes from Barbie (they really fit!) to Men's size 13. Plain or hand decorated they are great for gardening or decoration. Lots of sawdust! Delftware began being made by potters in the city of Delft in the 13th Century. It is known for its delicately hand-painted blue and white porcelain. This is the only U.S. factory that is producing replica Chinese porcelain and it's just beautiful! While you're having your wooden shoes or small souvenir personalized, be sure to take the time to watch the artist use Delft colored paints to decorate plain pieces.

DUTCH VILLAGE

Holland - 12350 James Street (US 31 and James Street) 49424. Phone: (616) 396-1475. www.dutchvillage.com. Hours: SAturdays & Sundays 9:00am-5:00pm. (late April - Mid-October). Open daily each summer. Admission: $10.00 adult, $9.00 senior, $7.00 child (4-15). Note: Café. Ice cream shop. Specialty shops.

You'll feel like you're in Europe (Netherlands) as you see the quaint Dutch Style buildings, canals and flower gardens. Klompen Dancers perform to the music of the Amsterdam Street Organ and wooden shoe crafters are working in their shops with old tools that shape logs into shoes. Demonstration every 15 minutes! In the museum, you can learn how the famous Dutch cheeses of Gouda and Edam are made (then, sample some!). There are museums and historical displays (w/ 20 minute movie about the Netherlands) plus the kids favorite spot (and Michele's when she was little)...STREET CARNIVAL - Wooden Shoe Slides, Dutch Chair Swing, and antique Dutch pictured carousel. There's also a farmhouse with "pet and feed" animals, Dutch dancing lessons, "Street Cleaning" and something very different - Walk Your Goat!

HOLLAND STATE PARK

Holland - 2215 Ottawa Beach Road (west off US 31 on Lakewood Rd.) 49424. Phone: (616) 399-9390. www.michigan.gov/holland. Admission: $8-$10.00 per vehicle. Drawn to the beaches and swimming along with the beautifully well-kept, bright red, lighthouse is the reason most come. The park is divided into two separate units; one along Lake Michigan and the other along Lake Macatawa. The pier along the north side of the channel provides an excellent place for shore fishing. Charter boat services are available in the area to take people out on Lake Michigan. Ice fishing is a popular activity during the winter months. Almost 150 campsites, boating, and bicycle trails are also available.

SAUGATUCK DUNES STATE PARK

Holland - 2215 Ottawa Beach Road (Off US 31 north) 49424. Phone: (269) 637-2788. www.michigan.gov/saugatuckdunes. Admission: $8-$10.00 per vehicle. Over 2 miles of secluded shoreline along Lake Michigan. Winding throughout the park, Saugatuck Dunes has 13 miles of sandy hiking trails. The southern portion of the park is mostly made up of the coastal dune natural area. The Lake Michigan beach is a 0.6 mile hike from the picnic parking area. In addition, the park has fresh water coastal dunes that are over 200' tall. The park's terrain varies from steep slopes to rolling hills. Swimming, winter sports, and dunes, of course.

TULIP TIME

Holland - (800) 822-2770. www.tuliptime.org. 8 miles of tulips (6 million red, yellow and pink blooms), Klompen Dancers, fireworks and top entertainment. To start the festival, the town crier bellows "the streets are dirty" and youngsters begin cleaning with brooms and pails. Volksparade is next with the Kinder Parade of 5000 children dressed in costume. There are Dutch treats like pigs in blankets and pastries galore (the Queens Inn Restaurant is open), a Muziekparade and Kinderplasts - music, clowns, puppets, petting zoo, arts & crafts for kids. Admission charged to some events. (begins week before Mother's Day in May).

DUTCH WINTERFEST

Holland – Downtown. www.holland.org. Experience an old time Christmas celebration with all the Dutch trimmings! Open-air European market, Sinterklaas Eve, Parade of Lights, ice sculpting competition, specialty shopping, and more! (mid-November thru early December)

Ionia

IONIA STATE RECREATION AREA

Ionia - 2880 West David Highway (I-96, Exit 64) 48846. Phone: (616) 527-3750. www.michigan.gov/ionia.   Admission: $8-10 per vehicle.

Rolling hills, babbling brooks, open meadows, forested ridges, a lake nestled in the hills and a river winding its way through woods and fields. Dog field trials and training are frequent during the year. As birds are released for that sport which includes horse use, please be a good sports person and voluntarily stay clear of that activity. Shore and boat fishing is available on Sessions Lake and the Grand River. Stream fishing is available on Sessions Creek and Tibbits Creek. There are 3.5 miles of hiking trail loops within the park that traverse woods, streams, lake shore, meadows and river bottom areas. Camping/ cabins, boating, swimming, bicycle trails and winter sports.

Ludington

LUDINGTON CITY BEACH

Ludington - North Lakeshore Drive 49431. Phone: (231) 845-0324. www.ludington. mi.us/departments/parks/index.html. Hours: Daylight (summers). FREE.

A great summer place to cool off featuring swimming and miniature golf.

LUDINGTON STATE PARK / BIG SABLE POINT LIGHTHOUSE

Ludington - M-116 49431. Phone: (231) 843-8671 or (231) 843-2193 (boat rental). www.michigan.gov/ludington.   Admission: $8-10 per vehicle.

Over 300 campsites or cabins, plenty of beaches (one with surfing waves), and extensive hiking trails are big hits here. Lots of dunes here and a great canoe trail, boating, swimming, and fishing. Many love the cross-country skiing and the nature center. The Great Lakes Visitor Center, an outdoor interpretive facility, is a very popular attraction at Ludington. It offers interesting displays, slide presentations, videos and live programs. One of the more popular hands-on exhibits is "Night Visitors," featuring taxidermy mounts of nocturnal animals common to the area. A huge satellite map of the Great Lakes covers an entire wall. (open daily summers 10:00am-5:00pm, weekends only in spring and fall).

BIG SABLE POINT LIGHTHOUSE - on M116 (2 miles north of the State Park entrance - 231-845-7343 or www.bigsablelighthouse.org). The light from Big Sable is the last Michigan beacon seen by ships passing southward to

Chicago, and it is the first one spotted on the trip upbound. The lighthouse is a 1.5-mile walk from the campground along a wooded trail that parallels the Lake Michigan shoreline. The lighthouse is open daily, 10:00am-6:00pm, May 1 through October 30. Small tour admission.

S.S. BADGER

Ludington - 701 Maritime Drive (off US 31, Ludington exit into town. Follow signs for car ferry) 49431. Phone: (800) 841-4243. www.ssbadger.com. Hours: Depart times vary (usually morning departure from Michigan, afternoon departure from Wisconsin). Call for details (early May - early October). Be sure to call or visit their website for information on travel packages. Admission: (round trip) $128.00 adult, $117.00 senior (65+), $39.00 child (5-15), add $62.00 each way vehicle transport. Ages 4 and under are FREE. (All rates are per person, round trip and subject to change). One way rates available, too. Note: ROUND TRIP MINI-CRUISES without vehicle, returning within 48 hours, $89.00 adults, children (5-15) FREE. (Call for details). Staterooms are available and are a great place to catch a nap or have quiet time for young children. $49 each way.

Ready for a giant cruise on a giant lake? You have to experience the S.S. BADGER. With the excitement and romance of a sea voyage, plus uninterrupted time with family and friends....the journey is as much fun as the destination.

The Badger has expanded their focus on family amenities designed to appeal to passengers, children and even pets. Parents have more time to enjoy the cruise while their children have entertaining things to do. The expanded children's program (best for school-aged) includes a KidsPort playroom, face painting, a free activity book (coloring prizes), and always Badger Bingo and

Ready to board our ship...still powered by coal...what a fun day!

trivia for prizes. The Badger has also added a few new perks for pets including a special bandanna, treats and ventilated kennels. Adults head for the spacious deck areas ("steel beach") for walking or relaxing in the fresh air (a great place to avoid motion sickness, if you're prone – they also offer Sea Bands), two food service areas (serving really good food, beverage and snacks), private staterooms for naps and private bathroom (extra fee), and satellite televisio, or quiet rooms (place for reading or comfortable cat napping). The Main Lounge and Midship is where kids gravitate to. They watch movies in the

theatre; browse in the nautical ship's store (even have travel games for kids to purchase); but mostly participate in the Activity Director's games – like "Badger Bingo". Kids can also navigate and track the steamship's progress over open water. Make a vacation out of it - what an adventure on the sea and in port exploring!

WHITE PINE VILLAGE

Ludington - 1687 South Lakeshore Drive 49431. www.historicwhitepinevillage.org. Phone: (231) 843-4808. Hours: Tuesday-Saturday 10:00am-5:00pm (Early May to mid-October). Sunday & Holidays 1:00-5:00pm in the summer. Reduced winter hours. Admission: $6.00-$9.00. Slightly higher admissions for special events (i.e. Brunches, pioneer dinners)

A reconstructed 1800's village that features over 20 buildings including a courthouse, hardware store, fire hall, schoolhouse, chapel, and logging and maritime museums. The Exhibit Building has numerous antique transportation vehicles. They have an old-fashioned ice cream parlor, too. Outside are two more wooden boats and railroad carts used for moving heavy rail freight. Along with the automobiles are various tools from the era of the corner garage during the early days of the automobile repair business.

Mears

HART-MONTAGUE TRAIL STATE PARK

Mears - 9679 West State Park Road (along US31) 49436. Phone: (231) 873-3083.

A paved, 22-mile trail passing through rural forested lands. It showcases the beauty of Oceana county - from patchwork fields of asparagus, cherries, apples to marshlands...all with no motor vehicles. Picnic areas and scenic overlook areas are available along the trail.

MAC WOOD'S DUNE RIDES

Mears - West Silver Lake Drive (US 31 to Shelby Road exit east to B15 north) 49436. Phone: (231) 873-2817.   www.macwoodsdunerides.com.   Hours: Daily rides 9:30am-Dusk (Memorial Day-Labor Day). Daily rides 10:00am-4:00pm (mid-May - Sunday before Memorial Day & Labor Day - early October). Admission: $17.00 adult, $11.00 child (3-11).

Got Dunes? Well, ride on or from the Dunes of Lake Michigan as you spend some lazy days along US 31. Maybe start at Mac Woods Dune Rides. Your guide takes you on smooth, perfect sand dunes with easy dips and more than one gorgeous view of Silver Lake

A thrill ride for sure....just right!

and Lake Michigan. Even drive through Lake Michigan! Nearly 70 years ago Malcolm "Mac" Woods created the thrill of dune buggying. Today, your modern vehicle is a multi-passenger, modified, convertible truck "dune scooter". Hang on as you begin a fun and educational 40 minute, 8-mile ride that helps you understand the dunes and why people have come to love this sport. By the way, do you know what fulgurites are? Find them here!

SILVER LAKE STATE PARK

Mears - 9679 West State Park Road (US 31 exit Shelby Road west) 49436. Phone: (231) 873-3083.   www.michigan.gov/silverlake.   Admission: $8-$10 per vehicle.

Lots of campsites along the dunes is one draw but dune buggy riding is considered the best here. The dune ridges and valleys are mostly windblown sand and lack trees, scrub brush, and dune grass. The dune area is sometimes compared to a desert. Silver Lake State Park contains more than four miles of Lake Michigan shoreline and boasts a large sandy beach. Look for the Little Sable Point Lighthouse (great for pictures at sunset or dawn) and participate in swimming, boating, fishing, and hiking trails on and off dunes.

For updates & travel games visit: **www.KidsLoveTravel.com**

LITTLE SABLE POINT LIGHTHOUSE - 115 foot high and one of the tallest working lighthouses on Lake Michigan, it's visible for nine miles. In continuous operation since 1874, it is a guardian to ships that pass the Dunes. Open for tours each summer. Wednesday-Sunday 10:00am-5:00pm. $1.00-$2.00 admission. (must be 36" or taller)

WEST MICHIGAN SAND DRAGWAY

Mears - 7186 W. Deer Road (Take Hart Exit West off of US-31 - follow signs - 2 Miles down Deer Rd.) 49436. Phone: (231) 873-2778. www.sanddragways.com.

Sand Drag Race programs include top fuel dragsters, funny cars, 4 X 4's ATV's dune buggies, Jr. Dragsters, Jr. ATV's and Mighty Midgets. Tickets: $7.00-$13.00 (age 11+). May-early October.

SIERRA SANDS AT THE DUNES

Mears (Silver Lake) - (7990 W Hazel Road, 231-873-1008 or www.sierrasands.com. US 31 to Shelby exit to B15 around the east side of Silver Lake). Want to stay near Silver Lake? With friendly owners and amenities like: a heated outdoor pool and whirlpool, a playground, kiddie and mini-suites available, a Backyard! With tether ball, basketball, horseshoes, a campfire pit and plenty of lawn – this is an oasis from concrete, boring hotels. Just a short walk to town shops and restaurants and game centers. Plus, they offer discounted admission to amusements, bike rentals, water sport rentals, dune riding and horseback riding – order them right from the front office. Their packages are so fun. Most are around $150.00 per night.

Muskegon

LAKESHORE MUSEUM CENTER

Muskegon - 430 West Clay Avenue 49440. www.lakeshoremuseum.org. Phone: (231) 728-4119. Hours: Monday-Friday 9:30am-4:30pm, Saturday-Sunday 12:30-4:30pm. Educators: worksheets: www.muskegonmuseum.org/worksheets.html

LAKESHORE MUSEUM: History of Muskegon County with features of Lumbering, Industry and Wildlife, Native Americans, and a favorite kid spot - Hands on Science Galleries with Body Works. The Coming to the Lakes exhibit examines why various groups of people have migrated to this region for the last 10,000 years. Educational Gift Shop.

HACKLEY HOSE COMPANY NO. 2 - (231) 722-7578. Wednesday-Sunday Noon-4:00pm (May-October). $3 admission. Tour a replica Fire Barn, complete with fire-fighting equipment artifacts, horses stalls, firemen's living room.

Youngsters can sit up in an old pumper. (Wednesday-Sunday, noon-4:00pm)

SCOLNIK HOUSE: A historic house of the Depression Era where kids can see how families "made do" or try talking on a party line. (Wednesday-Sunday, noon-4:00pm)

MUSKEGON LUMBERJACKS HOCKEY

Muskegon - 955 Fourth Street (L.C. Walker Arena) 49440. Phone: (231) 726-3879. www.muskegonlumberjacks.com. Admission: $8.50-12.50.

International Hockey League professional team plays here October - April. The Muskegon Sports Hall of Fame is located in the Arena. Meet Furious Fred, the team's mascot and join the Hot Shotz Kids Club.

PORT CITY PRINCESS CRUISES

Muskegon - 1133 West Western Ave (Mart Dock, 560 Mart Street, off US-31 Bus onto Seaway Dr. - Downtown) 49440. Phone: (231) 728-8387 or (800) 853-6311. www.portcityprincesscruises.com.   Admission: General $20.00. Special prices for seniors and children 10 and under. Theme/Meal cruises extra.

A sightseeing tour of Muskegon Lake and if the weather is good a brief look at Lake Michigan.

S.S. MILWAUKEE CLIPPER

Muskegon - 2098 Lakeshore Drive 49440. www.milwaukeeclipper.com. Phone: (231) 755-0990. Hours: Saturday & Sunday, 1-5:00pm (Memorial Day-Labor Day Weekends) Admission: $7.00 adult, $5.00 student (age 6+).

Enjoy a guided tour of this 1904 361-foot vessel (built 7 years before the Titanic), the last American passenger ship left on the Great Lakes. Inside is the antique cafeteria, a model ship display, staterooms, a soda bowl (guess what that is?), a giant pilot house, a theatre and the newly discovered Children's playroom.

HOFFMASTER STATE PARK

GILLETTE DUNE CENTER

Muskegon - 6585 Lake Harbor Road (I-96, exit 4 west - Pontalune Road) 49441. Phone: (231) 798-3711 or (231) 799-8900 center.   www.michigan.gov/hoffmaster. Hours: Center: Saturday 10:00am-4:00pm (fall, winter, spring). Open Daily in the summer. Center closed in December and January. Park is open 8:00am - Dusk. Admission: $8-10 per vehicle. Note: Winter hosts cross country skiing, sledding, and snowshoeing. Campsites on shaded dunes. Fishing, boating, and swimming.

P.J. Hoffmaster State Park features forest covered dunes along nearly 3 miles of Lake Michigan shore. Its sandy beach is one of the finest anywhere. There are ten miles (16 km) of hiking trails, including the Dune Climb Stairway on the tallest dune. At the top, an observation deck offers a panoramic view of the dunes and Lake Michigan. Three miles (5 km) of trails are groomed in the winter for cross-country skiing.

A focal point of the park is the GILLETTE VISITOR CENTER. The Center has exhibits and hands-on displays. See a multi-media presentation that illustrates and explains both

Sand...sand...and more sand... for miles around...

dormant and living dunes. Nature trails to observation decks (one is handicap and stroller accessible). Towering dunes with a dune climbing stairway to the top overlook (it's a workout). The Center has lots of live turtles and frogs, similar to ones that live in dune environments. The favorite for our kids was the giant crystal of sand and the samples of different types and color of sand found around America. Do you know what 3 things are needed to form dunes?

USS SILVERSIDES SUBMARINE MUSEUM/ USCGC MCLANE)

Muskegon - 1346 Bluff at Pere Marquette Park (Southside of Channel Way) 49443. Phone: (231) 755-1230. www.silversidesmuseum.org. Hours: Daily 10:00am-5:30pm (June-August). Daily 10am-4pm (rest of year). Admission: $10.50-$15 (age 5+). FREE for Active Military. Online discount coupons. Museum only: $6.00. Note: Watch out if you're claustrophobic. Difficult to take pre-schoolers around on poor footing, cramped quarters.

The Silversades is a restored, famous WW II submarine that was once used for sinking ships. No other WWII sub remains that sank more ships. At Great Lakes Naval Memorial & Museum, you can open up to the thrill of going back to WW II and taking part in an authentic submarine experience. Go through the sub's compartments and see how sailors work and live in such cramped quarters (for up to 2 months). Explore decks, engine rooms, and battle stations. Also, a Camp Aboard program is available for a real fun time!

MICHIGAN'S ADVENTURE AMUSEMENT PARK & WILDWATER ADVENTURE

Muskegon - 4750 Whitehall Road (I-96 to US-31) 49445. Phone: (231) 766-3377. www.miadventure.com. Hours: Daily 11:00am-9:00pm. (Memorial Day weekend - Labor Day weekend). Hours vary slightly throughout the season. Call or visit website for complete schedule. Admission: General ~$28.00 (under 2 Free). Admission is good for both parks. Season passes available. Parking $8.00.

Summer...thrill rides, waterparks and food...right? Michigan's largest amusement park awaits your family for a day (or 2) of summer's best. With over 40 rides with names like Mad Moose, Big Dipper, Wolverine Wildcat, and Shivering Timbers (the 3rd largest wooden roller coaster in the country), you can be sure that your day will be fun-filled! Don't worry there are also some "calmer" rides (7 are made just for younger children) including the Zachary Zoomer, a special scaled down coaster just for younger children. A tree house and play areas are also included for younger children. Wildwater Adventure admission is also included (the state's largest waterpark) with the Lazy River water tube ride, a wave pool, the Grand Rapids family water ride, and Michigan's longest waterslide.

HAMPTON INN OF MUSKEGON

Muskegon - 1401 East Ellis Rd 49444. (US 31 at Sternberg exit) www.hampton-inn.com/hi/muskegon or 231-799-8333. Set in Muskegon near rich forests and stunning beaches, this hotel is close to a variety of popular attractions, including PJ Hoffmaster State Park, The Lakes Mall, and Michigan's Adventure Theme Park. Their clean space, complimentary deluxe breakfast bar, warm indoor pool and whirlpool and location right near the mall and major routes is great.

New Era

COUNTRY DAIRY

New Era - 3476 S. 80th Ave. (US 31 to New Era exit. Take MI 20 east) 49446. Phone: (231) 861-4636 or (800) 243-7280. www.countrydairy.com. Tours: summers at 9am, 10:30am, noon, and 1:30pm Monday-Saturday. Also Saturdays during September and October at Noon and 1:30pm. Tour Prices: $6 adult/$3 child (3-16) Note: Farm Store and Deli serving Ice Cream (made on premises) for dessert.

Come visit the ShowBarn, which houses 50 top-producing, prize-winning Holstein cows. Start at Moo School and then take a guided, tractor-pulled wagon tour of a "working" dairy farm and milk processing facility. On your tour, you will be able to see how cows are milked, how milk is bottled or (on certain days) turned into cheese and ice cream. At the close of your tour, you can sample their famous Premium Chocolate Milk, or try some "Moochies" (cheddar cheese curds). Spiced Monterey Jack cheese (many varieties) is their specialty

> Ice cream combinations here all sound yummy - ex. Blue Moo, Apple Crisp, Cowfetti or Super Cow.

FREE ICE CREAM SOCIAL

New Era. Country Dairy. www.countrydairy.com. (231) 861-4636. The small town of New Era, population 600, welcomes around 3000 people each year for its annual free ice cream social. The workers at Country Dairy devote the day to greeting their guests with good old-fashioned country hospitality. They offer free tours of their processing plant, hayrides and many children's activities. Of course the main attraction is always the free ice cream tent! Guests are encouraged to try all 17 flavors of premium ice cream that are produced right there on the farm, with milk from their own cows. (first Saturday in July)

⊠

Newaygo

NEWAYGO STATE PARK

Newaygo - 2793 Beech Street (US131, exit 125 West) 49337. Phone: (231) 856-4452. www.michigan.gov/newaygo.

Newaygo State Park is a 99-site rustic campground, which sits atop 20-foot embankments overlooking the Hardy Dam Pond, a six-mile flooding of the Muskegon River. The park caters primarily to campers, anglers and recreational boaters/swimmers. The campground is nestled in oak and poplar forests and is noted for its large, private sites and scenic beauty. There is a 20-30 foot forested buffer between sites, and each site is provided with a picnic table and a fire ring

.

North Muskegon

DUCK LAKE STATE PARK

North Muskegon - 3560 Memorial Drive (US-31, take the Whitelake Drive (Duck Lake State Park) exit, west and go a half-mile to Whitehall Road) 49445. Phone: (231) 744-3480. www.michigan.gov/ducklake. (Day use park only). Admission: $8.00 per vehicle.

Duck Lake State Park is a 728 acre day use park, located in Muskegon County. Featuring a towering sand dune, the park stretches from the northern shore of Duck Lake to Lake Michigan. A sandy beach on Duck Lake is available and a boardwalk around the end of Duck Lake provides access to Lake Michigan for swimming. A paved path provides a pleasant stroll through the woods and along the Duck Lake shoreline. The park is closed to motor vehicle traffic in the winter, but accessible by skis and snowmobiles. The White Lake area, about five miles north, includes restaurants, shopping, marinas and free weekly summer concerts. Day use boating and fishing docks.

MUSKEGON STATE PARK

North Muskegon - 3560 Memorial Drive (US-31 to M-120 exit) 49445. Phone: (231) 744-3480. www.michigan.gov/muskegon. Admission: $8.00 per vehicle.

Features over 2 miles of shoreline on Lake Michigan and over 1 mile on Muskegon Lake. The vast expanse of Great Lakes sand beach ranks among the most beautiful in the world. Forested dunes join miles of Great Lakes shoreline. Twelve miles of marked hiking trails can be found in the park. The trails are a diverse series of loops that meander through a variety of landscapes, from flatland to bog; from lowland to the top of scenic sand dunes. The sports lodge is the focal point for winter activities at Muskegon State Park. Check out their luge runs. Camping, hiking trails, boating, fishing, swimming, and winter sports.

MUSKEGON WINTER SPORTS COMPLEX

North Muskegon - 462 Scenic Drive (Inside Muskegon State Park) 49445. Phone: (231) 744-9629 or (877) TRY LUGE. www.msports.org. Hours: Complex: 10am-10pm daily. Also Friday night, Saturday, Sunday beginning mid-December thru winter. Weekday leagues. Admission: Park vehicle pass is $8.00. Lesson & Open Time passes $25.00 - 40.00. (Includes coaching, sled, track use & helmet). Group rates and season passes. Skating/Skiing Use/Rentals: $3.00-$8.00. Note: Since size and physical ability are key factors in being able steer the sled, they allow anyone 48" or taller and from 8 years old on up to participate.

Are Mom and Dad ready to re-live their glory days of winter fun? A New 700 foot ice skate trail traverses through the woods! The unique ice skating trail actually runs through the beautiful woods of Muskegon State Park. Very unique and much more scenic. Of course there is the normal winter fun of ice skating and cross-country skiing trails, but that's only where the fun begins. The luge tracks (ice covered with banked turns) allow beginners and advanced sledders to go at their own pace (starting at different ascents on the tracks). You receive quality instruction and only advance as you master introductory slides. Speeds range from 25 - 45 MPH! Hang on!

Youth Wintersportsfest
22 Sports - 3 days - 3000 participants. This is for the novice as well as the conditioned athlete. www.wintersportsfest.com. Lots for the spectators to see.

Pentwater

MEARS STATE PARK

Pentwater - West Lowell Street (US-31, take the Pentwater exit and go west on Lowell Street) 49449. Phone: (248) 869-2051. www.michigan.gov/mears. Admission: $8.00 per vehicle.

Located on Lake Michigan with a several hundred yards of white sandy beach. Paved campsite lots are surrounded by fine sand, and a swimming beach is adjacent to the harbor pier. The existing park land was once owned by Charles Mears, an early settler of Pentwater. Shore fishing is very popular at Pentwater Lake in the fall, and anglers can expect to catch steelhead, perch, trout and smelt. Fishing from piers adjacent to the park is also a popular year-round activity. During the winter, Pentwater Lake provides excellent ice fishing. There is an interpretive trail about one mile in length that winds around to the top of Old Baldy, a wooded and sand-blown dune that provides an excellent view of the Lake Michigan shoreline, the town of Pentwater and the boat harbor

.

Rothbury

DOUBLE JJ RESORT

Rothbury - 5900 South Water Road (US 31 to Exit 136 - East) 49452. Phone: (800) DOUBLEJJ or (231) 894-4444. www.doublejj.com. Admission: Prices are all inclusive for standard activities offered at that time of year. Meals are included in weekly rates (avg. $500). Call or visit website for weekend, one-day festival and 3-day rates (start at only $99.00!) Note: The Double JJ Resort includes a number of accommodations including suites, condos, studio rooms, and cabins. Family cabins, tent camping, RVs, covered wagons or teepees, too.

Did you know that Michigan has "Dude Ranches"? Well...Double JJ is actually more than a dude ranch. Daily rides are offered and staffed by experienced "cowpokes" who will teach you all the skills along the way. There is even a rodeo at the end of the week where you can test your newly acquired talent. There is something for all ages. Adults and children (with supervision) can learn separately at there own pace. Some of the summer attractions and fun include a swimming hole with 145-foot waterslide, a petting farm, riding center, Wild West Shows for the adults in the dance hall (kids have their own shows), fishing, hot tubs, pools, and an award-winning 18-hole golf course. Winter activities include mushing, treking, snowshoeing, snowmobiling and cross-country skiing. Aaahhh...the life of a cowboy!

GOLD RUSH INDOOR WATER PARK: The Gold Rush is a medium-sized park with a Western motif. The park features the Miner's Plunge bowl ride, the Thunder Canyon family raft ride, a lazy river, some body and tube slides, and an indoor/outdoor whirlpool spa. Like most water parks, it also offers a family interactive play center with small slides and a tipping bucket. Only open to overnight guests. 9:00am-9:00pm or 10:00pm daily.

FALL FESTIVAL

Rothbury - Double JJ Ranch. www.doublejj.com. Old-fashioned hayride, pumpkin patch, corn maze, petting farm, Wild West Stunt Shows, cider and craft barn. Admission. (weekends end of September thru October)

⊠

Shelby

SHELBY MAN-MADE GEMSTONES

Shelby - 1330 Industrial Drive (off US 31) 49455. www.shelbygemfactory.com. Phone: (231) 861-2165. Hours: Showroom: Monday-Friday 9:00am-5:30pm. Saturday Noon-4:00pm. Admission: FREE.

In a 50 seat theatre you can learn the fascinating manufacturing process of how man can actually create gemstones such as diamonds, rubies, and sapphires. They are the largest manufacturer in the world of simulated and synthetic gemstones in the world. See how they can process smaller gems into larger ones at a much lesser cost. If your kids are into rocks (especially pretty colored ones, like our daughter) they'll love this place!

Whitehall

WHITE RIVER LIGHT STATION MUSEUM

Whitehall - 6199 Murray Road (US-31 to White Lake Dr. exit (west) to South Shore Dr., turn left and follow Museum signs) 49461. www.whiteriverlightstation.org. Phone: (231) 894-8265. Hours: Tuesday-Friday 11:00pm-5:00pm. Saturday-Sunday Noon-6:00pm (Summer). Close one hour earlier in September and October. Small admission fee.

At one time, the Muskegon/White Lake area was known as "The Lumber Queen of the World". Shipping over the Great Lakes was the primary means of transporting this lumber. This historic lighthouse was built in 1875 and your family can still climb the old spiral stairs to the top for a view of White Lake and Lake Michigan. Made of Michigan limestone and brick, it features photographs, paintings, artifacts and maritime stories.

NE CHAPTER AT A GLANCE

Alpena * Jesse Besser Museum

Atlanta * Clear Lake St Pk

Carp Lake * Wilderness St Pk

Cheboygan

* Aloha St Pk * Cheboygan St Pk

* Cheboygan Cty Historical

East Tawas

* Corsair Ski Area

* Tawas Point St Pk

* Tawas Point LIghthouse

* Perchville USA

Fairview * MI Ausable Valley RR

Gaylord

* Call of the Wild Museum

* Ostego Lake St Pk

* Alpenfest

Grayling

* Bottlecap Museum * Forestfest

* Grayling Fish Hatchery

* Hartwick Pines St Park

* Skiline Ski Area

* Wellington Farm Pk

* Ausable River Fest

Harrisville

* Negwegon St Pk * State Park

* Sturgeon Point Lighthouse

Houghton Lake * Tip Up Town USA

Indian River * Burt Lake St Pk

Mackinac Island

* Fort Mackinac St Hist Pk

* Mackinac Island Carriage Tours

* Mackinac Island St Pk

* Original Butterfly House

* Wings of Mackinac

* Grand Hotel * Mission Point Resort

Mackinaw City

* Colonial Michilimackinac St Hist Pk

* Ice Breaker Mackinaw

* Historic Mill Creek

* Mighty Mac Bridge & Museum

* Mackinac Island Ferrys

* Mackinaw Trolley Tours

* Old Mackinac Point LIghthouse

* Thunder Falls Family Waterpark

* Ironworkers Fest

* Mackinaw Fudge Fest

Onaway * State Park

Oscoda

* Iargo Springs

* Ausable River Queen

Ossineke * Dinosaur Gardens

Presque Isle * Lighthouse Museums

Rogers City

* Hoeft St Pk

* Presque Isle Cty Hist Museum

* Thompsons Harbor St Pk

Knoebe's Apple Farm

Roscommon

* North Higgins Lake St Pk

* South Higgins Lake St Pk

* Rifle River Rec Area

Chapter 3
North East

Mackinaw City

Mackinac Island

Cheboygan

23

27

CHEBOYGAN

Rogers City

PRESQUE ISLE

Presque Isle

Gaylord

MONTMORENCY

Alpena

OTSEGO

ALPENA

75

Grayling

OSCODA

ALCONA

23

CRAWFORD

Harrisville

ROSCOMMON

IOSCO

East Tawas

OGEMAW

27

UW

UE

NW

NE

CW

CE

SW

SE

A Quick Tour of our Hand-Picked Favorites Around...

North East Michigan

Michigan is defined not only by its waters but also by the forests once used for logging. Rivers and lakes for water sports, and thousands of miles of hiking trails thread their way among some 100 species of trees. The Mackinaw State Forest and Huron National Forest dominate the majority of Northeast Michigan. Four state parks—situated along the shores of Lake Huron - await fishing, camping and watersports enthusiasts. There are two different routes to cover this region – one, north on I-75, the other, north on US 23.

Starting along I-75, and just northeast of Grayling is **Hartwick Pines State Park**, where visitors can participate in a number of outdoor activities and learn about Michigan's logging history at the Hartwick Pines Logging Museum. Some call it an "outdoor cathedral of nature," walking along the Old Growth Forest Foot Trail as it winds through the forest behind the Visitor Center (full of "talking" trees and loggers).

If you take the scenic route along US 23, be sure to take your time and stop at several lighthouses along the way. Probably the best overall maritime town to visit for lighthouse exploring is **Presque Isle**. Climb the steps and hear the stories of storms and hardships of keepers. Alpena, also located on Lake Huron, is the center of commerce and culture in this sparsely populated region of Michigan. For a break from recreation, visit the **Besser Museum**. Where else can you find a Picasso, a Planetarium, and Indian artifacts all in one place in Northeast Michigan?

Whether you take US 23 or I-75, they both end up in the same magical place – Mackinaw or Mackinac (pronounced Mac-eh-naw). European fur traders and settlers established a stockade village on the Straits of Mackinac, a key strategic point in the Upper Great Lakes. This settlement is now preserved in time as **Colonial Michilimackinac**. Outside of the settlement, today's Mackinaw City offers visitors a 'resort town' environment that allows walking to most every attraction on the mainland. In the mix of old and new there are 3 other National Historic Sites: Old Mackinac Point Lighthouse, Historic Mill Creek, and **Fort Mackinac**. When it's time to return to the present you will find a Family Waterpark, parks, beaches, and over 100 shops and dining to delight you... all within the backdrop of the **Mighty Mackinac Bridge**. Can't decide what to do first? We highly recommend the **Mackinaw Trolley** Tours to get an overall picture of the area. Let your kids ring the trolley bell!

For a little slower pace, take a ferry over to **Mackinac Island**. Since motor vehicles aren't permitted on the island, we suggest you take a guided carriage tour or rent bicycles for a 5-6 mile self-guided tour around the entire island. Your kids will like the adventure of being on an island with no fear of getting run over – just cobblestone streets and coastline roads sprinkled with carriages and bikes. Many young families may just opt to day trip here but if you stay the night and want to make it special – the Grand is grand and Mission Point is full of activities for kids.

Sites and attractions are listed in order by City, Zip Code, and Name. Symbols indicated represent:

 Festivals   Restaurants   Lodging

Alpena

JESSE BESSER MUSEUM

Alpena - 491 Johnson Street (Off US 23 near Alpena General Hospital) 49707. Phone: (989) 356-2202. www.bessermuseum.org. Hours: Monday-Saturday 10:00am-5:00pm.. Admission: $5.00 adult, $3.00 senior and child (5-17). Notes: Planetarium extra. Planetarium programs are Saturday at 2:00pm (Under age 5 not admitted to Planetarium).

Mostly local history with a re-created 1800's street of shops and cabins. If you come during a festival or special event weekend, make sure you see the display on the role of concrete in the area. The concrete block-making machine was perfected here in a land rich with limestone. Other permanent exhibits include: Gallery of Man, Lumbering and Farming, a Focult Pendulum, Area Fossils and Restored Historic Buildings. Where else can you find a Picasso, a Planetarium, Indian artifacts and a Street of Shops all in one place in Northeast Michigan?

MICHIGAN BROWN TROUT FESTIVAL

Alpena - Downtown and Alpena Mall. (800) 4-ALPENA or www.alpenami-browntrout. com. The Great Lakes' longest continuous fishing tournament. Anglers vie for top prizes and all can enjoy Art On the Bay, a Kid's Carnival, Fish Pond, and FREE concerts. (mid-to-end of July)

Atlanta

CLEAR LAKE STATE PARK

Atlanta - 20500 M-33 (M-33 nine miles north of Atlanta) 49709. Phone: (989) 785-4388. www.michigan.gov/clearlake. Admission: $8.00 per vehicle.

Located in elk country, Clear Lake State Park is a quiet, secluded retreat offering a sandy beach and a shallow swimming area that is ideal for children. The 133-acre Clear Lake is spring fed and has a depth of 100 feet. A variety of fish species have been planted and the lake is excellent for trout and smallmouth bass. Two paved launch sites provide access to the spring-fed lake. Camping, hiking, and winter sports.

Carp Lake

WILDERNESS STATE PARK

Carp Lake - 898 Wilderness Park Drive (west of Mackinaw City by CR 81) 49718. Phone: (231) 436-5381. www.michigan.gov/wilderness. Admission: $8.00 per vehicle.

Wilderness State Park offers visitors a variety of year-round recreational activities within its over 10,000 acres. Wilderness areas and 26 miles of beautiful Lake Michigan shoreline (some for swimming) provide great places to observe nature from the numerous trails throughout the park. The park's 250 modern campsites are divided into two units, the Lakeshore and the Pines. Six rustic cabins and three rustic bunkhouses are additional options for accommodations within the park. More than 16 miles stretch across the East Boundary, South Boundary, Nebo, Sturgeon Bay, Swamp Line and Big Stone trails. These trails are shared with all bicycles, including mountain bikes. Boating, fishing, too.

Cheboygan

ALOHA STATE PARK

Cheboygan - 4347 Third Street (M-33 South) 49721. www.michigan.gov/aloha. Phone: (231) 625-2522. Admission: $8.00 per vehicle.

The largest freshwater lake in Michigan (Mullett Lake) is here. Aloha State Park offers modern camping on beautiful Mullett Lake. Whether fishing, boating, swimming or picnicking, Aloha is close to many of Michigan's most famous travel attractions at the Straits of Mackinaw. Mackinaw to Hawks Rails to Trails runs through Aloha State Park. The primary surface of the trail is gravel. During the summer this trail is non-motorized and used for hiking, equestrian, and biking. During the winter months the trail is groomed for snowmobiling. Campsites are near the Park's boat launch for those traveling this route.

CHEBOYGAN COUNTY HISTORICAL MUSEUM

Cheboygan - 404 South Huron Street 49721. www.cheboyganhistorycenter.org. Phone: (231) 627-9597. Hours: Tuesday-Saturday 1:00-4:00pm. Admission: $500 adult (18+).

The county sheriff used to call this place home from 1882 - 1969 - it even was the area jail complete with 8 cells. Today, these cells have become exhibit areas featuring local history including: lumbering, farming, and lifestyle. Walking down the corridor of REAL jail cell displays intrigues the kids. See a recreated late 1800's "parlor room", a barber shop (look for old-fashioned curling irons), bedrooms, and even a schoolroom. Look for the old TV's and record players. The log cabin on site was part of a Native American village on Burt Lake built in the late 1800's.

CHEBOYGAN STATE PARK

Cheboygan - 4490 Beach Road 49721. www.michigan.gov/cheboygan. Phone: (231) 627-2811. Admission: $8.00 per vehicle.

Cheboygan State Park is open all year for a variety of activities. A system of well-marked trails through the park provides access to scenic Lake Huron vistas, glimpses of rare wildflowers and the lake shore species. Modern camping, rustic cabins, and teepees are all available within the park. The Little Billy Elliot Creek flows through the park and is known for its trout. Fishing is also plentiful in Duncan Bay. Several well-marked cross-country skiing trails provide expansive winter vistas of the Lake Huron shoreline and inland natural areas. One of the main highlights of the park is the Cheboygan Point Light or the Duncan Bay Beach.

East Tawas

CORSAIR SKI AREA

East Tawas - 218 West Bay Street 48730. Phone: (989) 362-2001 or (800) 55-TAWAS. www.n-sport.com/crosscountryskiing.html.   Admission: Donation to pay for trail grooming.

A cross country ski area with over 35 miles of groomed trails. Visit their warming cabin for a well deserved and welcome respite after an invigorating day of skiing. All skill levels. Rentals are available in town. Great picnic area and hiking in summer and fall. Help your kids try their luck at trout fishing in the Silver Creek.

TAWAS POINT STATE PARK

East Tawas - 686 Tawas Beach Road (3 miles east of town off US 23) 48730. Phone: (989) 362-5041. www.michigan.gov/tawaspoint.   Admission: $8.00 per vehicle. Additional $2.00 per person for lighthouse tour (only open summers).

Check out the 1876, 70 foot lighthouse, TAWAS POINT LIGHTHOUSE. The lighthouse is open to the public for viewing by appointment or on special occasions. The lighthouse stands 70 feet above Lake Huron and the walls at the base are 6 feet thick. The Coast Guard station adjacent to the park on Lakeview Drive was also built in 1876 and is the only surviving example of the First Series Life Saving Stations built on the Great Lakes. The park overall has been referred to as the "Cape Cod of the Midwest". Mini-Cabins and campsites, beach, birding (best in May), nature trails, boating and fishing are there, too.

PERCHVILLE USA

East Tawas - (800) 55-TAWAS. www.tawas.com. Ice and shorelines. Ice fishing contests for all ages, ice demolition derby, all-you-can-eat perch dinners, and the annual Polar Bear Swim where adults cut a giant hole in the frozen bay, jump in and swim. Children's ice/snow games. Admission. (first or second weekend of February)

☒ _____

Fairview

MICHIGAN AUSABLE VALLEY RAILROAD

Fairview - 230 South Abbe Road (I-75 exit 202 north. Off SR33, 3.5 miles south of the blinker light in town) 48621. www.michiganausablevalleyrailroad.com. Phone: (989) 848-2229. Hours: Weekends and Holidays 10:00am-5:00pm. (Memorial Day-Labor Day). Also Fall Color tour first two weekends of October. Tours: 1.5 mile trip takes approx. 18 minutes. Admission: $6.00 (ages over 2). Note: Quaint depot and gift shop where you can purchase tickets and fresh, hot popcorn.

This ¼ scale train offers visitors a calm, scenic tour which travels through a jackpine forest (Huron National Forest) and overlooks the Comins Creek Valley. You'll get to pass through a 115 foot wooden tunnel and over two wooden trestles (one of them is 220 feet long). Some passengers get a glimpse of wildlife such as deer, hawks, heron, beaver and maybe even elk or bear!

Gaylord

CALL OF THE WILD MUSEUM

Gaylord - 850 South Wisconsin Avenue (I-75 exit 282, then east on Main Street, then south on Wisconsin) 49735. www.gocallofthewild.com. Phone: (989) 732-4336 or (800) 835-4347. Hours: Daily 9:00am-9:00pm. (mid-June-Labor Day), Daily 9:30am-6:00pm. (Rest of year). Admission: $4.50-$7.00. Note: Also at location are Bavarian Falls Adventure Golf, Go Carts, Krazy Kars Tot Ride. Gift shop.

The museum is full of dioramas of over 60 North American Animals in natural settings. As you look over displays of elk, moose, black bear, timber wolves, etc., you'll learn about their behavior and habitat and sounds. The Michigan History area has stories recounted by an early fur trapper named Joseph. The Four Seasons Display of Michigan changes as you watch. They have an observation beehive there, too. Before you begin your adventure into the museum, make sure you pick up an activity sheet to help you discover a little more as you go through. Once you are finished going through the museum, you can turn in each activity sheet for a prize.

OSTEGO LAKE STATE PARK

Gaylord - 7136 Old 27 South (off I-75 south, Take I-75 to the village of Waters, Exit 270, and go west to Old 27. Go north on Old 27 five miles to park) 49735. www.michigandnr.com/parksandtrails/ParksandTrailsInfo.aspx?id=482. Phone: (989) 732-5485. Admission: $8.00 per vehicle.

"The Alpine Village." The park is shaded with large oak, maple and pine. The park encompasses 62 acres and provides more than a half mile of sandy beach and large sites near or within sight of the lake. For those without a boat, the park has an accessible fishing pier. The Otsego Lake Park Store offers hand-dipped ice cream, soda, candy, pizza, subs along with T-shirts and sweatshirts. The store is open from Memorial Day weekend to Labor Day weekend. Camping/ mini cabin, boating, swimming (mid-April to early November).

ALPENFEST

Gaylord - Downtown. www.gaylordalpenfest.com. (800) 345-8621. The featured activity is a Swiss tradition of the burning of the Boogg - where residents place all their troubles on slips of paper and throw them into a fire. Many parades and the world's largest coffee break. (third week in July)

Grayling

BOTTLECAP MUSEUM

Grayling - 231 Michigan Avenue (uptown Grayling, Dawson & Stevens Classic 50's Diner) 49738. www.bottlecapmuseum.com.

Lunch and dinners are served in this 50s motif restaurant and museum. More than 7,000 pieces of Coca-Cola memorabilia once housed in Sparr have been placed in the diner. The oldest pieces in the collection are bottles dating back to the 1890s. Among the original owners favorite pieces is a driver's hat from the 1930s. While  you're waiting on your burgers and fries, take a look at the various displays behind glass around the store.

GRAYLING FISH HATCHERY

Grayling - North Down River Road (I-75 to exit 254) 49738. Phone: (989) 348-9266. www.graylingfishhatchery.com. Hours: Daily Noon-6:00pm (Memorial Day-Labor Day). Admission: $3 adult, $2 child (5-12), $12.00 family.

It's always fun to watch kid's eyes light up at a "fish farm". See 11 ponds that contain more than 40,000 trout. See fish ranging from tiny aquarium size (2 inches long) to several pounds (28 inches long), and yes, you can even buy some to take home (priced by the inch). Fish food is available from dispensers for a nominal fee and is a great way to really bring the fish to life. Entertainment and demos every Sunday at 2:00pm.

HARTWICK PINES STATE PARK

Grayling - 4216 Ranger Road (I-75 exit 259 - on M-93) 49738. Phone: (989) 348-2537 center or (989) 348-7068 park. www.michigan.gov/loggingmuseum. Hours: Park open 8:00am-10:00pm. Museum buildings 9:00am-4:00pm (May-October) and for special events. Logging Museum is closed November - April. Admission: $8.00 per vehicle admission to park. Museum is free. Note: Bike trails, Braille trails, hiking, camping, fishing, picnic areas, winter sports, small gift shop. Summers-living history programs along the Forest Trail.

Some call it an "outdoor cathedral of nature", walking along the Old Growth Forest Foot Trail as it winds through the forest behind the Visitor Center. A paved trail through the forest leads visitors to the 300-year-old Monarch pine, a remnant of the ancient forests that once covered most of northern Michigan. Along the 1¼ mile long trail, you can stop at the Logging Museum (open May-October only). Depending on the event, you'll see logging wheels and other logging equipment, a steam sawmill, plus logger's quarters in use. Be sure to stop in the Michigan Forest Visitor Center before your walk out into the pines. See the history of logging - both past cut and run phases - and modern conservation forestry. The audiovisual show gives you a great overview. The self-guided tour takes the visitor on a journey through time that begins with the Ice Age and ends with a look at how Michigan's healthy forest lands of today are growing more each year than is harvested. Did you know, today, there is more paper recycled than made from trees cut down? Find hands-on exhibits on computer (Forest Management Simulation), dioramas (Reading the Rings, Sounds of Birds), and the talking "Living Tree"... or talking Loggers and Rivermen displays. Their guides and programs have a great reputation.

FOREST FEST

Grayling - Hartwick Pines State Park, (I-75 & M-93). (989) 348-2537. Renaissance Forester performance of logging songs, visit by Smoky Bear, displays of DNR fire-fighting equipment, a tree giveaway, pine walks and Logging Museum (second Saturday in August)

SKYLINE SKI AREA

Grayling - 4020 Skyline Road (I-75 to exit 251) 49738. Phone: (989) 275-5445. Hours: Thursday evenings, Friday-Sunday & Holidays 10:00am-9:00pm.

Skyline Ski Area in Grayling, Michigan is an intimate ski resort geared primarily toward beginning and intermediate skiers. The resort features a peak elevation of 1,516 feet and a modest vertical drop of 210 feet, making it an ideal place for youngsters to learn to ski or snowboard.

The resort offers 11 lifts and 10 trails that feature all-natural snow that's groomed daily. The trails and slopes are carved from Michigan's woodlands, consisting primarily of Aspen and Poplar stands, making for scenic views, especially from the resort at the summit.

WELLINGTON FARM PARK

Grayling - 6940 S Military Rd. (I-75 49738. www.wellingtonfarmpark.org. Phone: (989) 348-5187. Hours: Friday, Saturday, Sunday 9:00am-5:00pm (Memorial Day weekend thru October). Seasonal festivals throughout the year focus on old-fashioned farming themes. Admission: $5.50-$7.50 per person.

Wellington Farm, USA is a 60-acre open-air interpretive museum designed to provide an educational opportunity for visitors to experience life as it was in rural mid-America during The Great Depression. Located in the former Michigan Central Depot, the museum details local history from Camp Grayling military history to lumbering and fire fighting. You can walk through historic buildings, see them in operation when scheduled, and usually be fortunate enough to sample some freshly prepared food/goodies of Depression-era inside the sumptuous Summer Kitchen. The museum also has a railroad caboose, a farm shed, a trapper's cabin and a display dedicated to the greatest archer of all time - Fred Bear. Watch audio visual tapes of some of the area's old-timers telling family histories and stories of the early days.

PUMPKIN & APPLE FEST

Grayling - Wellington Farm Park, (I-75 to exit 251). www.wellingtonfarmpark.org. (888) OLD-FARM or Visit the pumpkin patch, watch cider-making,   corn-husking, wood-carving, milling and blacksmithing demos. Punkin Chunkin – catapult pumpkins, corn maze, hayrides. Admission. (weekends in October)

AU SABLE RIVER INTERNATIONAL CANOE MARATHON & RIVER FESTIVAL

Grayling to Oscoda - Downtown & along Au Sable River. www.ausablecanoemarathon. org. (800) 937-8837. Called the world's toughest spectator sport - why? Probably because it's tough to follow canoes by land and a good chunk of the race is through the night until daybreak. Because the kids might only be able to catch the beginning or end of this canoe race, downtown areas are prepared to fill the time with family activities like Youth Canoe Races, Children's Fishing Contest, a Festival Parade and Dance, and a tour of Camp Grayling - the nation's largest National Guard training facility. (last full weekend in July)

Harrisville

HARRISVILLE STATE PARK

Harrisville - 248 State Park Road (US-23 South of M-72) 48740. Phone: (989) 724-5126. www.michigan.gov/harrisville. Admission: $8.00 per vehicle.

Harrisville State Park features a campground/mini-cabins and day-use area nestled in a stand of pine and cedar trees along the sandy shores of Lake Huron. The park is within walking distance of the resort town of Harrisville. Over ½ mile of Lake Huron frontage with Cedar Run Nature Trail, boating, fishing, swimming, bicycle trails, and winter sports.

NEGWEGON STATE PARK

Harrisville - 248 State Park Road Take US-23 12 miles N. of Harrisville to Black River Road. 48740. www.michigan.gov/negwegon. Phone: (989) 724-5126. Note: Small gift shop.

A rustic, undeveloped area for hiking. Please use caution when visiting Negwegon as the roads into the park are often so sandy that a four-wheel drive vehicle is needed. No camping, no services.

STURGEON POINT LIGHTHOUSE

Harrisville - Sturgeon Point Road (5 miles north of Harrisville State Park entrance, off US 23, Lakeshore Drive, follow signs) 48740. Phone: (989) 724-5056. www.alconahistoricalsociety.com Hours: Daily 10:00am-4:00pm (Memorial Day-September). Lighthouse Tower Open: Noon-3:00pm on Friday, Saturday & Sunday.

An 1869 lighthouse. Tour the restored lighthouse keeper's house, and the tower on weekends. The stark contrast of the white painted bricks against the bright red trim makes the building very photogenic. Sitting on the shore end of a long and rocky submerged finger of land that juts into Lake Huron, it is plain to see why a lighthouse was needed here.

Houghton Lake

TIP-UP TOWN, USA

Houghton Lake - www.tip-up-townusa.com. (800) 248-LAKE. Chilly festival. Ice fishing with tip-up rigs (hence, the name of the town), parade and games such as ice softball, snow mobile racing or snow eating contests. Admission. (last two weekends in January)

Indian River

BURT LAKE STATE PARK

Indian River - 6635 State Park Drive (I-75 exit 310 west to SR 68 to Old US 27) 49749. Phone: (231) 238-9392. www.michigan.gov/burtlake.   Admission: $8.00 per vehicle.

Burt Lake State Park is open from April to November (depending on the snowfall). It is located on the southeast corner of Burt Lake with 2,000 feet of sandy shoreline. Shoreline fishing is available on the northern boundary of the park along the Sturgeon River. Great beaches on the state's third largest lake, the park has numerous campsites and cabins, boating and rentals, swimming, and winter sports.

Mackinac Island

FORT MACKINAC STATE HISTORIC PARK

Mackinac Island - (on the bluff above downtown Mackinac Island) 49757. Phone: (906) 847-3328. www.mackinacparks.com. Hours: Daily 9:30am-6:30pm or later (mid-June to mid August). Daily until 4:30pm (early May to mid-June and mid-August to early October). Admission: $11.00 adult, $6.50 youth (5-17). Combo tickets for Fort Mac, Colonial Michi and Mill Creek are available at great discounts. Note: Food available at Tea Room (lunch). Pets are welcome. Educators: lesson plans on Kids & Teachers page.

Your carriage is greeted by a period dressed soldier inviting strangers to visit. Children and families will want to see the short audio visual presentation in the Post Commissary Theater. It's quick and simple but enough to "pull you in". Next, if it's close to the top of the hour, be sure to check out the kid-friendly, wonderfully amusing, cannon firing and rifle firing demonstrations. Maybe volunteer to help the soldiers (check out the funny, pointed hats). The Post Hospital and Officer's Quarters (costumes/hands-on or "Hanging with Harold") and Blockhouses (short narrative by an animatronic figure) will intrigue the kids. In the new exhibit space, Military Medicine, you can hear through a giant stethoscope, visit with a virtual Post Surgeon on rounds, and take a look at a frostbitten foot! On your way in or out of the complex, be sure to visit the Soldier's Barracks exhibits featuring "Mackinac: An Island Famous in These

Regions". Mackinac Island history from Furs (touch some) to Fish (step on a dock and listen to the fishermen come into port) to No Cars (1898 law) to Fudge! Oh, by the way, be sure to check and see if your ancestor was a Victorian soldier at Fort Mackinac. Well done, folks.

MACKINAC ISLAND CARRIAGE TOURS

Mackinac Island - (Across from Arnold Ferry Dock - Main Street, Downtown) 49757. Phone: (906) 847-3307. www.mict.com. Hours: Daily 9:00am-5:00pm (mid - June - Labor Day). Daily 9:00am-3:00pm (mid-May to mid-June and Labor Day to October 1st). Daily 9:00am-2:00pm (rest of October). Admission: $24.50 adult, $10.00 child (5-12). Tours: 1 hour & 45 minutes. YOu also have on/off privileges at several "hot spots".

Step Back In Time...

Since motor vehicles aren't permitted on the Island, this is one fun way to leisurely see the sites. It keeps the island quaint to hear the clip-clop sound of carriages - we think you'll agree!

It's guaranteed you'll hear amusing stories of the history (past & present) of the island. The multi-seated carriages stop at all of these highlights: Arch Rock (which story of formation do you believe?), Skull Cave, the Governor's Mansion, Grand Hotel, Fort Mackinac, Surrey Hill shops and snacks (including Wings of Mackinac Butterfly House), and the horse's stable area. Look for several "parking lots" full of bikes and carriages! We recommend this tour on your first trip to the island.

MACKINAC ISLAND STATE PARK

Mackinac Island - 49757. www.mackinacparks.com. Phone: (906) 847-3328. Hours: Park open 24/7. Visitors Center open every season 9:00am-4:00pm, except winter. Admission: FREE for center. Tours of historic homes require fee of $3-$5 (age 5+). Tours: Summers - guided tours w/ costumed interpreters. Beaumont Memorial (dedicated to study of human digestion), Blacksmith, Biddle House (crafts), McGulpin House, Indian Dorm are off premises but part of package fee in the summer. Many archeological digs take place every few years. Note: Visitors Center located downtown on waterfront. Maps of numerous different trails to bike and/or walk (and easy-reading history of places you'll see) is available on many ferries or at the Visitors Center.

Most of Mackinac Island is preserved as a state park. Stretching eight miles around the island's perimeter, M-185 is a scenic shoreline road and the nation's only state highway without motor vehicle traffic. There are 70 miles of roads and trails within Mackinac Island State Park, most of which are wooded inland trails for hikers, bikers and horseback riders in spring, summer and fall. There are 1,800 acres under canopies of cedars, birches and crossings of creatures like butterflies. The prehistoric geological formations, Arch Rock and Sugar Loaf, are natural limestone wonders that tower over the Straits. These can be viewed from below on biking trails or from a walking overview. Fort Holmes features a panoramic view of the Fort Mackinac and the Straits of Mackinac at the island's highest point - 320 feet above Lake Level. Look for historic caves and nature trails around most every turn.

ORIGINAL BUTTERFLY HOUSE

Mackinac Island - 1308 McGulpin Street (Huron Street north to Church Street west to McGulpin) 49757. Phone: (906) 847-3972. www.originalbutterflyhouse.com. Hours: 10:00am-7:00pm (Summer), 10:00am-6:00pm (Labor Day- late October). Admission: $8.50 adult, $4.00 child (4-11).

See several hundred live butterflies from Asia, Central and South America and the United States in free flight. You will be amazed at the size of the insects that live in the tropical regions of the world. 14" Walking Sticks, and 6" Centipedes along with the world's largest Cicada and Heaviest Bug are on display, while live reptiles and amphibians living in their natural habitats help keep things fun for the kids. Kids of all ages will love the new interactive displays and our "Turtle Adventure Park". A great setting of tropical gardens. One of America's first butterfly houses featured in popular magazines.

WINGS OF MACKINAC

Mackinac Island - (Surrey Hill Shops, just past Grand Hotel) 49757. Phone: (906) 847-WING. www.wingsofmackinac.com.

The all-glass Conservatory holds beautiful lush plants surrounded by hundreds of butterflies, dancing around you to gentle instrumental music. See exotic butterflies from around the world including: White Peacocks, Long-Tailed Skippers, Painted Ladies, Spice Bush Swallowtails, Graphium Decolors, Ruddy Daggerwings, Blue Morphos, Tiger Swallowtails and Monarchs. Curators available to answer questions. Admission: $4-$7.50 (age 5+).

LILAC FESTIVAL

Mackinac Island - www.mackinacislandlilacfestival.org (800) 4-LILACS. Lilacs were first planted by French missionaries a couple of hundred years ago and the bushes still bloom full of white and purple flowers each year. Dancers, famous fudge, Grand Lilac Parade (100+ horses pulling lilac-theme floats with clowns and marching bands. (June)

GRAND HOTEL

Mackinac Island - (from the ferry docks, head west one-half mile). (906) 847-3331 or (800) 33-GRAND or www.grandhotel.com. At 660 feet, Grand Hotel's Front Porch (full of white rockers) is the world's largest. Self-guided grounds tours are $10.00 per person if not a hotel guest. The kitchen staff of 100 serves as many as 4,000 meals per day. Their gourmet food is unforgettable! Ask to take a Kitchen Tour to see how they do it. Kids won't believe the large number of plates, pies and potatoes they use. (Kitchen tours by pre-arrangement only or at special events). Recreational activities include: golf, tennis, croquet, bocci ball, swimming (outdoor pool), bicycling, saddle horses, carriage tours, duck pin bowling and a game room. Children's Programs (day or evening-3 hours)

include "kids-style" lunches or dinners and fun group games, arts and crafts or a hike or tour. Rebecca's Playroom is open daily for families to enjoy games, crafts, videos and play when they are not conducting a paid program. Off-peak or special family rates begin at around $400.00 per night (includes full breakfast and five-course dinner and gratuities). Watch the movies "Somewhere in Time"

Wow...the front porch is over 600 feet long!

(Christopher Reeve/Jane Seymour) or "This Time for Keeps" (Esther Williams) before your visit to get the feel for the place. If you forget, they have a TV/VCR in every room and a copy of "Somewhere in Time" ready to watch. Remnants of these movies are found throughout the grounds (i.e.. Esther Williams pool or "Is it you?" twin trees). Believe it or not, this place is not stuffy...just casually elegant...best for a special treat or occasion.

MISSION POINT RESORT

Mackinac Island - (from the ferry docks, head east one-half mile). Phone: (906) 847-3312 or (800) 833-7711. www.missionpoint.com. This is truly a "family-friendly" resort and with the features they keep adding...it's a destination to stay at for a few days. You can just hang out around the grounds with amenities like: outdoor heated pool, tennis, croquet, horseshoes, video arcade/ game room and lawn bowling. Or, sign up for a one hour Island sail or Ferry tour. Now, rent bikes or in-line skates and explore the 8 mile Island trail. They have four eateries and kids 12 & under eat FREE (most

A great way to see the island... and the best part, no cars!

restaurants). They have hayrides, picnic games, poolside bingo and Sundae parties, too. Probably the best feature is their children's program: Mac The Moose Kid's Club, open to all youngsters ages 12 and under. Character meets, parties and tuck-in services are available for a fee. The Discovery Club Center has themes like "Space Day", "Nature Day", "Under the Sea", or "Wild West Day". They have a Tweeners club, too (ages 11-14). Rates: Start at $149.00 per night. Open May - October.

Mackinaw City

COLONIAL MICHILIMACKINAC STATE HISTORIC PARK

Mackinaw City - 102 Straits Ave (Downtown under the south side of Mackinac Bridge - Exit 339 off I-75) 49701. Phone: (231) 436-5563. www.mackinacparks.com. Hours: Daily 9:00am-4:00pm (May to early October). Extended hours until 6:00pm (mid-June to mid-August). Admission: $11.00 adult, $6.50 youth (5-17). Combo tickets for Fort Mac, Colonial Michi and Mill Creek are available at great discounts. Note: Many festivals are held here including encampments and Colonial weddings. Pets are welcome. Educators: Lesson Plan: http://www.mackinacparks. com/Userfiles/File/CM_Adventure_JP.pdf.

"Join the Redcoats. Watch a Dig. Dance a Jig". In the Summer, costumed docents (in character) demonstrate musket /cannon firing, cooking, blacksmithing, barracks living, church life, and trading. Pies cook near fireplaces, chickens roam free, and an amusing soldier leads you on a tour of the village. Originally occupied by the French, then the British, even the Indians - an audiovisual program will explain the details. Archeological digs are held in the summer to look for ongoing significant finds. What you see today on this site is a reconstruction of how the fortified village appeared in the 1770s, based on evidence gathered during the nation's longest archaeological excavation! Be sure to check out the updated "Treasure From the Sand" exhibit as it takes you to a

Famous explorers in Michigan that looked a lot like our family!

unique underground tunnel display of subterranean artifacts recovered. In the Soldiers Barracks hands-on building: Dress up, stir the pot, lie in a bunk, try on coats, play a game or go into the "Black Hole" - a dark "time-out". Many areas of this park engage the kids interest - how cool to play (and learn) in a real fort!

HISTORIC MILL CREEK

Mackinaw City - South US 23 (5 minutes southeast of town) 49701. Phone: (231) 436-7301. www.mackinacparks.com. Hours: Daily 9:00am-5:30pm (mid-June to mid-August). Daily 9:00am-4:30pm (May to mid-June) & (Labor Day to late September). Admission: $8 adult, $4.75 youth (6-17). Good combo rates when add Fort Michilimackinac, Old Lighthouse or Fort Mackinac. Note: Cook house Snack Pavilion. Museum Store. Forest trails with working beaver dam. Educators: http://www.mackinacparks.com/Userfiles/File/Historic_Mill_Creek.pdf.

As you walk along wooden planked paths, notice the different tree names - Thistleberry, Ironwood, etc. You'll have an opportunity to see a replica 18th century industrial complex - the oldest sawmill yard to provide finished lumber - in the Great Lakes Region. Water-powered sawmill and sawpit demos are given daily (Summers -lumberjack demos). Participants can help demo old & "newer", easier techniques to saw wood (which would you rather do?). There's also a reconstructed millwrights' house on site along with a museum. The audiovisual orientation is only 12 minutes long and is a great way to understand Michigan lumber history. Did you know a local amateur historian discovered this site, accidentally, in  1972? Creatures of the Forest is a naturalist outdoor "forest" talk - dress up as a beaver (why the raincoat?) and learn how creatures and trees coexist. New last year is the high ropes nature experience. Soar like an eagle down the Eagle's Flight Zip Line. Walk through the treetops on the Forest Canopy Bridge. For the youngest adventurers, exercise body and mind by exploring the Water Power Station and fostering interaction in the Forest Friends Children's Play Area. Now they have something for toddlers through teens.

ICE BREAKER MACKINAW

Mackinaw City - 131 S. Huron Ave (Chief Wawatam railroad dock) 49701. Phone: (231) 436-9825. www.themackinaw.org. Hours: Daily 9am-5pm (mid May - early October). Daily til 7pm each summer. Admission: $11.00 adult, $6.00 child (6-17) Note: Recommended to wear closed-toe shoes.

When commissioned, Mackinaw was the most powerful and capable icebreaker in the world. During World War 2, the Mackinaw had a crew of 140 and broke ice 24 hours. She is still the standard by which other icebreakers are measured. Hop aboard and take a look around. What jobs did seamen perform on board? How do you navigate an ice breaker? Note the narrow spacing in the ship's steel ribs that distinguish her as an icebreaker.

MACKINAC BRIDGE MUSEUM AND "MIGHTY MAC" BRIDGE

Mackinaw City - 231 East Central Avenue (Downtown within view of bridge) 49701. Phone: (231) 436-5534. www.mackinacbridge.org. Hours: Daily 8:00am-Midnight (May-October). Bridge open 24 hours. FREEBIES: Kids Corner page online.

Go to the upstairs museum at Mama Mia's Pizza (donations only). Watch the all new digitally re-mastered movie covering the history and construction of

A mega-bridge that is 5 miles long - wow!

the Mackinac Bridge back in the mid-1950's. Why build the longest bridge ever - the "bridge that couldn't be built"? When you see the black & white photos of the long lines, staging cars to get on ferry boats to cross over the lake to the Upper Peninsula, you'll see the reason. On display, are the original spinning wheels that spun and ran cable (41,000 miles of it!) across the bridge; the original wrench (9-10 feet long) used to tighten anchor bolts on the towers; and most interesting, the hard hats of the numerous iron workers. Now, pay the $2.50 toll and cross the 5 mile long steel super-structure! On a windy day the bridge bows or swings out to the east or west as much as 35 feet...you won't feel it though...really!

The Mackinac Bridge is the 3rd longest suspension bridge in the world!

BRIDGE WALK

St. Ignace to Mackinaw City. www.mackinacbridge.org. This annual crossing draws an average of 50,000 participant walkers. Starting in St. Ignace, the walkers head south across the Mackinac Bridge to the other side in Mackinaw City. This is the only time civilians are allowed to walk over the bridge. If you complete the 5 mile walk, you'll receive a Bridge Walk Certificate and enjoy a celebration in town. (800) 666-0160. (Labor Day - September)

MACKINAC ISLAND FERRY SERVICES

Mackinaw City - (Stops/Dock Pickups are clearly marked) 49701. Call for season schedules. Rain or shine. (early May - mid to late October). Note: Budget $24.00 for adults, about 1/2 price for kids. (Round Trip)

- ❑ ARNOLD LINE FERRY. www.arnoldline.com. (800) 542-8528. Smooth trips, large ships, comfortable seats and cabins. Restrooms.

- ❑ SHEPLER'S FERRY. (800) 828-6157 or www.sheplersferry.com. Fast trips with very courteous and efficient staff. Restrooms. Narrative on the way over.

- ❑ STAR LINE FERRY. (800) 638-9892 or www.mackinacferry.com. Newest fleet. Most scheduled daily departures. Restrooms.

MACKINAW TROLLEY TOURS

Mackinaw City - (pickup at hotels) 49701. www.mackinawtrolley.com. Phone: (231) 436-7812. Tours: off peak season general transport tours of the city only: Narrated $3 historical tour is priced just right for everyone looking to see Mackinaws timeless historical sites.Note: During your tour, if you climb Castle Rock, you earn a sticker! This is a wonderfully organized tour with amusing stories and enough stops along the way to keep the kids attention from wandering. Try a different trip each visit! Kids get to ring the trolley bell, too.

Here are some of the best trolley tours for families:

- ❑ HISTORICAL TOUR OVER THE BRIDGE: Ride through history on the Mackinaw Trolley as they narrate happenings and events along the way. Fort Michilimackinac area, Old Mackinac Point Lighthouse, Train and Car Ferry Docks, The Mackinac Bridge, Father Marquette's Mission and Grave Site at St. Ignace, Indian lore at Ojibwa Museum and the magnificent view from Castle Rock. 2½ hours. Departs 10:00am daily (mid-May to mid-October). Additional departure at

1:00pm during summer. Rates $7-$16 (age 3+). A similar MI History tour is available to student groups.

❏ LIGHTHOUSES OF NORTHERN LAKE HURON: Visit the Great Lakes Shipwreck Museum at Whitefish Point on Lake Superior to see artifacts and exhibits of shipwrecks, including the famous Edmund Fitzgerald, and many other ships that went down in the cold waters of Lake Superior. Tour the original Whitefish Point Lighthouse, and then venture along the Lake Superior shore line and through the Hiawatha Forest to climb and explore the famous Point Iroquois Lighthouse and tower. Lunch included. 5 ½ hours (late June-late September). Rates $35.00.

❏ DISCOVER MACKINAW: Climb aboard and witness why Mackinaw is a unique Great Lakes experience. Explore Old Mackinaw Point, one of the few remaining castle-like lighthouses. Imagine plying the Straits aboard the USCG Cutter Mackinaw nicknamed, "The Guardian of the Great Lakes". Savor the delicacies available during your tour of a distinctly Mackinaw industry - a local fishhouse (available exclusively on this tour) 2.5 hours. Rates: $13-$17.

❏ FALL COLOR TOUR: See Northern Michigan's brilliant fall colors and visit a scenic working farm producing 100 acres of pumpkins, gourds, Indian corn, and vegetables. Pick a pumpkin or a bucket of gourds right out of the field. Ride down back roads to Lakeshore Drive's famous tunnel of trees and view Michigan in all of her glory. (mid-September to mid-October). Rates $7.00-$16.

OLD MACKINAC POINT LIGHTHOUSE

Mackinaw City - (just east of the Colonial Michilimackinac Visitor's Center in Mackinaw City near the south end of the Mackinac Bridge) 49701. Phone: (231) 436-4100. www.MackinacParks.com. Hours: Daily 9:00am-4:00pm (mid-May to early October). Extended until 5:00pm in summer. Admission: $6.50 adult, $4 youth (5-17). Combo tickets for Fort Mac, Colonial Michi and Mill Creek are available at great discounts. Tours: tours to the top of the lighthouse tower include 4 stories via 51 steps and an 11-rung vertical ladder through a narrow access opening. You should be over 4 ft tall and wear shoes that have no chance of falling off your feet while climbing the stairs and ladder (no bare feet or flip-flops).

Recently re-opened for the first time in over 50 years, the entire first floor of the structure and the tower is open for touring. Visitors will see original artifacts from the station, including the brass and glass Fresnel lens that lit the Straits of

Mackinac for more than 60 years. Built in 1892, the light guided ships through the dangerous straits until the navigation lights from the Mackinac Bridge rendered it obsolete. Take a peek at the restored, fully furnished kitchen of the keeper's dwelling in its 1910 appearance. Hands-on exhibits let you test your nighttime navigation skills, light up a miniature Fresnel lens, and try on a lighthouse keeper's clothing. Guides in historic costumes are stationed within the lighthouse to provide historical information, conduct tours of the grounds and lead small groups up the tower. Enjoy a panoramic view of the Mackinac Straits with unique photographic perspectives of the Mackinac Bridge and Mackinac Island.

THUNDER FALLS FAMILY WATERPARK

Mackinaw City - (off I-75 exit 337 or 338 and turn right) 49701. Phone: (231) 436-6000. www.thunderfallswaterpark.com. Hours: Open daily 11:00am-8:00pm (summer). Admission: General Admission Rates: $18-$24.95. Twilight Special (Starts at 3:30pm) $16.95.

Visit one of Michigan's largest and newest Waterpark attractions, Thunder Falls Family Waterpark. Discover your favorite among 12 slides or enjoy the leisurely pace of our Lazy River. Cool off and relax in Michigan's best wave pool by riding the 4 foot waves, or enjoy the arcade, lounge areas, food court and interactive children's play areas. Water temperatures are comfortably heated.

IRONWORKERS FESTIVAL

Mackinaw City - Mackinac Bridge. www.ironfest.com. Ironworkers from around the world come here annually to test their skills in the column climbing, knot tying, rivot toss and spud throw. The prize is the coveted gold belt buckle. Also a celebration of the building of the Mackinac Bridge in 1957. (800) 666-0160. (second weekend in August)

MACKINAW FUDGE FESTIVAL

Mackinaw City - Downtown. www.mackinacislandfudgefestival.org or (800) 666-0160. "Fudgies" from this state and neighboring states and countries come to taste and judge the area's famous fudge. Numerous "fudge-related" events include eating contests (got milk?). (last long weekend in September)

Onaway

ONAWAY STATE PARK

Onaway - 3622 North M-211 (M-211 six miles north from the City of Onaway) 49765. Phone: (989) 733-8279. www.michigan.gov/onaway.   Admission: $8.00 per vehicle.

One of the oldest State Parks in Michigan is located on the southeast shore of Black Lake. The park covers 158 acres of rugged land, including sand cobblestone beaches, large unique rock outcroppings and a diversity of trees including a stand of virgin white pines. Known for game fishing, they also have camping, hiking trails, boating, and swimming. Just 10 miles east of the park is the picturesque Ocqueoc Falls, the largest waterfall in Michigan's Lower Peninsula. The nearby city of Onaway has been designated the "Sturgeon Capital of Michigan."

Oscoda

AU SABLE RIVER QUEEN

Oscoda - West River Road (6 Miles West Of Oscoda) 48750. Phone: (989) 739-7351 or (989) 728-3775. www.ausableriverqueen.net. Admission: $7.00-$12400 (age 5+). Prices can be slightly higher for fall color tours.

An authentic paddle wheel boat that has been touring this section of the river for over 40 years hosts you for a relaxing and narrated 19 mile trip. "Captain Roger" teaches about the area's history and wildlife along the journey. Glass enclosed decks and a snack bar are also available.

IARGO SPRINGS

Oscoda - (Au Sable River Road Scenic Byway) 48750. Phone: (800) 235-4625. Hours: Daily, year-round.   FREE admission. www.us23heritageroute.org/iosco. asp?ait=av&aid=28

What once was a spot for tribal ceremonies (the Chippewas believed that the spring had medicinal qualities), today is a great place to take the family into nature. The clear, cool waters of Iargo Springs run from the banks into the waters of the AuSable River below. Be sure to tell your kids not use up too much energy as you descend the 294 steps down the banks to the spring (don't worry, there are benches to rest on the way back up!). A new nature boardwalk (with a 30' tall observation deck) and interpretive center provides a spectacular panoramic view of the AuSable River.

Ossineke

DINOSAUR GARDENS PREHISTORIC ZOO

Ossineke - 11160 US 23 South 49766. Phone: (989) 471-5477 or (877) 823-2408. www.dinosaurgardensllc.com. Hours: Daily 9:00am-4:00pm (mid-May to Labor Day). Hours extended during summer break. Weekends only in September. Admission: $3.00-$5.00 per person. Note: Miniature golf. Snack bar.

An 80-foot long, 60,000 pound Brontosaurus is one of the many thrills that awaits your kids at this unique family tradition. A mixture of dinosaurs and cavemen with Christianity, as you're greeted by a Christ statue holding the world in his hand. Original owner Paul Domke spent some 38 years creating and sculpting 26 full scale dinosaurs that are "exploring" the forest of trees inside this attraction. A monstrous T-Rex in one exhibit is battling a Triceratops. Several scenes show cavepeople locked in mortal combat with giant snakes and Mastodons. A big-headed Aptosaurus is entered via a staircase. Inside the belly you'll find a heart-shaped Jesus - "The Greatest Heart." Storyboards and sound effects accompany each exhibit to help bring them to life. This is a great way to see the size and scale of the creatures that once walked the earth. They have some other activities to do on their online Kids Page.

Presque Isle

PRESQUE ISLE LIGHTHOUSE MUSEUMS

Presque Isle - 4500 East Grand Lake Road (US 23 to CR638) 49777. Phone: (989) 595-9917. www.presqueislelighthouses.org . Hours: Daily 9:00am-6:00pm. (Mid-May to Mid-October). Reduced hours for 1905 House (summers only, closed Mondays). Admission: $1.50-$2.50 (age 6+). Gifts shops

OLD LIGHTHOUSE: Supposedly haunted old lighthouse and keepers' house full of artifacts. Built in 1840, you can visit with the "lightkeeper lady" inside the keeper's cottage (so-o cute!). Kids can make noise blowing a foghorn or ringing a giant bell (or as George called it when he visited with his family when he was 2 years old…the Bongy Bell!). Any age can climb the minimal 33 stairs to the top of the lighthouse for a great view.

NEW LIGHTHOUSE: An 1871 lightkeepers' quarters and a larger, more classical lighthouse. At 113' high, New Presque Isle is one of the tallest lighthouses that shines on the Great Lakes. It has a Third Order Fresnel lens and a focal plane of light that is 123 feet above lake Huron. It's a challenge to climb the some odd 133 steps - but what a rush!

GREAT LAKES LIGHTHOUSE FESTIVAL

Presque Isle - Old and New Presque Isle Lighthouses. (800) 4-ALPENA. www. lighthousefestival.org. Plan to make it annually to tour and climb the famous short & spooky Old Presque Isle Lighthouse or the three times as tall - New Lighthouse. Keeper's quarters are open too. U.S. Coast Guard exhibits recall tales of disasters and valiant rescues. Some Admissions. (mid-October)

Rogers City

HOEFT STATE PARK

Rogers City - 5001 US-23 North   49779. www.michigan.gov/hoeft.   Phone: (989) 734-2543.   Admission: $8.00 per vehicle.

Contains 300 heavily wooded acres with a mile of sandy Lake Huron shoreline in the 654 total acres of park. The park features 4 ½ miles of trails that run through the forest and along the shoreline that is perfect for hiking or cross-country skiing. The moderating effect of Lake Huron causes temperatures to be less extreme during both summer and winter and also causes up to two weeks delay in season changes compared to a few miles inland. The park also has mini-cabins available that sleep four people. Visitors can also enjoy swimming in Lake Huron, a picnic area and shelter, a playground, and boating and fishing.

PRESQUE ISLE COUNTY HISTORICAL MUSEUM

Rogers City - 176 Michigan Street   49779. Phone: (989) 734-4121.   www. thebradleyhouse.org Hours: Tuesday-Saturday Noon-4:00pm. (May thru mid-October). Admission: Donations.

This house was the home of the president of Michigan Limestone & Chemical Company, the largest industry in this community. The restored Bradley House contains exhibits based on local history. In various theme rooms on three floors, see a re-created general store or Victorian parlor. Displays include marine, lumbering and American Indian artifacts.

THOMPSON'S HARBOR STATE PARK

Rogers City - US23 North   49779. Phone: (989) 734-2543.   www.michigan.gov/ thompsonsharbor.   For the rugged outdoorsman in the family, explore over 6 miles of trails in an area that is located on the Lake Huron shoreline. Adjacent to the Presque Isle harbor. Park roads are undeveloped. Call ahead for driving conditions. No camping. No services.

KNAEBE'S MMMUNCHY KRUNCHY APPLE FARM

Rogers City - 2622 Karsten Road, 49779. http://mmmunchykrunchyapplefarm.com. (989) 734-2567. Saturdays. Watch them press cider, then slurp some along with homemade donuts, apple pies or caramel apples. In October, they have goat and pony rides for kids. School Tours weekdays by appointment, and always kritters to visit. Kidyard and picnic tables. (September / October)

Roscommon

NORTH HIGGINS LAKE STATE PARK

Roscommon - 11252 North Higgins Lake Dr. (I-75 or US 27 exits - 7 miles west of town via US 27 and Military Road) 48653. Phone: (989) 821-6125 or (989) 373-3559 (CCC Museum). www.michigan.gov/northhigginslake. Hours: Park open dawn to dusk. Museum open summers 11:00am-4:00pm. Admission: $8.00 per vehicle.

Over 400 acres available for camping/cabins, picnicking, hiking, boating, fishing, swimming, and winter sports. Most people find the Civilian Conservation Corps Museum is the reason for their trip here. During the Great Depression, many men without work were enrolled to perform conservation and reforestation projects throughout Michigan. CCC planted trees, taught and practiced fire fighting, constructed trails, built bridges and even built buildings (some are still standing). Housed in replica barracks, the museum has displays of highlights and techniques of their work. Interpretive, outside walks are available too.

SOUTH HIGGINS LAKE STATE PARK

Roscommon - 106 State Park Drive (I-75 at Roscommon Road south, exit 239) 48653. Phone: (989) 821-6374. www.michigan.gov/southhigginslake Admission: $8.00 per vehicle.

Voted some of the most beautiful lakes in the world, this park caters to families. The park contains almost one mile of shoreline along Higgins Lake, which is a large spring-fed body of water known for its clarity and fishing potential. The beaches are family-friendly and there's plenty of camping sites. As the second largest campground in a state park, the park's 400 modern camp sites are situated in a hardwood-shaded area. The park is very popular during the summer months and reservations must be made early. Hiking trails, fishing, and winter sports are there too. For information on canoe and boat rentals call (989) 821-5930.

Rose City

RIFLE RIVER RECREATION AREA

Rose City - (Take I 75 to Exit 202 (Alger/Rose City) and go 20 miles N. on M-33 to Rose City) 48654. Phone: (989) 473-2258. www.michigan.gov/rifleriver. Admission: $8.00 per vehicle.

Rifle River Recreation Area is a wilderness located within the AuSable State Forest. Includes Devoe Lake and Grousehaven Lake, Lupton. Fisheries research is being conducted on Jewett Lake. This lake is closed to fishing without a permit which is available at park headquarters. All lakes are closed to boats with motors. Canoe launching sites are located in several places along the Rifle River in the park. The 14 miles of pathways meandering throughout the park offer hiking, biking, cross country skiing and snowshoeing. Numbered posts keyed to the map will help keep you oriented while on the pathways. There is an observation tower that gives sightseers a fantastic scenic view of the recreation area. Camping/cabins, swimming and winter sports.

Chapter 4
North West

Beaver Island

EMMET [31]

Petoskey

Charlevoix

CHARLEVOIX

Boyne

Leland

ANTRIM

LEELANAU

[31] US

[131]

Empire [72]

[31] US Traverse City

BENZIE

GRAND TRAVERSE

KALKASKA

MANISTEE

WEXFORD

[131]

MISSAUKEE

Cadillac

[31]

A Quick Tour of our Hand-Picked Favorites Around...

North West Michigan

Northwest Michigan is a popular vacationing spot for those interested in sandy beaches, outdoor recreation and natural history. With Lake Michigan on its western side, and a series of small, inland lakes and forest (like **Huron-Manistee National**) scattered throughout, Northwest Michigan is surrounded by nature.

The cherry capital of the U.S. and a tour through the **Traverse City** area will introduce you to some of the treasures of this regional cultural center. The Grand Traverse Region has long been known as a favorite vacation spot. The beauty of its clear water, rolling acres of fruit trees, and sand dunes has established the Traverse City Area as a relaxing, hospitable place. This is another Michigan, one that time happily forgot - a peninsula of small hamlets that ends in the quiet majesty of the **Sleeping Bear Dunes** National Lakeshore. The ever-popular Dune Climb is a challenge, but so worth it! (remember, climbing down is much easier than climbing up!) The Leelanau Peninsula, which juts out into Lake Michigan is a paradise of outdoor activities - swimming, hiking, fishing and canoeing.

The Petoskey stone can be found in Michigan from the shores of Traverse City across the state to Alpena. **Petoskey State Park** is a wonderful place to set up base camp for your search of the fossilized coral stones. Early spring is a good time to look for the stone after the ice has melted along the shore. Why Petoskey Stone? The city of Petoskey was named after an Ottawa Indian chief, Chief Pet-O-Sega. "Pet-O-Sega" means the "Rays of the Rising Sun". The eye of the stone is seen as the sun, and the lines or tentacles are seen as the rays radiating from the sun. The stone was named Petoskey because of the abundance of them found on the shores of Little Traverse Bay. In 1965 the State of Michigan adopted the Petoskey stone as Michigan's state stone.

Each year, Michigan's maritime climate guarantees snow-laden winds from the Great Lakes all winter long – making Michigan the winter sports capital of the Midwest. Dozens of **Ski Areas** and resorts, and 1000s of miles of groomed snowmobile or cross-country ski trails. If you absolutely have to get away from the snow, come indoors to a few assorted **Waterparks.**

Sites and attractions are listed in order by City, Zip Code, and Name. Symbols indicated represent:

 Festivals

Restaurants   Lodging

NW CHAPTER AT A GLANCE

Acme * Music House

Alanson * Oden State Fish Hatchery

Bellaire * Shanty Creek Ski Resort

Beulah * Platte River Fish Hatchery

Boyne Falls * Boyne Mtn & Avalanche

Cadillac

* Huron-Manistee Natl Forests

* Mitchell St Pk

* North Amer Snow Fest

Cedar * Sugar Loaf Resort

Charlevoix

* Beaver Island Boat Co

* Fishermans Island St Pk

* Young St Pk

Cross Village *Legs Inn

Empire * Port Oneida Fair

Harbor Springs

* Boyne Highlands * Nubs Nob

Interlochen * State Parkt

Kaleva * Bottle House Museum

Manistee

* Orchard Beach St Pk

* Little River Band Ottawa powwow

* Natl Forest Fest

Northpoint

* Leelanau St Pk

* Grand Traverse Lighthouse

Petosky

* Kilwins Candy Kitchens

* LIttle Traverse Hist Museum

* Petoskey St Pk

Thompsonville * Crystal Mtn Resort

Traverse City

*Tall Ship Manitou

* Great Wolf Lodge

* Pirates Cove Adventure Pk

* Dennos Museum Ctr

* Old Mission Peninsula Lighthouse

* Sand Lakes Quiet Area

* Traverse City St Pk

* Natl Cherry Fest

* Sleeping Bear Dunes

Acme

MUSIC HOUSE MUSEUM

Acme - 7377 US 31 North (8 miles north of Traverse City) 49610. Phone: (231) 938-9300. www.musichouse.org. Hours: Monday-Saturday 10:00am-4:00pm, Sunday Noon-4:00pm (May-November). Plus Holiday hours, Friday-Sunday (December). Admission: $11 adult, $4 child (6-15)

Guided tours feature major instruments being played and explained. Rare antique musical phonographs and music boxes. Tinkertune's Musical Instrument Petting Zoo is a circus of musical sound. Students in groups can enjoy and enhance the sound track for a silent movie.

Alanson

ODEN STATE FISH HATCHERY

Alanson - 8258 South Ayr Road (off of US-31 (northside of road) just west of Oden) 49706. www.michigan.gov/dnr/0,1607,7-153-10364_28277-22423--,00.html. Phone: (231) 347-4689.

The new Oden State Fish Hatchery complex was completed in 2002 and is one of the most advanced fish culture facilities of its kind. This facility is the brown and rainbow trout broodstock station and is a major rearing facility for those two species. The facility has a state of the art effluent treatment system. The old hatchery has been transformed into a Great Lakes watershed interpretation area, featuring a MICHIGAN FISHERIES VISITOR CENTER that includes a replica of a fish transportation railcar. The railcar has a historic recreation of the interior of the original railcar, a watershed interpretive area and an interactive computer with hands-on learning opportunities concerning our watersheds and other aspects of fish culture. A trout stream was constructed in old raceway complex and shows the public how a degraded stream can be repaired. It includes a viewing chamber to allow the public to see what happens underwater in a stream. What are raceways for fish?

Bellaire

SHANTY CREEK RESORT SKI AREA

Bellaire - One Shanty Creek Road (off M-88) 49615. Phone: (231) 533-8621 or (800) 678-4111. www.shantycreek.com.

A resort that features 41 runs, ski lessons, and equipment rentals.

Accommodations include a new slopeside hotel and spa. An Arnold Palmer designed golf course awaits your golfing skills in the summer. Great children's ski school. Big Air ramps/landings. Monster Energy Park. Tubing park. Snowmobiling. Babysitting is available.

Beulah

PLATTE RIVER STATE FISH HATCHERY

Beulah - 15120 US-31 49617. Phone: (231) 325-4611.   www.michigan.gov/dnr. (click on Fishing) Hours: Monday-Friday 8:00am-4:00pm (year-round).

Fish hatcheries are always a family favorite. The entire family will enjoy this guided tour, which also includes watching the big chinook and coho salmon run up the Platte River. The new information center, hatchery building, lower weir harvest facility and the upper weir egg-take station are the best places to learn. The Visitors Center provides information on the importance of medium sized rivers to the Great Lakes, the salmon story, how watersheds work and how a hatchery operates. Best time to visit is in the fall when thousands of salmon can be seen.

Boyne Falls

BOYNE MOUNTAIN & AVALANCHE BAY INDOOR WATERPARK

Boyne Falls - (off US 131) 49713. Phone: (231) 549-6001 or (800) GO-BOYNE. www.boyne.com/boynemountain/ or www.avalanchebay.com. Hours: Resort is open year-round. Summer is golf, Winter is skiing. Indoor waterpark open all year. Admission: Lodge packages vary. Admission to waterpark begins at $25.00 per person (age 3+).

Where else can you ski and waterpark at the same time?

MOUNTAIN RESORT: One of the Lower Peninsula's finest resorts, Boyne Mountain 40+ runs, many new trails, rentals, ski lessons, outdoor pool and slopeside lodging/cabins. A children's ski program and baby sitting are also available.

AVALANCHE BAY WATERPARK: Attached to the New Mountain Grand Lodge and Spa luxury hotel, Avalanche Bay Indoor Waterpark is BIG, WET, and fully enclosed providing a great year-round family aquatic adventure. Themed as a Swiss-Austrian village, Avalanche Bay Indoor Waterpark will transport guests to a winter wonderland enjoyed at a comfortable 84 degrees! Slides, rides, kid's pools, climbing wall, lazy river, even a surf simulator – there is something for everyone at Avalanche Bay. The Vertigo Cannonbowl tube slide sends riders into a giant bowl, around-and-around you go until flushed into the pool below! And for the little ones, Fritz the mascot and his furry friends will be at Avalanche Bay.

Cadillac

HURON-MANISTEE NATIONAL FORESTS

Cadillac - 1755 South Mitchell Street (over 960,000 acres in the northern part of the Lower Peninsula) 49601. www.fs.fed.us/r9/hmnf/hmindex.htm. Phone: (800) 821-6263. Hours: Open 24 hours daily. Admission: $3.00 per carload per day or $5.00 per carload per week.

Popular activities here are swimming in Lakes Huron and Michigan, cross-country skiing, snowmobiling, trout fishing, modern and rough camping, boating and bicycle trails. Popular spots within the forests are:

THE NORDHOUSE DUNES - one mile of undeveloped shoreline along Lake Michigan. One of the few wilderness areas in the U.S. with an extensive lake shore dunes ecosystem. Most of the dunes are 3500 to 4000 years old and some stand about 140 feet (43 m) higher than the lake. There are many small water holes and marshes dotting the landscape and dune grass covers many of the dunes. The beach is wide and sandy, excellent for solitary walks and sunset viewing.

THE LODA LAKE WILDFLOWER SANCTUARY - one mile trail through marsh, forest and orchards. Over 40 miles of trails for hiking along the Manistee River.

THE RIVER ROAD SCENIC BYWAY - runs 22 miles along the south bank of the Au Sable River. View reservoirs, bald eagles, salmon, the Canoeists Memorial and the Lumberman's Memorial and Visitors Center of logging.

TUTTLE MARSH WILDLIFE AREA - Managed 5000 acres of fox, deer, coyote, muskrat, beaver, otter and weasel.

MITCHELL STATE PARK

Cadillac - 6093 East M-115 (3 miles north of US 131) 49601. Phone: (231) 775-7911. www.michigan.gov/mitchell. Hours: Center open daily 10:00am-6:00pm (May-November). Weekends only the rest of the year. Admission: $8.00 per vehicle. Note: Camping and cabins, boating and rentals, fishing, swimming, and winter sports.

The park is 245 acres and is situated between Lake Mitchell and Lake

Cadillac and provides an excellent opportunity to view a variety of wildlife on the outskirts of Cadillac. A historic canal connects the two lakes and runs directly through the park. The quarter-mile canal is a popular place for children to shore fish in the park, and in the evening, many fish for bullheads.

The Visitor's Center is also called the Carl T. Johnson Hunting & Fishing Center. A full size Michigan elk mount is on display in the exhibit hall, as well as other wildlife species which have been "brought back" by the efforts of sportsperson's organizations. With the push of a button, visitors can hear the call of the elk or other species featured in the wildlife exhibit. Exhibits include a wall-length aquarium and trapping and conservation efforts. Many come here for the birding too. You may see great blue heron, yellow finches and mallards.

NORTH AMERICAN SNOW FESTIVAL

Cadillac - (800) 225-2537. Ice sculptures are a feature, but at the North American Snow Festival in Cadillac, snowmobiles rule. The city plays host to Michigan's largest snowmobile shindig and it takes place on Lake Cadillac with as many as 10,000 sleds. Lake Cadillac, Lake Mitchell and the Cadillac Armory for Radar Run, Grudge Race, Pond Hockey, Ice Sculptures, kids races and Fun Run. (last weekend in January)

Cedar

SUGAR LOAF RESORT

Cedar - 4500 Sugar Loaf Mountain Road (off M-72) 49621. Phone: (231) 228-1553 or (800) 952-6390. Hours: Resort is open year-round, but skiing is usually from December-March. Golf in summer.

20 runs, an excellent kids' ski schools (toddlers and up), rentals, lessons, and a restaurant. Indoor pool and spa with attached fitness center, and a heated outdoor pool.

Charlevoix

BEAVER ISLAND BOAT COMPANY

Charlevoix - 103 Bridge Park Drive 49720. Phone: (231) 547-2311 or (888) 446-4095.. www.bibco.com.   Admission: $21.00 adult, Basically Half Price-child (5-12). Rates are roundtrip. Vehicle transport also available. May thru October.

PASSENGER AND CAR FERRY SERVICE - from Charlevoix to Beaver Island, the Great Lakes' most remote inhabited island. Beaver Island has beautiful scenery & intriguing history. The Island is home to two lighthouses. Packages include round trip cruises and possible escorted island tours of museums and island lunches. Call for schedule and information (April-December).

REGULAR ISLAND TOUR (1 ½ hours) - This tour focuses on the northern end of the island and the harbor area. View the picturesque village of St. James including its lighthouse on Whiskey Point, shops, museums and churches. The tour then proceeds to the west side of the island to see spectacular Donegal Bay with views of High, Whiskey, Trout and Garden Islands. Finally you will visit Protar's home and tomb and hear the intriguing history of this fascinating man. (May - October).

FISHERMAN'S ISLAND STATE PARK

Charlevoix - Bells Bay Road (off US-31 southwest) 49720. Phone: (231) 547-6641. www.michigan.gov/fishermansisland.   Admission: $8.00 per vehicle.

Fisherman's Island State Park is not actually an island, but a 2,678-acre park that features a park road that travels for two and one-half miles along the Lake Michigan shoreline. The park encompasses a tiny island, Fisherman's Island, located a short distance offshore from the picnic area. Located just south of Charlevoix, it features a rustic campground with some of the sites nestled in the dunes along the lakeshore. The park road travels through the campground to the picnic area with access to the beach and miles of hiking trails. Camping, hiking, fishing, swimming and bicycle trails.

YOUNG STATE PARK

Charlevoix - 2280 Boyne City Road (US-131, west on M-75) 49720. Phone: (231) 582-7523. www.michigan.gov/young.   Admission: $8.00 per vehicle.

Young State Park is located at the east end of beautiful Lake Charlevoix. The park spans over 560 acres in Charlevoix County and is a mix of gently rolling terrain, lowlands, and cedar swamp. Mirror Pond provides a good fishing site for children. The pond is stocked with sunfish and rock bass. The park concession now rents canoes, kayaks, and camping equipment and features gourmet coffees and homemade baked goods along with many other items needed by campers and beach goers. Camping, hiking, boating and rentals, fishing, swimming and winter sports.

Cross Village

LEGS INN

Cross Village - M-119 (US 31 to Carp Lake Village to Gill Road west through Bliss

Township to Cross Village) 49723. Phone: (231) 526-2281. www.legsinn.com. Hours: Daily, Lunch and Dinner. (mid-May to mid-October).

Included on the State Historic Register, this restaurant's roof line is ornamented with inverted cast-iron stove legs. The fantasy-like atmosphere of this medieval looking stone, timber and driftwood landmark was created by one man, Polish immigrant, Stanley Smolak. The original Polish owner was also inducted into the Ottawa Indians tribe locally. His sculptures and whimsy decorating using tree trunks will intrigue you. The authentic Polish cuisine is the specialty, but delicious American dishes are also served. Indoor/Outdoor dining but no A/C. Casual dress. Moderate prices. Children's Menu.

Empire

PORT ONEIDA FAIR

Empire - Rural Historic District of Sleeping Bear Dunes National Lakeshore. www.leelanau.com/fair. Journey into the past at the Port Oneida Fair, a two-day celebration of Michigan's rural traditions. The Port Oneida Fair features demonstrations and interactive displays of activities, both work and play, that could be found in Michigan in the 19th and early 20th centuries. As a part of touring the district's one-room schoolhouse, historic farms and original homesteads, visitors can witness timber framing, blacksmithing and quilt making, experience a Civil War Encampment, take a ride on a horse and wagon, watch a team of oxen at work in the field or learn about life in the early 1900s from an original resident. Family programs like games, music and live entertainment will take place throughout both days. Food and refreshments will be available and picnic areas will be provided. A free shuttle service will transport visitors between the five historic event sites. (second weekend in August).

Harbor Springs

BOYNE HIGHLANDS

Harbor Springs - 600 Highlands Drive (I-75 exit 282, west on M-32) 49740. Phone: (800) GO-BOYNE or (231) 526-3000. www.boynehighlands.com.

WINTER: Besides great family skiing (on your choice of 44 slopes), this resort offers a large heated outdoor pool that is warm even when the outside temperature is below zero. Babysitting, rentals, slopeside lodging (inn and cottages), children's activities and lessons are also available. Horse Drawn Wagon rides at Boyne are a great way to bring the family together singing songs or to provide a romantic nightcap to a perfect evening.

SUMMER: Boyne has 8 challenging golf courses, award winning restaurants, tennis, breathtaking views from chairlifts rides, swimming, shopping, nationally acclaimed dinner theatre, fishing, boating, biking, and more.

YOUNG AMERICANS DINNER THEATRE: talented young performers, ages 15-21, come together from across the nation and make Boyne Highlands their summer home. The show features all styles of music from the past 100 years along with various numbers from the Broadway hits of yesterday and today. They present this unique music and dance experience while serving as your waiters and waitresses. Dinner shows $25.00-$45.00.

NUB'S NOB

Harbor Springs - 500 Nub's Nob Road 49740. Phone: (800) SKI-NUBS or (231) 526-2131. www.nubsnob.com.

Nub's Nob Ski Resort near Harbor Springs was voted #1 for terrain parks and #4 for grooming by SKI Magazine. This snow sport hot spot in northwest Lower Peninsula is known for stellar snowboard half pipes and the state's first super pipe. It also boasts 248 acres of skiing on 53 slopes, and 28K of cross-country trails, including a 2K loop lit at night. Keeping it all in top condition are 242 snow guns. Also, for the beginners, be sure to check out the Midwest's only Free LEARN-TO-SKI & SNOWBOARD AREA (all ages) complete with its own chairlift and a newer Thrill-filled Terrain Park.

Interlochen

INTERLOCHEN STATE PARK

Interlochen - M-137 (South of US 31) 49643. www.michigan.gov/interlochen. Phone: (231) 276-9511. Admission: $6.00-$8.00 per vehicle.

Interlochen State Park is situated between two well-known fishing and swimming lakes: Green Lake and Duck Lake. Camping on the beach of the lake with bathhouses and boat rentals is popular especially in the summer. Hiking trails, fishing, boating, bicycle trails, and winter sports are available.

In 1928, the National Music Camp was established on the property adjoining the northern boundary of the park. The Interlochen Center for the Arts is adjacent to the park. Renowned musicians perform concerts year round. Schedules can be obtained online or by phoning (231) 276-7200, or (231) 276-9221.

Kaleva

BOTTLE HOUSE MUSEUM

Kaleva - 14451 Wuoksi (next to Bethany Lutheran Church) 49645. Phone: (231) 362-3793. Hours: Saturday Noon-4:00pm (Memorial Day weekend-Labor Day weekend). Other times by appointment.

Over 1500 articles of historical interest housed in the beautiful and unique building well known as the "Bottle House." The home was built with over 60,000 soft drink bottles in 1941. It is listed on the Michigan Register of Historical Sites, Ripley's Believe it or Not and the National Register of Historic Sites.

Manistee

ORCHARD BEACH STATE PARK

Manistee - 2064 Lakeshore Road (US 31 to M-10 north) 49660. Phone: (231) 723-7422. www.michigandnr.com/parksandtrails/ParksandTrailsInfo.aspx. Admission: $8.00 per vehicle.

Orchard Beach State Park is situated on a bluff overlooking Lake Michigan. Lots of reasonable camp site rentals on the dunes, great beaches with swimming, hiking trails. A stairway leads from the campground to the beach and self-guided hiking trails are adjacent to the park.

Around Manistee: Be sure to ride the trolley on a historic tour of Manistee; there is no better way to become acquainted with the city and to learn a little about its unique history. Manistee was a lumbering town and has preserved the Victorian atmosphere with its Victorian Village shopping district and lumbermen's homes. The harbor has two piers where fishing is good all year long. Two excellent beaches flank the harbor, along with playgrounds, picnic facilities, public restrooms and concessions. Fishing in Lake Michigan and Manistee Lake is terrific year round. During August and September, fishing reaches a feverish pitch as coho and chinook salmon come in for their spawning run. Later in the year, steelhead make their fall run. Charter boats, dock rental and good launching facilities all are available.

LITTLE RIVER BAND OF OTTAWA INDIANS POW-WOW

Manistee - Little River Gathering Grounds (US 31 & M22). (231) 723-8288. 300+ tribes are together to display Native American singers, dancers, crafts and food. (first weekend in July)

NATIONAL FOREST FESTIVAL

Manistee - Downtown. (800) 288-2286 or www.manisteecountychamber.com/forestfestival. Visit the open houses of the Lymon Building and Water Works with local history artifacts, parades, dances, midway, boat parade and fireworks. (4th of July week)

⊠

Northport

LEELANAU STATE PARK / GRAND TRAVERSE LIGHTHOUSE

Northport - 15310 North Lighthouse Point Road (north of Traverse City on M-22 through Northport and take M-201 eight miles north) 49670. Phone: (231) 386-5422. www.michigan.gov/leelanau or www.grandtraverselighthouse.com. Admission: $8.00 per vehicle to park. $4 adult, $2 child (6-18) to lighthouse.

The word Leelanau is the Indian word for "A Land of Delight" and could not better describe the area. Along the shorelines, Petoskey stones can be found. Camping/cabins, hiking trails, fishing, swimming and winter sports.

GRAND TRAVERSE LIGHTHOUSE tours along coastal dunes are a big draw (daily afternoons May thru October, and November weekends). The Lighthouse has been guiding ships and sailors since it was built in 1858. Today, one can tour the restored lighthouse resembling a keeper's home of the 1920's and 30's. Exhibits on area lighthouses, foghorns, shipwrecks and local history are located in the Lighthouse and Fog Signal Building. The restored air diaphone foghorn is demonstrated throughout the year, and visitors can climb the tower for a spectacular view of Lake Michigan. (Summer Hours: Daily 10am-5pm. May, Sept., Oct. Noon-4pm) Experience the blast of the foghorn. (Summer Saturdays). Enjoy coffee, pastries, & sandwiches in the Lighthouse Gift & Camp Store.

Petoskey

KILWIN'S CANDY KITCHENS

Petoskey - 355 North Division St. 49770. Phone: (231) 347-3800. www.kilwins.com. Admission: FREE Tours: Monday-Friday 10am-3pm. Note: Retail store sells over 300 types of mouth-watering candy.

When first arriving, you'll probably park your car where the sign reads, "Chocolate Lovers Parking - All Others Will Be Towed". This is just the right kind of invitation to let you (and the kids) know that you are in for a real treat. Northern Michigan seems to have a real taste for fudge and candy and Kilwan's is one of the area's most respected candy-makers. Get "close to the action" on this tour and see all of the various production processes. The kids will love watching 2 workers stretching 3 foot slabs of peanut brittle!

LITTLE TRAVERSE HISTORICAL MUSEUM

Petoskey - 100 Depot Court (Waterfront at Bayfront Park) 49770. Phone: (616) 347-2620. www.petoskeymuseum.org. Hours: Monday-Friday 10am to 4pm. Saturday 1:00-4:00pm (May-October). Admission: $3.00 adult (over 18). FREE for children.

Housed in an old railroad depot, you'll find information about the area's Okawa Indians and pioneer times. Exhibits about Ernest Hemingway (Much of the exhibit revolves around the time when Hemingway lived in the Petoskey area as a young man) and Civil War author Bruce Catton. Display of Petoskey stones, too. It is located at Bay Front Park, with it's magnificent view of Little Traverse Bay, and the "Million Dollar Sunsets".

PETOSKEY STATE PARK

Petoskey - 2475 M-119 (north of US 31, 1.5 miles N. on M-119) 49770. Phone: (231) 347-2311. www.michigan.gov/petoskey. Admission: $8.00 per vehicle.

Old Baldy Trail includes a stairway that leads up Old Baldy, a stable dune that is one of the attractions in the park. After climbing the dune, the view that is available of the bay is breathtaking. The mile-long sand beach is famed for its "million-dollar sunsets." The Portage Trail winds through very diverse terrain where a nature lover may find different species of plants and wildlife. Campsites along Little Traverse Bay with a great beach and trails in and out of wooded dunes. There's well developed nature trails and in Spring, sort through Winter's debris for Petoskey stones (designated Michigan state stone). Look for the coral fossils in the stones and you've probably found one. Boating and winter sports are also available.

> The Oden Fish Hatchery is a short drive from the park and one of the most advanced facilities of its kind. For anyone interested in how brook and brown trout are raised, this is the premier destination.

Thompsonville

CRYSTAL MOUNTAIN RESORT

Thompsonville - 12500 Crystal Mountain Dr. (off M-115) 49683. Phone: (231) 378-2000 or (800) 968-7686 Adventure Center. www.crystalmtn.com. Hours: Resort is open year-round. Skiing usually December-March. Golf and waterpark in summer.

WINTER: Crystal Mountain is a "family-friendly" resort that offers 34 runs with a children's "learn to ski" program, indoor and outdoor pools, restaurant, and slopeside rooms.

SUMMER: THE PARK AT WATER'S EDGE. One-acre outdoor waterpark complex with large pool with zero-depth entry. Lap lanes, water playground (water cannon, lily pad walk, water basketball and volleyball court, a tumble pail, crawl tube), hot tub and a sand play area. Around $10.00 per person admission. Cottages feature 22 two-and three-bedrooms. Also, Saturday chairlift rides for a great view and supervised tube or canoe trips on the Platte River. Bike rentals and planned family games and recreation available as packages.

Traverse City

TALL SHIP "MANITOU"

Traverse City - 13390 SW Bay Shore Drive (Grand Traverse Bay - West arm) 46984. Phone: (231) 941-2000 or (800) 678-0383. www.tallshipsailing.com. Admission: Varies by length of "get-away "starting at $299.00 per person. 2 hour sails range from $22.00-42.00 adult/ Half price child. Call or visit website for sailing schedules and rates. (Summer). Kids like the Moomer Ice Creat Sails best.

Several schooners similar to those that traveled the seas more than 150 years ago sail Midwest waters. The Manitou (114') ship offer tours during the summer months and accommodations in September. From port, she offers fun-filled 2-hour outings, three to four times a day throughout the sailing season. Her bright white sails and hull are a most popular sight on the sparkling waters of West Grand Traverse Bay. Aboard the schooners, passengers can participate as part of the crew, helping set the sails and taking turns at the wheel. Or they can just relax and appreciate the scenery, as the wind does the work. "Manitou" is one of the largest sailing ships on the Great Lakes, similar in design to vessels that sailed one hundred years ago. She was built specifically for passenger service, making her one of the most comfortable windjammers afloat. If you want to spend the night aboard ship, The Manitou departs on two- to five-day sailings (some especially for families). Stops include islands and shore towns. You can dine at buffets on deck and on hearty family-style fare in the main cabin. Up to twenty-four passengers can enjoy the pleasure and thrill of sailing aboard "Manitou."

GREAT WOLF LODGE

Traverse City - 3575 North US 31 South 49684. www.greatwolflodge.com. Phone: (231) 941-3600.

A Northwoods themed year-round resort with family-sized suite lodging; a huge indoor waterpark (waterslides, a family boat ride, indoor/outdoor pool, children's pool, lazy river, whirlpools and interactive water fort); an arcade and restaurant. Great Wolf Resorts has combined an American favorite – ice cream – and the hospitality industry's latest trend – spas catered to tweens – to create Scooops™ Kid Spa. ME! Bath's exclusive ice cream-themed products begin with an ice cream bath fizz, shower sherbet scrub, sundae topping foot mask and moisturizing body icing. MagiQuest™ – a live-action adventure game, and Howl In One – an outdoor miniature golf course are the newest draws (fees for these activities run $5.00-$25.00). This all-in-one resort draws you in to stay in the backwoods, modernly rustic setting. Your stay includes passes to the indoor waterpark, evening storytimes and Cub club activity room. The décor in the lobby and suites are so comfortable. Packages start at $169.00 per family per night.

SNOWLAND

Traverse City - Great Wolf Lodge. www.greatwolflodge.com. The lodge is decorated in a winter scene. It snows 3x daily, hot cocoa and live music, clock tower sing along, Rowdy the Reindeer Storytime. Attend the North Pole University for Elves. Admission (includes lodging and indoor waterpark passes). (month-long in December)

PIRATE'S COVE ADVENTURE PARK

Traverse City - 1710 US-31 North 49684. www.piratescove.net. Phone: (231) 938-9599. Hours: Daily 10:00am-11:00pm (summer). Reduced hours in May, September and October. Admission: $6.95-$12.95 per activity (age 4+). Rides use tokens that can be purchased.

Adventure Miniature golf in a fun-filled setting of lavish landscaping and delightful pirate themes. Putt your way over footbridges, under waterfalls, and through mountain caves. Sharpen your putting skills on Blackbeard's Challenge Course, Captain Kidd's Adventure or The Original Course. A fun park for kids of all ages. Electric cars entertain the youngest kids while go-carts and waterslide (must be 42" tall to use) help keep the older kids entertained. Specially designed to be ridden in your street clothes—if you dare! Maybe try a bumper boat pond with squirt gun-equipped boats. New zipline.

DENNOS MUSEUM CENTER

Traverse City - 1701 East Front Street (On campus of Northwestern Michigan College) 49686. Phone: (231) 995-1055.   www.dennosmuseum.org.   Hours: Monday-Saturday 10:00am-5:00pm, Sunday 1:00-5:00pm. Closed on major holidays. Admission: $6.00 adult, $4.00 child (under 18).

A regional hub for arts and culture, this dramatic building features three rotating exhibition galleries, a sculpture court, a gallery of Inuit Eskimo art, as well as the 367-seat Milliken Auditorium, a 32-seat video theater, and a museum store. The museum's permanent display of sculpture, prints and drawings by the Inuit artists of the Canadian arctic is one of the largest and most historically complete collections anywhere. Highlights of the Discovery gallery include several unique interactive exhibitions including Recollections and Elastic Surgery, The Sound Wall, A Laser Harp and Anti-Gravity mirror plus numerous exhibitions related to light and color. The gallery also features a Hubble Space Telescope theater with ongoing transmission of programming from NASA and the Space Telescope Institute.

OLD MISSION PENINSULA LIGHTHOUSE

Traverse City - (along M-37) 49686.

View this 19th Century lighthouse and step back in time as your kids stand at the geographical point that is exactly halfway between the Equator and the North Pole. Beach shoreline nearby.

SAND LAKES QUIET AREA

Traverse City - (M-72 to Broomhead Road - South) 49686. Phone: (231) 922-5280. Hours: Always open (year-round). Free admission.

This adventurous place is so "quiet" (as the name implies) because all motor vehicles are banned from the 10 miles of trails that feature fishing and camping. Make your plans to hike in and camp and see how Michigan must have looked to the early pioneers and Native Americans. (Note: Trails are not stroller accessible).

TRAVERSE CITY STATE PARK

Traverse City - 1132 US-31 east 49686. www.michigan.gov/traversecity. Phone:
(231) 922-5270. Admission: $8.00 per vehicle.

Traverse City State Park is a 47-acre urban park that features a quarter mile
of beautiful beach on the Grand Traverse Bay. The park is only two miles from
downtown Traverse City, one of the most popular resort towns in Michigan.
Almost 350 campsites opposite Grand Traverse Bay with bridge to beach and
close to attractions. Powerboating and sailboating are popular Traverse Bay
aquatic activities. Kayaks and hydrobikes are available for rent. There is a
paved bike trail, which is accessible through the park, and runs east and west,
parallel to the park. Along with biking, the TART Trail provides multiple uses
for hiking, cross-country skiing and other trail recreation.

NATIONAL CHERRY FESTIVAL

Traverse City - (800) 968-3380 or www.cherryfestival.org. Cherry treats, three parades,
two air shows, turtle races, band contests, mountain-bike rides, live performances and
beach volleyball to begin with. There's also a Very Cherry Luncheon, Cherry Pie Eating
Contest, cherry grove tours and fireworks above Grand Traverse Bay. (begins right
before/after July 4th for eight days)

SLEEPING BEAR DUNES NATIONAL LAKESHORE

Traverse City (Empire) - 9922 Front Street (SR 72) (I-75 to M-72 exit, head west.
35 miles along northwest Lower Peninsula shores) 49630. Phone: (231) 326-5134.
www.nps.gov/slbe. Hours: (Visitor's Center) Daily 8:00am-6:00pm (Summer). Daily
9:00am-4:00pm (rest of year).
Admission: $10.00 per week /
per vehicle or $5.00 per person
per week. Note: Visitor's Center
in Empire has nice slide show to
understand area better. Canoeing/
Rafting: www.theriverglenarbor.
com. The Homestead Resort:
www.thehomesteadresort.com.

*An easy climb down...but take your time
on the way back up...*

The name of the shore comes
from Chippewa Indian stories of
a mom and her two bear cubs
separated by a forest fire. The

cubs now stand for the North and South Manitou Islands - still stranded. Among the dunes are rugged bluffs, ghost forests, and exposed bleached trees. From late April through early November, take the Pierce Stocking Scenic Drive route to view the dunes. On South Manitou Island, climb the 100 foot lighthouse or view the wreck of a freighter or the Valley of Giants (white cedar trees). The islands are accessible by ferry from Leland. The Maritime Museum at the Coast Guard Station in Glen Haven displays maritime area history and is open summers only. A daily re-enactment of a Life-Saving Service rescue is the highlight of every afternoon (specifically directed toward kids!). The ever-popular Dune Climb is a challenge, but so worth it! (Remember, climbing down is much easier than climbing up!). The climb is one of those things you must do in a lifetime - at least once! Be sure to take pictures once you arrive on a high summit. Ranger-led walks, campfire programs and other activities are available in July and August. Fishing, canoeing, hiking and cross-country skiing are favorite activities here.

Mom & Daniel...
barefoot fun!

GREAT LAKES CHILDREN'S MUSEUM

Traverse City (Greilickville) - 13240 S. West Bayshore Drive (across from Heritage Harbor, on M-22) 49684. Phone: (231) 932-GLCM. www.greatlakeskids.org. Hours: Tuesday-Saturday 10:00am-5:00pm, Sunday 1:00-5:00pm. Holiday Mondays, too. Admission: $5.00 per person (age 2+).

A hands-on interactive children's museum focused on the Great Lakes and water. Exhibits include kid-sized lighthouse & keepers quarters, a sailboat, and a periscope. A child can pilot a Great Lakes freighter or navigate the Lakes on the navigation wall. The In the Great Lakes Thoughts Flow area, visitors can interact directly with moving water, channeling and redirecting it in hundreds of different ways. In the Water Cycle children can go up the sunshine climb as they evaporate, condense in the cloud chamber, slide down as precipitation, and then go into the groundwater tunnel. There are over 30 exhibits & activities awaiting...most related to water and navigating water travel.

Chapter 5
South East

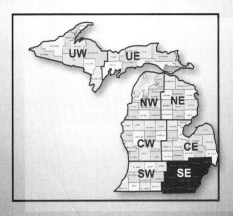

A Quick Tour of our Hand-Picked Favorites Around...

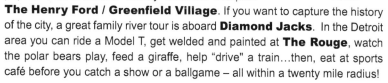

South East Michigan

Detroit, the largest metropolitan area in Michigan, boasts one of the Midwest's great **Zoos**, the home of the Motown sound, a revitalized theater and arts district, homes & factories of the "Auto Barons," major league sports, and America's most popular indoor/outdoor history museum complex – **The Henry Ford / Greenfield Village**. If you want to capture the history of the city, a great family river tour is aboard **Diamond Jacks**. In the Detroit area you can ride a Model T, get welded and painted at **The Rouge**, watch the polar bears play, feed a giraffe, help "drive" a train...then, eat at sports café before you catch a show or a ballgame – all within a twenty mile radius!

Want a farm setting near the city? Try a day trip to a real farm at **Calder Dairy** (Detroit area) or a research facility at **MSU's Dairy Plant & Children's Garden** (East Lansing). Kids will delight exploring the Pizza Garden as their appetite builds for yummy homemade ice cream later at the dairy. Buy your heaping cones first, and then venture through the self-guided mezzanine tour of the giant vats and flavor stations of the ice cream production plant. Before you leave the Lansing area, every Michigander must promise a visit to the **Michigan Historical Center**, downtown. It takes the best of every historical place in the state and interactively allows you to learn by having fun. Want more interaction? Try **Impression 5** science museum where you can make slime and explore science.

Just a ways west of metro Detroit is a sleepy town called Chelsea. Not so sleepy to factory tour hounds like us – two wonderful tours are located here – **Jiffy Mix** and the **Chelsea Teddy Bear Factory**. Muffins and a new teddy bear sound like a tea party in the makings. Day trips don't get any better than this!

With all the city influences abundant is this region, you may not think there is a place for nature. Well, there are scattered recreation areas around big cities. Camping, fishing and mountain bike trails can be found at Pontiac Lake State Recreation area in Pontiac, Pinckney State Recreation area in Pinckney and Maybury State Park in Northville. Look for "beach" parks, too

A QUICK GLANCE AT THE SOUTH EAST CHAPTER

Albion * Wild Swan Theater

Ann Arbor

* Ann Arbor Hands-on Museum

* Dominos Farms *U of M Museums

* PowWow * Parker Mill

Belleville *Natl Strawberry Fest

Brighton

* Island Lake Rec Area

* Mt Brighton Ski Area

* Brighton Rec Area

Brooklyn

* Walker Tavern

* MI Internatl Speedway

Carleton * Calder Dairy Farm

Chelsea

* Jiffy Mix Tour

* Chelsea Teddy Bear Co

* Waterloo Rec Area

Dearborn

* Automobile Hall of Fame

* Ford Rouge Factory Tour

* Greenfield Village & The Henry For

Detroit

* Detroit Sports Teams

* Mus of African-American History

* Detroit Historical Museum

* Detroit Instit of Arts (DIA)

* MI Science Ctr * Detroit Zoo

* Belle Isle * Pewabic Pottery

* Dossin Great Lakes Mus

* Histoirc Fort Wayne

* Motown Historical Mus

* Ford Field Tours *Hockeytown

* Chrysler Mus * Rainforest Cafe

* Cranbrook Art & Science

* Morley Candy Makers

* Marvins Marvelous Mechanical

* Diamond Jacks River Tours

* Greenmead Historical Pk

* Motorsports Mus & Hall of Fame

Dexter * Spring Valley Trout Farm

Dundee * Splash Universe Riverrun

East Lansing

* MSU Attractions

Hanover * Buffalo Ranch

Holly *Rec Area *Seven Lakes St Pk

Jackson *Environ Educ Ctr *Cascades

Lansing

* MI Hist Mus *Fenner Nature Ctr

* Lansing Lugnuts *Potter Park Zoo

* Woldumar Nature Ctr *Impression 5

* MI State Capitol *Planet Walk

* RE Olds Transportation *MI Princess

Milan *Clean Water Beach *Dragway

Monroe *River Raisin Battlefield

Onsted/Irish Hills

Plymouth *Hist Mus *Orchard/Cider Mill

Waterford *St Parks *The Fridge

*Nature Ctr

Ypsilanti

*Rolling Hills Park

*Country Fair Wkends

Ann Arbor

WILD SWAN THEATER

Ann Arbor - 416 West Huron Street (performances at Towsley Auditorium) 48103. Phone: (734) 995-0530. www.wildswantheater.org. Admission: $8.00-$12.00 for single tickets.

A professional theater company that performs for family audiences using dance, masks, puppets and music. Productions like "Winnie the Pooh" or "Peter Rabbit" and other famous storybook tales come to life for the kids. Mostly matinees. Study guides for each production available online.

ANN ARBOR HANDS-ON MUSEUM

Ann Arbor - 220 East Ann Street (between 4th & 5th Avenue - Downtown) 48104. Phone: (734) 995-5439. www.aahom.org. Hours: Monday-Saturday 10:00am-5:00pm, Sunday Noon-5:00pm. Thursdays til 9pm are half price. Admission: $10.00 general (age 2+). Note: Explore Store. Education related materials online.

Your kid's eyes will light up with amazement as you explore over 250 exhibits on 4 floors in this old firehouse. Watch your skeleton ride a bicycle as you explore human movement, play a song on a walk-on piano, "be one" with a green screen, touch fossils, have bubble fun, climb walls, and whisper across the room to a friend (and they can hear you) are just a few of offerings. Learn "How Things Work" with gears, pulleys and air movement or play a laser harp in "Light & Optics". "Waste 2 Watts" shows how new environmentally friendly technology can turn our trash into electricity. Let the little ones find their own space in the "Preschool Gallery". Now it's cool to be a Geekiac! (Remember Mom & Dad...you came for the children...but learning sure is fun!).

DOMINO'S PETTING FARM

Ann Arbor - 24 Frank Lloyd Wright / Earhart Road (I-94 to US-23 North. Take US-23 North to Plymouth Road exit (exit 41) 48106. www.pettingfarm.com. Phone: (734) 998-0182.   Hours: Monday-Friday 9:30am-4:00pm, Saturday & Sunday 10:30am-5:00pm. Admission: $5.50-$7.00 per person (age 2+). Winter rates (December 1 - February 28) are $3 per person. Hayride included. Weekend pony rides are $5.00 extra. Note: Picnic area. Domino's Pizza available. FREEBIES: farm bingo and animal facts online.

First pass a herd of buffalo or cows grazing on the grounds of the Domino's Pizza World Headquarters. Across the street is Domino Farms, an early 1900's depiction of Michigan farm life. The Petting Farm has 100+ chickens, goats, sheep, peacocks, pot-bellied pigs, and miniature horses. Take a hayride to buffalo fields and stop and get a close look at their shy, huge faces! Many animal  demonstrations throughout the day. Kids may get to hold a baby goat, pet a sweet chicken (so soft!), and spend some time with tiny black lambs. The staff carry the baby animals around and come alongside your kids to gently orient them to each animal. One of the cleanest farms you'll ever see. Nice outdoor activity to enjoy with a picnic.

UNIVERSITY OF MICHIGAN MUSEUMS

Ann Arbor - (I-94 to State Street Exit) 48109.   www.umich.edu/museums.php

SPORTS MUSEUM - 1000 South State Street - (734) 647-2583. Captures the spirit of 100+ years of athletic competition with emphasis on the Rose Bowl, Big Ten and U.S. Olympics. Located in the nation's largest college stadium. Only open for special events..

MUSEUM OF NATURAL HISTORY - 1109 Geddes Avenue - (734) 764-0478. Michigan birds and animals. Face to face with prehistoric allosaurus conquering a stegosaurus or a mastodon from Michigan. Evolution of whale's skeletons. Daily until 5:00 pm. Suggested donation $6.00. Planetarium.

MUSEUM OF ARCHEOLOGY - 434 South State Street - (734) 764-9304. 100,000+ artifacts from ancient Egypt, Greece and Rome. See a mummy child! Open Daily until 4:00pm, except Mondays.

STEARNS MUSICAL COLLECTION - 1100 Baits Drive - North Campus. (734) 763-4389. 2000+ musical instruments on display from around the world. Open until 4:00pm weekdays.

BOTANICAL GARDENS - 1800 North Dixboro Road - (734) 998-7061. Tropical, warm-tempered or desert plants. Nature trail. Prairie. Daily, except Monday 10:00am - 4:30pm. Admission FREE.

POW WOW

Ann Arbor - U of M, Crisler Arena. (734) 647-6999 or www.umich.edu/~powwow/. For several decades now, more than 1000 champion Native American singers, dancers, artisans and drummers gather for competitions. Nearly 12,000 people attend this event. Admission (1weekend in March)

ANN ARBOR STREET ART FAIR

Ann Arbor - Burton Carillon Tower on North University Ave. www.artfair.org. (734) 994-5260. 1000+ artisans from across the nation set up booths. There are face-painting experts, beginner watercolor stations with try-it easels, Family art activity center, magicians, jugglers, and lots of American and ethnic food. (third long weekend in July)

PARKER MILL

Ann Arbor - 4650 Geddes, (east of US-23). (734) 971-6337. Sunday tours. FREE admission. This restored 1800's gristmill is one of the country's few remaining completely functional mill and log cabin. Picnicking is recommended. (September / October)

Belleville

NATIONAL STRAWBERRY FESTIVAL

Belleville - Wayne County Fairgrounds and downtown, (I-94 Belleville Road exit south into town). (734) 697-3137 or www.nationalstrawberryfest.com. If they're ripe, local farms can be visited heading in or out of town (Rowe's or Potter's). The festival draws 100,000 berry lovers, mostly families. A family circus, kids carnival and games, pony rides, and a parade Saturday. (Father's Day Weekend in June)

Brighton

ISLAND LAKE RECREATION AREA

Brighton - 12950 East Grand River (I-96, exit 151) 48116. Phone: (810) 229-7067. www.michigan.gov/islandlake. Admission: $8.00 per vehicle.

Island Lake Recreation Area is a 4,000-acre park in Livingston County that offers an "up north" experience without leaving southeast Michigan. Island Lake is the only balloon port in the state park system. Balloons usually take off in the early morning or late evening, depending on the wind and weather. Two beaches are available for day use, one at Kent Lake and one at Spring Mill Pond with more than 100 feet of sandy beach. The pond is spring feed, so the water stays cool and clear all summer. A canoe livery offers relaxing trips down the scenic Huron River. Hiking trails, beaches, boating, fishing, swimming, bicycle trails, winter sports and cabins available.

MOUNT BRIGHTON SKI AREA

Brighton - 4141 Bauer Road (I-96 - Exit 145) 48116. www.mtbrighton.com. Phone: (810) 229-9581.

A "family friendly" attraction that offer 26 runs of various skill levels. Snowboarding, lessons and rentals are available.

BRIGHTON RECREATION AREA

Brighton - 6360 Chilson Road (I-96 exit 147 head west) 48843. Phone: (810) 229-6566. www.michigan.gov/brighton Admission: $8.00 per vehicle.

The area has a combination of high, irregular ranges of hills, interspersed with a number of attractive lakes. Beaches, swimming, and trout fishing are most popular here. Bishop Lake beach has been totally remodeled and is now universally accessible. Opened in the spring of 2006, new features include a beach house, beach area, picnic areas, and a sand volleyball court. Vending machines are available at the beach house. Bird watching is a popular recreation activity at this location. Other features include hiking, winter sports, modern and rough camping, boating and bicycle trails.

Brooklyn

WALKER TAVERN STATE HISTORIC COMPLEX

Brooklyn - 13220 M-50 (US 12 & M-50) 48230. www.michigan.gov/walkertavern. Phone: (517) 467-4401. Hours: Wednesday-Sunday 10:00am-5:00pm (Memorial Day - Labor Day). Closed MIS race weekends. Admission: FREE Note: On most Sundays thru September, you can shop at a real farmers market. Settling a State - Kids Activities and Teacher Lesson Plans.

In the mid-1800's, the journey between Detroit and Chicago (by stagecoach) was a 5-8 day event (one-way, can you imagine?). Two roads played an important part in Michigan's early development. They crossed at Cambridge Junction, where Sylvester and Lucy Walker assisted travelers at their tavern. This farmhouse tavern was the original stopping point (along what is now known as US 12) where travelers could have a meal, relax, or spend the night. Discover how life was in the 1840's with realistic exhibits that show a barroom, dining room, parlor and kitchen. The Visitor's Center also features a movie about a young boy's travels from New York to Chicago in the 1840's. Located in the Cambridge Junction Historic State Park. No camping.

MICHIGAN INTERNATIONAL SPEEDWAY

Brooklyn - 12626 US 12 (1 mile west of M-50) 49230. Phone: (517) 592-6666 or (800) 354-1010 tickets. www.mispeedway.com. Hours: Call or visit website for current schedule. (Summer) Admission: $15.00-$100.00 per person.

Gentlemen (and ladies) start your engines! The thrill of world class professional motorsports is alive and well in Michigan. This speedway is a D-shaped, 2-mile oval that offers high-banked (18 degree) turns to a variety of racing vehicles including NASCAR, CART, and the NASCAR Craftsman Truck Series. Also see the fastest 400 mile race, the annual Michigan 400 or Winston Cup series.

Carleton

CALDER DAIRY FARM

Carleton - 9334 Finzel Road (I-275 - Telegraph Road Exit (south), to Stoney Creek Road - West to Finzel Road South - follow signs) 48117. Phone: (734) 654-2622. www.calderdairy.com. Hours: Daily 10:00am-7:00pm. Winter hours vary. Admission: FREE Note: Farm Store and Ice Cream Shop. Main Store - watch milk arriving and fed through series of pipes for processing.

See how luscious ice cream is made - right from the Brown Swiss Cow's milk! Calder Dairy has 37 flavors of New England Style Ice Cream which is hand

packaged on the farm. At the farm: Pet the Holstein and Swiss Cows plus numerous other animals that you're likely to see on a farm (pigs, ducks, sheep). They make creamy ice cream, chocolate milk, eggnog, plus milk right from the cows - fresh in glass bottles. (Calder's Dairy also continues to make home deliveries of bottled milk as it has since it opened. Their trucks are unmistakable with big Holstein black markings and the Calder logo).

Check out the milking machines behind the store to see cows milked by the dozen. Come out and help feed the baby calves at 3:00 pm daily and then watch the 'girls' being milked at 4:00 pm every day. Their "Viewing Room" has recently been renovated and now contains great informational posters and fun interactive activities for all ages.

Take a tour in a hay wagon (horse driven) and you'll see fields of llamas, deer and bright peacocks. A family of ducks and geese can be fed corn that can be purchased right here at the store. At the end of your visit to the land of "Babe", be sure to buy a generous souvenir cup of fresh ice cream!

Chelsea

"JIFFY MIX"- CHELSEA MILLING

Chelsea - 201 West North Street (I-94 west to Chelsea exit - north - follow signs) 48118. Phone: (734) 475-1361. www.jiffymix.com. Hours: Monday-Friday 9:00am-3:00pm. Closed Holidays. Tours require advance reservations. Admission: FREE Note: Souvenir box of Jiffy Mix given with recipe booklet.

Chelsea Milling calls itself a complete manufacturer: storing wheat, milling wheat into flour, producing mixes from the flour and even making the little blue boxes.

In a time when manufacturing tours are minimal or eliminated, this is a good, old-fashioned tour! Inside the world headquarters of the internationally known Jiffy Mix Baking Products, you'll begin in the auditorium with a slide show narrated by your tour guide.

JIFFY MIX TOUR (continued)...

Because they're veteran associates, they talk about each operator by name. Learn some history about the company including how they got the name "Jiffy". In 1930, Grandma Mabel Holmes named the famous, low-priced, blue and white baking mix boxes "Jiffy" after hearing cooks exclaim, "The muffins will be ready in a jiffy!". Their flour is from Michigan and is milled using silk material similar to your kid's blanket edging. You'll see the packaging process,

first in the slide show, then actually out in the factory. After you have a snack of Jiffy Mix cookies and juice, everyone wears a hair net and takes a 20 minute walking tour of the packaging process. It's neat to see waxed paper formed in a block, filled, boxed and then sealed. The sealing machine is a cute 8 legged machine. Did you know their #1 selling product is "Corn Muffin" mix? At the end of the tour you can choose from muffin or another mix box to take home... yummies there...yummies at home!

CHELSEA TEDDY BEAR COMPANY

Chelsea - 400 N. Main Street (downtown) 48118. www.chelseateddybear.com. Phone: (734) 433-5499. Tours: Saturdays at 11am, 1pm, and 3pm

What does *one hundred thousand* teddy bears look like...Well come and see 100,000 teddy bears in the huge warehouse and production facility located in the historic Clock Tower Complex. Visit Michigan's magical teddy bear destination with a trip to downtown Chelsea. Learn about teddy bear design and see their dressing/assembly stations - too cute. An on-site visit includes the "World's Largest Teddy Bear" standing over 10' tall and a 7' tall stuffed "happy" Grizzly Bear. Many antique teddy bears are on display along with a visual tour of the history of the teddy bear. Sneak in some more education

> Chelsea Teddy Bear Co. was founded in 2003 and is known for its personalized teddy bears sold to schools and the military. The U.S. Navy is the company's largest single customer.

learning about the eight species of live bears and discover where these bears live and how they survive.

WATERLOO RECREATION AREA

Chelsea - 16345 McClure Road (take I-94 to exit 157 (Pierce Road) and go north to Bush Road) 48118. Phone: (734) 475-8307. www.michigan.gov/waterloo. Admission: $8.00 per vehicle.

The lower peninsula's largest state park, it features cross-country skiing, horse rental and trails, modern and rough camping and cabins, beaches and boating, fishing, bicycle trails, and winter sports. There's also long hiking trails and an Audubon Society preserve adjacent.

Many visit often to the EDDY DISCOVERY CENTER (open Tuesday-Saturday 10:00am-5:00pm, Sunday Noon-5pm. Winter: wkends only. 734-475-3170), where you can view changing samples of geos from the Great Lakes, Michigan and the Midwest. The exhibits include: a "mad scientist lab" with interactive tests of mineral radioactivity, luminescence and computer microscopes; an interactive map of Michigan's bedrock with lift-door samples from prominent sites; and a "fossil graveyard" featuring lift-a-rock models of famous fossilized bones and teeth. Touch-screen computer mineral games challenge users to "where does it come from," and a model ice cave takes the visitor back to the Ice Age through blue-screen technology. There's also a collection station that has rotating rock and mineral collections. Outside, a quarter-mile paved rock walkway features large, outstanding samples of Michigan bedrock. There's also a slide show, hands-on activities and professional demonstrations. In the fall, watch apple cider making.

Dearborn

AUTOMOBILE HALL OF FAME

Dearborn - 21400 Oakwood Blvd. (Next to Greenfield Village) 48121. Phone: (313) 240-4000. www.automotivehalloffame.org. Hours: Wednesday-Sunday 9:00am-5:00pm. Closed major winter holidays. Admission: $4.00-$8.00 (age 5+).

To educate and encourage the next generation of industry participants, school groups can visit the Automotive Hall of Fame for only $2.00 each.

A 60-seat theatre giant-screen theatre features a short film, "The Driving Spirit", that takes an amusing look at the individuals responsible for the creation of the automotive industry (follow the "Spirit-ed" boy on this video journey and through the rest of the museum). Before you leave, be sure to start up a replica of the first gasoline-powered car, listen in on a meeting that led to forming the world's largest corporation, look into the Ransom Olds workshop, and visit a classic 1930's showroom. Hear about Whiz Kids and experience a modern factory setting of Eiji Toyoda.

FORD ROUGE FACTORY TOUR

Dearborn - (The Henry Ford Museum departures out front) 48124. Phone: (313) 982-6001. www.thehenryford.org. Hours: Monday-Saturday 9:30am-5:00pm. Open some holiday weekend Sundays and all summer Sundays (mid-April thru Labor Day), too. Closed Thanksgiving and Christmas Days. Admission: Timed tickets: $15.00 adult, $11.00 child (3-12). Reservations are suggested. Tours: While they cannot guarantee you will see the assembly line in full operation, you will still be able to visit the assembly line area temporarily suspended in mid-operation. FREEBIES: Activities for educators online.

You've already pre-purchased your timed ticket for the factory tour, now head over to the bus depot to depart at your assigned time. Motor coach rides over include audio and video presentations featuring key historic sites along the route. Tell the kids to look and listen. Your tour bus actually drives through the Steel Stamping Plant. Next, visitors are led to the Legacy Theater where you view a 12-minute film made from historic photos and films, which tells the story of both Henry Ford and the Ford Rouge complex (great Industrial Revolution learning here, parents).

See A Giant Industrial Lab...
in many fun ways!

A short walk away, visitors enter the next theater, the Art of Manufacturing. This 360-degree, multi-screen theatre-in-the-round gives viewers the sensation of actually being a part of the manufacturing process through the film which incorporates the traditional visual experience with sound, touch and scent (new car smell)! Visitors feel the heat of the blast furnace and the gentle mist of the paint shop. Get stamped and welded, too! Station Three, the eighty-foot high Observation Deck, offers an impressive view of the entire Rouge Center, including the world's largest living roof covering much of the Dearborn Truck Plant. Finally, visitors take a walkway to the Ford F-150 truck assembly plant for a panoramic, self-guided view of the modern industrial factory (stroller accessible). Along the one-third of a mile walk (with rest stops and potty breaks, if needed) through the plant, you'll see key points in the final assembly process. Meet actual team leaders (by video) and hopefully Bumper and Blinker are working hard installing windshields. Because it's both entertaining and industrial (not super technical), both parents and kids will enjoy this tour.

GREENFIELD VILLAGE

Dearborn - 20900 Oakwood Blvd. (I-94 to SR 39 north to Oakwood Blvd.) 48124. Phone: (313) 982-6100 or (313) 982-6150 info. www.thehenryford.org. Hours: Daily 9:30am-5:00pm (April 15 - early November). Friday-Sunday 9:30am-5:00pm (November-December). Open New Year's Day. Closed Thanksgiving and Christmas Days. Admission: $24.00 adult, $22.00 senior (62+), $17.50 child (5-12) for each museum. (Combo prices and additional attractions are available). Horse-drawn carriage rides, Model T rides, sleigh rides, steam train or steamboat rides available for additional fee. Note: Curriculum online (grades 4th-12th). Fast and slow paced dining options and snacks sold throughout the complex.

When a new road forced Henry Ford's beloved birthplace from its original location, Ford decided not only to move it, but to restore and refurnish it to match his boyhood recollections. The restoration received so much press that Ford was inundated with requests to save other buildings. Soon after, the idea for Greenfield Village was born. The American Experience examines so much of American history it's hard to believe it's all in one village. Henry Ford's was genius in choosing the best authentic and reproduced historic buildings. Greenfield Village Highlights:

- ❑ <u>HENRY FORD BIRTHPLACE</u> - he certainly loved and cherished his mother. See what he played with as a boy.

- ❑ <u>FORD COMPANY</u> - the hostess recommends you don't buy the model A, but wait for the Model C (better radiator).

- ❑ <u>COHEN MILLINERY</u> - try on hats of olden days.

- ❑ <u>GEORGE WASHINGTON CARVER - PEANUTS!</u> A great look at the possibilities of products made with peanuts. Carver helped find industrial uses for peanuts to help poor Southerners find new crops to grow and new uses for the crops they had. Summers, you'll often find "Mr. Carver" making some clever concoctions for you to try.

- ❑ <u>WRIGHT BROTHERS CYCLE SHOP & HOME</u> - just think of the boys "tinkering" around the shop.

- ❑

- ❑

❑ MATTOX HOUSE - "Recycling" before the word existed! Newspaper wallpaper, license plate shingles, and layered cardboard ceilings.

❑ EDISON'S MENLO PARK LAB - Learn about Edison's brilliant and showy sides. Using a loud child as a volunteer, they demonstrate a real Edison phonograph (it really worked) and souvenir piece of tin foil used as the secret to the phonograph's success.

❑ TASTE OF HISTORY RESTAURANT -Choose from favorites such as Abraham Lincoln's Chicken Fricassee or George Washington Carver's dish-of-choice. Or, try a Railroaders Lunch made with hobo bread just like 19th century railroad workers ate - round raisin nut bread filled with turkey and cheese. Sounds funny but it's really good!

The guides and actors really are skilled at engaging the kid's curiosity and use kids, not adults, as part of their demos.

HENRY FORD (THE)

Dearborn - 20900 Oakwood Blvd. (I-94 to SR 39 north to Oakwood) 48124. Phone: (313) 982-6001 or (800) 835-5237. www.thehenryford.org. Hours: Daily 9:30am-5:00pm. Closed Thanksgiving and Christmas Days. Admission: $14.00 adult, $13.00 senior (62+), $10.00 child (5-12). Combo discounts available for Rouge Factory tour or Greenfield Village. IMAX Theatre (800-747-IMAX) where you'll learn of fascinating innovations and interesting modern science ($8.50-$11.75

per movie). Educators: Themed itineraries & Curriculum online (grades 4th-12th): http://www.thehenryford.org/education/erb/ AmericanInnovationDuringIndustrialRevolution. pdf CAFÉ - Check out the Weiner Mobile (even make a Mold-A-Rama w/ the kids or grab a snack at the Weiner Mobile Café).

America's largest indoor-outdoor museum examines our country from rural to industrial societies. A special focus is placed on accomplishments and inventions of famous Americans. The Henry Ford Museum highlights:

Fun at the "Mold-A-Rama"

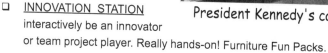

- ❏ <u>HOME ARTS</u> - evolution of home appliances. Were those the "good ole days"?

- ❏ <u>PRESIDENTIAL LIMOUSINES</u> - Among the nationally renowned artifacts of the Museum are the vehicles in which 20th-century American presidents traveled. The Kennedy limo is unforgettable.

- ❏ <u>MADE IN AMERICA</u> - production of goods made in the USA.

- ❏ <u>INNOVATION STATION</u> interactively be an innovator

President Kennedy's car...

or team project player. Really hands-on! Furniture Fun Packs.

- ❏ <u>YOUR PLACE IN TIME</u> - explore the 1900's from your own life history experiences. Kids find it silly to see what was considered "technology" years ago. For example, The Dymaxion House was built and sold in the mid-1900's as a solution to the need for a mass-produced, affordable, easily transportable and environmentally efficient house. The house was shipped in it's own metal tube and used tension suspension from a central

Home Sweet Home...it reminded us of a GIANT Hershey's Kiss ®

point. From the outside, it looks like a mutated Airstream or flying saucer! A Sales Rep greets you at the entrance and shares the features of the efficient home with your family – want to buy one?

- ❏ <u>HEROES OF THE SKY</u> - With a blend of education and entertainment, it literally allows visitors to become a wingwalker at the county fair, see just how far the Wright Brothers flew on their first flight, or test the principles of aviation as you prepare and test flight your special paper plane. Fifteen historic airplanes interpret storylines that bring to life the lofty accomplishments of America's pioneering aviators.

❑ WITH LIBERTY & JUSTICE FOR ALL - Lincoln's Chair (the rocking chair he was assassinated in) and Rosa Park's Bus (the one that started the Civil Rights movement). They will stop you in your tracks!

Compared to our visits as children years ago, we noticed a much more interactive, kid-friendly environment.

BEST WESTERN GREENFIELD INN

Dearborn (Allen Park) - 3000 Enterprise Drive, (I-94 exit 206 east). Phone: (313) 271-1600 or www.bestwesterngreenfield.com. Amenities: Spacious rooms (some w/ frig), large heated indoor pool & jacuzzi, fitness center, coffee makers, cookies at night, in-room VCRs, and Special price tickets available to The Henry Ford/Greenfield Village.

HOLIDAY INN EXPRESS HOTEL & SUITES

Dearborn (Allen Park) - 3600 Enterprises Drive (off I-94). www.ichotels.com. (313) 323-3500. The Family Suites have bunk beds w/ Redwing décor and the continental breakfast is massive. The indoor pool area is clean and kid-friendly, too.

Detroit

DETROIT SPORTS

❑ **DETROIT TIGERS BASEBALL**: Comerica Park. (313) 471-BALL or www.detroittigers.com. Major league baseball played April-September. Game's biggest scoreboard. Home runs - two huge tigers with glowing eyes growl and aquatic fireworks fountain performs. Outside - 30 hand-painted tigers on carousel and Italian Ferris wheel. Inside - main concourse has a visual tour of baseball and lifestyle history.

❑ **DETROIT LIONS FOOTBALL**: Ford Field. www.detroitlions.com. (248) 325-4131. NFL football (over 70 seasons) season runs September-December. Giant glass wall in new dome stadium.

❑ **DETROIT RED WINGS HOCKEY**: Joe Lewis Arena. (313) 396-7575 or www.detroitredwings.com. NHL top five team in the League play September-early April. Call or visit website for ticket availability.

❑ **DETROIT PISTONS BASKETBALL**: The Palace of Auburn Hills.

(248) 377-0100 or www.nba.com/pistons. NBA team with all star players. Kids Crew Post Game Shot nights.

- ❑ **DETROIT SHOCK WOMEN'S BASKETBALL**: The Palace of Auburn Hills. (248) 377-0100 or www.wnba.com/shock/. WNBA play in the spring.

DETROIT SYMPHONY ORCHESTRA

Detroit - 3663 Woodward Avenue #100 48201. Tickets: (313) 576-5111 or Office: (313) 576-5100.. www.dso.org.

Let your imagination run wild at Macy's Super Saturdays at The Max. Make a day of it with concerts and activities for all ages. It's a musical extravaganza the whole family will enjoy. Come early and enjoy KidZone FREE: Music instrument petting zoo, Balloon artists, Arts & Crafts, and Meet-n-greet with members of the DSO. Be sure to ask about "Young People Series".

MUSEUM OF AFRICAN-AMERICAN HISTORY

Detroit - 315 East Warren Avenue (off I-94 or I-75, next to Detroit Science Center) 48201. Phone: (313) 494-5800. www.thewright.org. Hours: Tuesday - Saturday: 9:00am - 5:00pm, Sunday: 1:00pm - 5:00pm. Admission: Adults $8.00 (18+), $5.00 senior (62+) and child (3-12). Note: Vending area.

A tribute to the history and culture of Detroit's African-American community. The exhibit, "And Still We Rise" traces the history and operations of the slave trade. Learn also that Detroit was one of the most active stops in the "Underground Railroad" (a network of safe stops that helped slaves escape from the south before the Civil War). Once reaching Detroit, they could cross the Detroit River into Canada. See the space suit worn by Mae Jemison, the first African-American woman to travel in space in 1992. Twenty-six interactive stations make up a three-dimensional "dictionary" designed for children from pre-school through fourth grade in A is for Africa. Other fun and educational exhibits trace the history of African music and how it transformed present American music including the famous Detroit's "Motown Sound".

AFRICAN WORLD FESTIVAL

Detroit - Philip Hart Plaza. (313) 494-5800. Sponsored by the Museum of African American History, this outdoor festival features cultural and educational programs, music, global cuisine, and storytellers at the Children's Village. FREE. (third long weekend of August)

KWAANZA

Detroit - Museum of African American History. www.thewright.org. (313) 494-5800. Weeklong during Kwaanza.   Kwaanza (first fruits) is an African celebration of the harvest and the fruits of the community's labor. Each day has a special focus: unity, self-determination, collective work and responsibility, cooperative economics, purpose, creativity and faith. (end of December)

DETROIT HISTORICAL MUSEUM

Detroit - 5401 Woodward Avenue (Woodward and Kirby. SR 1) 48202. Phone: (313) 833-1805. www.detroithistorical.org. Hours: Wednesday-Friday 9:30am-3:00pm, Saturday 10:00am-5:00pm, Sunday Noon-5:00pm. Admission: $6.00 adult, $4.00 senior (62+) or child (5-17). Children under 5 FREE. Parking is $3.00 per car Note: Motor City Online Curriculum Guide.

Newly renovated! After you've wondered through Frontiers to Factories: Detroiters at Work before the Motor City; and the Streets of Old Detroit, be sure to plan most of your time in the Motor City exhibits. See the first car in Detroit - a horseless carriage that was driven down Woodward Avenue. The Train-cam mini-train setup is a new feature where camera displays the view from the little train going around the town. Then, around the corner, you can crank up a Model T and then sit in it (great photo op!). The best part of this exhibit has to be the Body Drop! First, watch it happen on video (actual footage from a Ford Assembly plant). Then see the 70 foot section of actual assembly plant and the performance of the final steps of production. Some mannequins are in the pits below, some workers are above one floor as they "drop" the car body onto the chassis below. Did you know that Mr. Cadillac's full name is Antoine de la Mothe Cadillac? - No wonder they're so fancy!

DETROIT INSTITUTE OF ARTS (DIA)

Detroit - 5200 Woodward Avenue (off I-94 or I-75, Cultural Center) 48202. Phone: (313) 833-7900. www.dia.org. Hours: Wednesday-Sunday 10:00am-4:00pm, Saturday and Sunday til 5pm. Friday nights until 10:00pm. Admission: $8.00 adult, $6.00 senior, $4.00 child (6-17). Note: CaféDIA and the Kresge Court Coffee Stop.

A great place for kids of all ages to interact and explore. Most exhibits are "kid-friendly" and interactive and there is even a booklet: Animal & Creatures Abound, that encourages kids to "want to discover" the museum and its treasures. See exhibits such as "The American House", "The Spiral Staircase" and even "The Donkey" (which invites kids to hang, climb, and burn up excess energy) while at the museum. Fun, interactive computer programs also entertain and teach. The Great Hall features many suits of armor from the 13th to 18th century. But, above all, the masked mummy (kept safely in a display case) in the Egyptian art and artifacts exhibit is always a way to get the kids to say "wow" or "wooooo".

MICHIGAN SCIENCE CENTER

Detroit - 5020 John R Street (I-75 - Warren Exit) 48202. Phone: (313) 577-8400. www.sciencedetroit.org.   Hours: Monday-Friday 9:00am-3:00pm, Saturday 10:00am-6:00pm.Sunday Noon-6pm. Increased hours during school holidays and occasional Fridays. Admission: $16.95-18.95 per person (age 2+). IMAX is additional $5.00. Note: Café. Educators: online click Programs/Educator Guides & Events. THE FORMER DETROIT SCIENCE CENTER CLOSED. New ownership plans to reopen the facility, mostly intact, hopefully in 2013.

Just a block away from the Detroit Institute of Arts is another wonderful example of what learning "outside of the books" is all about. Located in the heart of Detroit's Cultural Complex (park once and visit maybe 4-5 museums), the museum still has the IMAX Dome Theatre and Digital Dome Planetarium plus new, dynamic exhibits. Space Laboratory takes you into the sky via space shuttle or telescope. Visitors can pedal a bicycle "at the speed of the space shuttle" to discover how long will it take to reach the moon, Mars and beyond and position each planet the correct scale distance from the sun. Motion Lab has a "stadium" Science Stage and lots of pulling, pushing physics comparing motion, speed and direction (little engineers thrive here). The Life Science Lab focuses on similarities between the rainforest and city ecosystems. The Matter and Energy Lab has a "caged" Sparks Theatre and exhibits exploring electricity, magnetism, energy conversion, etc. Power a light bulb with a hand-crank generator—then see how much less effort is required to light a fluorescent tube of the same intensity. Or, create a tornado! Surf the phenomena of everyday light and sound in the Waves and Vibrations Laboratory - just look for all the funky lights and sounds. There's even an area for the younger set to explore all the things their older siblings are playing with on a larger scale. Everyday objects become boats and water movers in a water feature surrounded by aquariums and plants. A quiet area provides families with a space where children can work on computers and infants can receive special care. Children can create treasures to take home in the Make and Take area, a space designed as a "science through art" studio. The Greenhouse introduces children to seeds, plants and how things grow.

BELLE ISLE

Detroit - 100 Strand Drive (I-75 to East Grand Blvd. Take MacArthur Bridge over to the Isle on the Detroit River) 48207. Phone: (313) 852-4075. www.detroitmi.gov/ DepartmentsandAgencies/RecreationDepartment/Belleisle.aspx Hours: Dawn to Dusk. See specific hours for special parks within the Isle. Note: FREE admission to Trails, Picnic areas, beach, Nature Center. Common to see many deer. There's also a wild animal hospital and playgrounds. In Winter: Ice skating and sledding • 30-foot ice sculpture.

The island is situated on America's busiest inland waterway and provides spectacular views of Detroit, Canada, freighter traffic and the Ambassador Bridge. Once on the island, you may get about by car or take a leisurely walk along the many miles of trails, paths and roadways that connect all of Belle Isle's points of interest. The well-used 1000 acre park and playground, still in site of the skyscrapers of Detroit offers:

- ❑ CONSERVATORY - (313) 852-4141. Hours: Daily 10:00am-5:00pm. FREE. The conservatory explores plants and flowers mostly in desert and tropical settings (ex. Cacti, ferns, palm trees, banana trees and orchids). It has a continuous display of blooming plants during the six major flower seasons of the year.

- ❑ DOSSIN GREAT LAKES MUSEUM - 100 Strand Drive (South Shore of Belle Isle). www.detroithistorical.org/aboutus/dossin.asp. (313) 833-1805. Hours: Saturday - Sunday, 11:00am-4:00pm. You're greeted by two Battle of Lake Erie cannons and the actual anchor recovered from the Edmund Fitzgerald shipwreck. The Miss Pepsi, one of the fastest hydroplane racing boats of all time. Stand in the pilot house of an ore carrier. As the marine radio sends out requests, turn the ship wheel to steer it on course or use the periscope. The 1912 Great Lakes Luxury Steamer Lounge Room is handsome (all oak carvings) - reminiscent of scenes in the movie "Titanic".

- ❑ BELLE ISLE BEACH AND WATERSLIDE - As the summer heats up, stay cool at the Belle Isle Water Slide, June 11 through Labor Day. Enjoy the slide all day for only $3.00.

HISTORIC FORT WAYNE

Detroit - (downtown, riverfront) 48207. www.historicfortwaynecoalition.com. Phone: (313) 833-1805. Hours: Saturday and Sunday 10:00am-4:00pm (Memorial Day-Labor Day weekends). Admission: secured parking is $5 per vehicle.

Enjoy special guided tours of the Historic Fort Wayne grounds at a price of

$3.00 per person. Leaving regularly from the Fort's Visitors Center, the tours will include the Star Fort built in the 1840s, the Commanding Officer's House, and the Spanish-American War Guardhouse. Secured parking is $5 per vehicle. Picnic lunches and coolers are permitted on the Fort grounds, which offer a nice view of the Detroit River, the Ambassador Bridge and Canada. However, alcohol, grills, pets and fishing are not permitted.

MOTOWN HISTORICAL MUSEUM

Detroit - 2648 West Grand Blvd. (M-10 to West Grand Blvd. Exit) 48208. Phone: (313) 875-2264. www.motownmuseum.com. Hours: Tuesday-Saturday, 10:00am-6:00pm. (Closed holidays) Admission: $10.00 adult, $8.00 child (12 and under).

In two homes that are next to each other, the music world was changed forever by Berry Gordy, composer and producer. The original recording studio "A" not only helped to build the "Motown" sound, but discovered and built the careers of the Stevie Wonder, the Temptations, the Four Tops, Diana Ross, and Marvin Gaye, just to name a few. A great stop in musical history.

PEWABIC POTTERY

Detroit - 10125 E. Jefferson Avenue (across from Waterworks Park and exactly 1.5 miles east of the Belle Isle Bridge) 48214. www.pewabic.org. Phone: (313) 822-0954. Gallery Hours: Monday-Saturday 10:00am-6:00pm. Admission: FREE. Tours: Self-guided tours of the pottery's kiln room and other production areas are from Monday-Friday 10am-4pm. Groups must call ahead to make reservations ($5 fee per person for 20 minimum group). Tours last approx. 1 hour.

Nationally renowned for its handcrafted ceramic vessels and architectural tiles and its unique glazes, Pewabic Pottery is located in the Detroit area. Being Michigan's only historic pottery, it continues to operate in a 1907 Tudor Revival building as a non-profit educational institution. The word Pewabic is derived from the Ojibwa (or Chippewa) word for the color of copper metal (or perhaps the clay from which copper came) and specifically referring to the "Pewabic" Upper Peninsula copper mine where Ms. Stratton walked with her father. They make a wide range of vases, candlesticks and unique embossed tiles. Four of the 13 People Mover stations are adorned with ceramic murals created at Pewabic. Guided Tours are suitable for children ages 12 years and older. Younger children appreciate a more interactive visit so we suggest a Pewabic Workshop or just a free look around visit.

FORD FIELD TOURS

Detroit - 2000 Brush Street (just south of I-75 (Fisher Freeway) and directly across Brush Street from Comerica Park) 48226. www.detroitlions.com/ford-field/ford-field-tours.html. Phone: 313-262-2100. Tours: each 25 person tour starts at Gate A or G and lssts one hour. Prices: $5-$7. Join public walk-up tours at 11:00am and 1:00pm on days marked on their website.

A behind-the-scenes glimpse at Detroit's crown jewel and the home of the Detroit Lions & Super Bowl XL. Get a peek at a Ford Field suite, an NFL locker room, walk down the tunnel to the field and stand on the turf for a player's view of the stadium.

INTERNATIONAL FREEDOM FESTIVAL

Detroit - Detroit Waterfront & Downtown Museums /Windsor Downtown Waterfront. Take the kids over the bridge or through the tunnel to Canada for the carnival rides, Canada's largest parade (July 1), or the Great Bed Race. On the U.S. side you'll find a children's carnival, food fair, tugboat race, international tug-of-war with Windsor, and finally fireworks on July 4th (said to be the largest pyrotechnic show in North America). http://detroitriverfront.org/riverdays/ (mid-June through July 4th)

GREAT LAKES STATE FAIR

Detroit (Novi) - Suburban Collection Showplace (46100 Grand River Ave) 48374. www.greatlakesstatefair.org (313) 369-8250. Open 10:00am - 10:00pm. This fair has a midway, baby animal birthing areas, champion animal contests, fair food, and free concerts daily by nationally famous artists. DNR Pocket Park (world's largest stove), pig races and children's theatre productions. Admission. (long Labor Day wkend)

AMERICA'S THANKSGIVING DAY PARADE

Detroit - (along Woodward Avenue from the Cultural Center to downtown). (313) 923-7400 or www.theparade.org. Buy a ticket for a grandstand seat ($15) or rent a room downtown along Woodward or get there early (6:00am) for free space streetside. Signaling the traditional kickoff to the holidays, you'll see floats, marching bands, giant balloon characters, and finally, at the finale, Santa and his sleigh. The parade starts at approximately 9:15am. Hob Nobble Gobble® includes entertainment, thrilling games and magnificent food as the celebration of a "Journey to a New Land!" moves the location of Hob Nobble Gobble® from Cobo Center to The Wintergarden at the Renaissance Center. Also spine-tingling experiences in Adventureland, Boogieland, Playland, Starland, Glamland, Paradeland and all the other lands of Hob Nobble Gobble® (day before Thanksgiving) -(Parade -Thanksgiving Day)

HOCKEYTOWN CAFÉ

Detroit - Downtown (2301 Woodward, 313-965-9500, www.hockeytowncafe.com. next to Fox Theatre,) near all the sporting action is a good stop for food and sports themed meals. The decor is highlighted by custom motorcycles themed after the Detroit Red Wings. You're greeted by the 1962 Zamboni (ice resurfacing machine) and while you're waiting on your food, take a stroll around and gander at the Statues, The Walk of Fame, or the Ring of Honor. Look for your favorite player's showcase. Both the outdoor video screen and televisions throughout the Hockeytown Café carry the live in-arena video and audio of Red Wings games directly on fiber optics from Joe Louis Arena. The kids meals are around the $5.00 range. The adult entrees were delicious and a great value. Ample, well-lit parking nearby in lots or garages. Many "kid-friendly" shows next door at Fox Theatre, too. Monday-Saturday lunch and dinner menu.

CHRYSLER MUSEUM, WALTER P.

Detroit (Auburn Hills) - 1 Chrysler Drive (northwest corner of Featherstone & Squirrel Roads on Daimler-Chrysler campus) 48326. Phone: (888) 456-1924 or (248) 944-0001. www.chryslerheritage.com. Hours: Tuesday-Saturday 10:00am-6:00pm, Sunday Noon-5:00pm. Admission: $8.00 adult, $7.00 senior (62+), $4.00 child (6-12). online discount coupon. Note: Kids Corner

The Museum contains 55,000 square feet and displays 75 vehicles. It tells the stories of Walter P. Chrysler and his love of trains, brothers John and Horace Dodge and their mechanical genius, and such industry notables as Carl Breer, Virgil Exner and Lee Iacocca. It covers everything from the Detroit Tank Arsenal to Roadrunners, Vipers and Prowlers. Several interactive displays explain brake systems, aerodynamics, power steering, platform team design and more. Interactive computer kiosks timeline the decades from 1920-1980 using vintage news footage, classic commercials and audio clips.

RAINFOREST CAFÉ EDUCATIONAL TOURS

Detroit (Auburn Hills) - 4310 Baldwin Road (I-75, exit 84 - Great Lakes Crossing) 48326. Phone: (248) 333-0280. www.rainforestcafe.com. Hours: Daily, Lunch and Dinner. Tours: usually begin at 10am and include lunch. must be scheduled.

A theme restaurant and wildlife preserve filled with live and mechanical animals; ongoing rainstorms (even thunder and lightning); a talking rainforest tree; giant "walk-through" aquarium (really cool!); hand-sculpted "cave like" rock everywhere. Preschoolers and younger love the fish tank but are a little uneasy with the motorized large gorillas and elephants (request seating on the other side of the dining room). Did you know they give Educational Group

Tours? What a "light-hearted" way to introduce your kids to the animals, plants and environs of the rainforest! The Fun Field Trip Adventure uncovers why elephants have big ears & why the Café's resident crocodile collects pennies for charity. What is your favorite fish in the coral reef? You can also include a group lunch afterwards in your plans (for an ~$8.00 per person fee). Nibble on Jurassic Tidbits and Paradise Pizza plus other kid-friendly food, drink and dessert. Although your food bill will be above moderate - it's the epitome of a theme restaurant.

CRANBROOK ART AND SCIENCE MUSEUMS

Detroit (Bloomfield Hills) - 1221 North Woodward Avenue (I-75 exit to Square Lake Road (West) to Woodward, I-696 exit - Woodward) 48303. Phone: (877) GO-CRANB. www.cranbrook.edu. Hours: Art: Wednesday-Sunday 11:00am-5:00pm. Science: Tuesday-Saturday 10:00am-5:00pm. Sunday Noon-4pm. Friday until 10:00pm. Admission: Science Museum: $12.50 adult, $9.50 seniors and children (2-12). Art museum: $2-$6.00 and children (12 and under) are FREE. Note: Picnic areas. Planetarium and Laser Shows. $4.00 extra. Live Bat Programs $4.00 extra. Café. Gift shop. Seasonal gardens with fountains, ponds and sculpture.

What makes Cranbrook an extraordinary place to visit is the wide selection of arts and entertainment it offers. Not only can you visit the Cranbrook Art Museum, but there is also the Cranbrook Institute of Science. The Cranbrook Institute of Science has programs for kids and adults, a planetarium and observatory, special group programs, summer camps and fun weekend events for the entire family throughout the year. Different areas to check out are: Our Dynamic Earth (15 foot T-Rex, woolly mastodon), Gem & Mineral Hall, Nature Place (live reptiles, turtles, and bugs - native to Michigan), Art (metalwork, realism sculpture "Body Builder", outdoor sculpture), Physics Hall (hands-on experiments about lasers and light, movement, water and air). The museum grounds feature a life-sized statue of a stegosaurus, as well as a koi pond.

MORLEY CANDY MAKERS

Detroit (Clinton Township) - Sanders Candy: 23770 Hall Road (I-94 to Hall Road M-59 Exit) 48036. Phone: (586) 468-4300 or (800) 682-2760. www.sanderscandy. com Admission: FREE.

One of Michigan's largest candy makers, this tour is sure to delight chocolate lovers of all ages. Both educational and fun, see Morley's cooking chocolate in huge copper kettles (gallons at a time). Much of that chocolate gets poured over the famous caramel used to make both vanilla caramels and, when mixed with fresh southern pecans, their spectacular Pecan Torties® ! Did you know chocolate doesn't like sudden temperature changes? How do they keep it from "turning"? The 70 foot long observation hallway is a great way to see all the candy making in action. Don't leave without your edible souvenirs!

MARVIN'S MARVELOUS MECHANICAL MUSEUM

Detroit (Farmington Hills) - 31005 Orchard Lake Road (I-696 exit Orchard Lake Road North) 48334. Phone: (248) 626-5020. www.marvin3m.com. Hours: Monday-Thursday 10:00am-9:00pm, Friday-Saturday 10:00am-11:00pm, Sunday 11:00am-9:00pm. Admission: FREE. Each device takes a quarter to operate. Note: Concessions. Modern pinball and interactive games are there too.

Something to play with everywhere here....

Pass back in time to an old-fashioned carnival full of antique slot and pinball machines, mechanical memorabilia and games. It's a very busy place with lights flashing and marionette music playing all around you. Here are some games that were really unique: a bulldozer mechanical game, Old Time Photos, Marionette and Clown Dancing Shows, and miniature carrousel and Ferris wheel. Marvin's is listed in the World Almanac's 100 most unusual museums in the U.S. Once you're inside, it's hard to know what game to play first! P.S. - Grandparents can get real sentimental here.

DIAMOND JACK'S RIVER TOURS

Detroit (Grosse Ile) - 25088 Old Depot Court (Rivard Plaza, foot of Woodward, downtown) 48138. Phone: (313) 843-9376. www.diamondjack.com. Hours: Thursday-Sunday (early June-Labor Day). Admission: $17.00 adult, $15.00 senior (60+), $15300 child (6-16). Tours: 2 hour leisurely narrated cruise departs at 1pm and 3:30pm. Note: Snacks and beverages available on board. Safest parking available at the Renaissance Center.

The 65-foot "mini-ship" cruises down the Detroit River around Belle Isle and back to Ambassador Bridge. This is the world's busiest international waterway

along the U.S. and Canadian shorelines. There's a good chance that large freighters and ocean ships will pass by. You'll see a great view of both the Detroit and downtown Windsor, Canada skylines and pass by (with stories told by captain) the historic Warehouse District, Mayor's Residence (if he's out back, he'll wave), Yacht Clubs, Islands, Bridges and a Fireboat. See the world's only marble Art Deco lighthouse or one of only two International Marine mailboats in the world. They told us the mailboat has its own zip code and delivers mail to the freighters by a pail on a pulley.

GREENMEAD HISTORICAL PARK

Detroit (Livonia) - 20501 Newburgh Road (jct. 8 Mile and Newburgh Roads) 48150. Phone: (248) 477-7375. www.ci.livonia.mi.us. Hours: Grounds open Daily 8:30am-4:00pm (May-October, and in December). Closed holidays. Admission: $2.00-$3.00 per person.

The 95 acre park site was the 1820's homestead of Michigan pioneer, Joshua Simmons. The Simmon's family lived in a modest frame house, while the barn, a building of primary importance, was the first major structure completed. Together, the buildings tell the story of farm life in rural Michigan. Eight historical buildings (some plain, some fancy) outline regional history, especially during scheduled events or Sundays. There is a wide variety of items exhibited in the general store. They have stocked the store with goods from the 1913 ledger. This building is a favorite of children of all ages, who enjoy shopping at its candy and trinket counters.

MOTORSPORTS MUSEUM & HALL OF FAME OF AMERICA

Detroit (Novi) - 43700 Expo Center Drive (current exhibit space) (I-96 - exit 162) 48375. Phone: (248) 349-7223. www.mshf.com. Hours: Until Further Notice, The Museum Is Open Only By Appointment. They have suspended public tour hours. Watch the website for updates of moving to new location.

If there is a racing fan in your family this is a "must stop". See over 40 vehicles including powerboats, motorcycles, "Indy style" racecars, NASCAR style racecars, dragsters, and even snowmobiles. Among the highlights are Art Arfons' Green Monster jet car and championship NASCAR stock cars driven by Darrell Waltrip and Dale Jarrett. Get their photo taken in the driver's seat of an actual Winston Cup racecar and then take the challenge of racing on the 4-lane scale slot car track or video simulation race car.

DETROIT ZOO

Detroit (Royal Oak) - 8450 West Ten Mile Road (I-75 to I-696 West - Woodward Avenue Exit) 48068. Phone: (248) 398-0900 info. http://detroitzoo.org. Hours: Daily 10:00am-5:00pm (April - October). Daily 10:00am-4:00pm. (November-March). Admission: $14.00 adult, $12.00 senior (62+), $9.00 child (2-14). $5.00 Parking fee. Note: Picnic areas and playground. Strollers and Adult roller chairs available for rent. Firagge Feedings (seasonal -$5 per person) offer personal food feedings off the new platforms!

Simply put...your family is in for a real day of adventure! The world's largest polar bear exhibit, the Arctic Ring of Life, is a lifelike trek to the North Pole's tundra, open sea and ice mountains. Start outside and curve around the exhibit to the spectacular 70 foot long clear tunnel (Polar Passage) which takes visitors underneath diving and swimming polar bears and seals. Their

antics will entertain you for most of the visit (plan 45 minutes to one hour just at this exhibit)! What a fun learning experience for the kids to see the Inuit peoples and their interaction with Arctic animals.

Here's a few of the other, constantly changing exhibits that you'll see: The Mandrill Exhibit (a very colorful baboon), The Wilson Aviary Wing (30 species of birds in a large free-flying building - much like an indoor jungle - there is even a waterfall), The Penguinarium (love that name! - see underwater views of these birds that cannot fly), The Chimps of Harambee (a forest setting with rock habitats...what a show!), and The Wildlife Interpretive Gallery (huge aquarium, theater, hummingbird and butterfly garden).

Visitors can now enjoy some of the most fascinating animals in a whole new way. Patrons will have the chance to get face to face with red kangaroos –

from inside the Australian Outback Adventure exhibit! Visitors move along a winding path bordered by knee-high cables on both sides, while the kangaroos are free to bound wherever they want. The simulated outback is complete with recreated settlement bulidings, termite mounds, and Aboriginal artifacts. Can you leap as far as the kangaroo can? And if all this wasn't enough...take an excursion on the famous Detroit Zoo Miniature Railroad (it transports over 500,000 passengers a year).

BEACH GRILL, THE

Detroit (St. Clair Shores) - (Jefferson Beach Marina Complex) - 24420 Jefferson (between 9 & 10 mile). (586) 771-4455. http://beachgrillrestaurantandresort.com/home. aspx Moderately priced meals and enjoy spectacular views of all the Great Lakes boats. Indoor/Outdoor dining. Trendy...yet family friendly. Kids menu $3.00-6.00. Open daily for lunch and dinner. More of a party crowd after dark.

WAYNE COUNTY LIGHTFEST

Detroit (Westland) - Hines & Merriman, (I-96 exit Merriman). www.waynecounty.com/parks/ (734) 261-1990. Nearly one million lights of arcs and tree-lined straights billed as the Midwest's largest holiday light show. More than 35 displays and a refreshment shelter, gifts, and visits with Santa. Admission $5.00 per car. Runs between (mid-November & January 1 - closed Christmas night).

Dexter

SPRING VALLEY TROUT FARM

Dexter - 12190 Island Lake Road (off I-94) 48130. www.springvalleytroutfarm.com. Phone: (734) 426-4772. Hours: Because of Michigan weather, the farm is open Spring and Fall on Saturdays and Sundays from 9:00am to 5:00pm. Memorial Day to Labor Day open Wednesday through Sunday from 9:00am-6:00pm. The farm closes end of September each year. Group tours available for ~$9/person.

Natural, organic (non-polluted water) fed trout in spring-fed ponds are waiting to be caught. There is even a Children's Trout pond reserved for little anglers under 10 years old. The environment is so perfect in these ponds, they can even guarantee a catch on every outing! They'll clean the fish and pack them in ice to take home. Fees charged ($4.00 per person to fish - age 5+ and a fee per pound of fish caught). Picnic/grilling areas. No license or equipment needed.

Dundee

SPLASH UNIVERSE RIVERRUN INDOOR WATER PARK RESORT

Dundee - 100 Whitetail Drive (Cabelas exit, US-23S. Exit 17 for M-50 toward Dundee/Monroe) 48131. Phone: 877-752-7482. www.splashuniverse.com. Hours: Waterpark Open 9:00am - 9:00pm every summer and school break. During School year: Friday nights, Saturday (9am-9pm) and Sunday (9am-6pm) Admission: Splash Universe RiverRun Indoor Water Park Admission Policy: Registered hotel guests receive passes to the water park as part of their room fees. Day passes ($20-$32.00) are available for the general public as well. A regional resident pays less for a day pass than someone from outside the area. Half-day and spectator only passes are available.

At 25,000 square feet, RiverRun is a comparatively small indoor water park, therefore more manageable - especially with the younger set in tow. While it lacks "thrill rides" like a water coaster or raft rides (more for tweens and teens), it does, however, offer the basic water slides, a lazy river, zero entry toddler play area, and an interactive water play station.

The 150-room hotel includes family suites and standard guest rooms. All rooms include a Fresh Start Breakfast. Kids Bunkhouse Suites start at $159 for a Family of 4! The resort also features over 70 bunk bed suites including a separate TV just for the kids in the bunk area, refrigerators, microwaves, and DVD players. In addition to the indoor water park, the resort offers an arcade, restaurant, and a gift shop. It also features the Adventure Quest Kids Clubhouse which provides crafts, storytelling, and other activities for younger children.

East Lansing

LANSING SYMPHONY ORCHESTRA

East Lansing - Bogue Street & Wilson (MSU Campus - Wharton Center for Performing Arts) 48824. www.lansingsymphony.org. Phone: (517) 487-5001 or (800) WHARTON.

Free Young People's Concerts and music for Broadway shows like "Beauty & the Beast". Hot Buttered Pops, Jingle Bell Pops, or Play Me A Story.

MICHIGAN STATE UNIVERSITY ATTRACTIONS

East Lansing - West Circle Dr. (Off SR 43) 48825. www.msu.edu/community/index.html.
Phone: (517) 355-7474.   Hours: Vary with museum. All sites closed on University holidays.

- ❑ <u>MUSEUM</u>: West Circle Drive. (517) 355-2370. Natural wonders of the Great Lakes, world cultures, animal diversity. 3 stories of special exhibits. Museum store. They offer numerous family programs focused on the history of inhabitants of Michigan.

- ❑ <u>KRESGE ART MUSEUM</u>: Culturally diverse art. FREE. (517) 355-7631.

- ❑ <u>BEAUMONT TOWER</u>: Site of Old College Hall - the first building erected for instruction in scientific agriculture. Recently renovated. Weekly carillon concerts.

- ❑ <u>FARMS</u>: Observe milking cows mid-afternoon. Also sheep, horse and swine areas. Weekdays only. (517) 355-8383. South Campus.

- ❑ <u>BUG HOUSE</u>: Natural Science Building. Farm Lane & East Circle Drive. (517) 355-4662. Noisy cockroaches, millipedes and giant grasshoppers.

- ❑ <u>ABRAMS PLANETARIUM</u>: Shaw Lane & Science Road. (517) 355-STAR. Small Admission. Weekend matinees are suggested for younger ones.

- ❑ <u>HORTICULTURE GARDENS AND GREEN HOUSE</u>: Bogue & Wilson Road (south end of campus). (517) 355-0348. American Trial Garden test site. Children's Garden - 63 theme gardens - garden emphasizes the important part plants play in children's daily lives, from the first cereal bowl in the morning to the last popcorn snack at night. Secret Garden (just like movie), Pizza Garden (wheat for dough, toppings and spices, tomatoes), Peter Rabbit Garden (bunny food favorites), Sensation Garden (guess which plant it is by smell), 2 Treehouses, and a Butterfly Garden. (517) 353-4800. Small Admission donation. Spring/Summer. Parking fee on weekdays. Our favorite garden for kids (in the state and midwest) is so colorful and artistically done (on a kid's level).

> Our favorite Midwest Children's Garden and University Dairy Plant are right here!

❑ DAIRY STORE AND PLANT. South Anthony Hall (Farm Lane & Wilson Road). (517) 432-2479 or http://dairystore.msu.edu/. Hours: Monday-Friday 9:00am-8:00pm, Saturday-Sunday Noon-8:00pm. Closed University holidays. Admission: FREE. Everything you ever wanted to know about "Cheddaring"! This is a great guided (in groups, pre-arranged) or self-guided (with simple explanations) observation deck tour of the pilot plant where students process milk making the famous Spartan cheese and ice cream. After you see the production facility, walk downstairs to the Dairy Store and buy a cone (their Junior cones are still 2 dips) or a light lunch.

EAST LANSING ART FESTIVAL

East Lansing - Downtown between Abbott and Mac Streets, 48823. (517) 337-1731. www.elartfest.com. Especially for kids are the performing dancers, storytellers, clowns and jugglers. Creative art project areas for kids include face painting and making a contribution to the Chalk Art Mural. Shuttles available from many parking sites nearby. (third weekend in May)

GREAT LAKES FOLK FESTIVAL

East Lansing - MSU Museum. **www.greatlakesfolkfest.net.** (517) 432-GLFF. Celebrating traditional visual and performing arts with musicians, dancers, craftspeople, storytellers, parades and lots of ethnic food. FREE. (mid-August weekend)

Fenton

APPLEFEST

Fenton - Spicer Orchards, (US-23 to Clyde Road exit). www.spicerorchards.com. (810) 632-7692. Take a hayride out to the orchards for apple picking, pony rides, Victorian Carriage House (storage for 10,000 bushels, a sorting machine, cider mill and shops) and other entertainment. Yummy cider and doughnuts. Apple Tours by appointment. Fee for some activities. (weekends in September and October)

Hanover

THE BUFFALO RANCH

Hanover - 12770 Roundtree Road (US-12 : Take Moscow Road North, Left (West) on Mosherville Road, Right (North) on Rountree Road) 49241. Phone: (517) 563-8249. www.horsesandbuffalo.net. Hours:Tuesday-Sunday 9:00am-5:00pm. Admission: Buffalo herd visit $5.00 per person. Horseback riding $20.00 per hour. Zipline ride $5.00. Mechanical Bull ride $5.00. FREE Bucking Barrel. Note: Be a cowgirl/ cowboy for the day (age 10+, $100.00) or Live on the Ranch overnight. Breakfast and lunch included. Group wagon rides $35. Ride horses, saddle and unsaddle horses, feed the horses. See and feed the buffalo. Dress casually.

Here's a visit that your kids are sure to tell their friends about! Take a hay wagon ride out into Gary Childs' pastures to see some of his more than 100 buffalo. The brave kids will usually get the opportunity to reach out and actually touch a live buffalo and feed corn cobs onto their huge tongues! (if the herd is cooperating that day). This ranch was also fortunate enough (1/40 million chance) to have given birth to a white buffalo...(which is a powerful Native American spiritual symbol). The calf died, but they have lots of pictures to show. Try a ride on the new mechanical bull or zip line while you're there.

Holly

HOLLY RECREATION AREA

Holly - 8100 Grange Hall Road (off I-75 exit 101) 48442. Phone: (248) 634-8811. www.michigan.gov/holly.   Admission: $8.00 per vehicle.

Approximately 10 miles of hiking and cross country ski trails are in the central portion of the recreation area. Although mountain bikes are prohibited on these trails, there is an extensive mountain bike trail system located in the Holdridge Lakes area of the park, ranging in terrain from easy to advanced. The rolling woodland and prairies that dominate this landscape, are featured in the development in the Holly Woods Disc Golf Course. Offering both 9 and 18 hole routes, this course offers a variety of challenges and fun for all skill levels. Camping, hiking, boating, fishing, swimming, winter sports.

SEVEN LAKES STATE PARK

Holly - 14390 Fish Lake Road (I-75, exit 101) 48442. www.michigan.gov/sevenlakes. Phone: (248) 634-7271. Admission: $8.00 per vehicle.

The dam, constructed by the developers, formed one large lake from seven small lakes (historically known as the DeCoup Lake) hence the name Seven Lakes State Park. Trail systems criss-cross the entire area. This trail system is used by hikers, cross country skiers, snowmobilers (when there is four or more inches of snow) and mountain bikers. About 230 acres of water with several miles of shoreline await the park user. Boat rentals of row boats, canoes, paddle boats and your-motor-on boats are available from mid-May to mid-September. Camping, hiking trails, fishing, swimming, bicycle trails, and winter sports.

MICHIGAN RENAISSANCE FESTIVAL

Holly - Festival grounds near Mount Holly, (I-75 north exit 106). www.michrenfest.com. (800) 601-4848. Beginning in mid-August and running for seven weeks, the "Robinhood-ish" woods of Holly take you back to the sixteenth century. See knights in shining armor, strolling minstrels or Henry VIII characters. If you like, your family can dress as a lord or lady. Don't dress the kids too fancy though, all the food served is eaten with only your hands and fingers (ex. Giant turkey legs, cream soups served in bread bowls). Watch a mock jousting tourney, run from the friendly dragon, see jugglers and jesters, listen to storytellers, and best of all, ride on human-powered fair rides (it's hilarious). Admission $6.00-15.00 depending on age. Discount coupons available at area supermarkets. (mid-August weekend for seven weekends through September)

 _____

Howell

MICHIGAN CHALLENGE BALLOONFEST

Howell - Howell High School area, (I-96 exit 133). www.michiganchallenge.com. 60,000 or more folks will share space with you watching skydiving, stunt kites, music, fireworks, and spectacular balloon launch flight competitions. There's also a carnival for the kids and bright balloon glows in the evening. Admission by carload ($10.00) or by entire weekend per person (slightly more). (third or fourth weekend in June)

 _____

Irish Hills

MCCOURTIE PARK

Irish Hills (Somerset Center) - (US 12 and US 127 - 11/2 miles west - enter from South Jackson Road) 49282. www.michigan.org/ property/mccourtie-park.

Walk over 17 concrete bridges (each a different style), visit the underground apartments and garages, see the giant birdhouse and their tree chimneys. All of this concrete! Until you get up close, it will fool you - it looks like wood! Herb McCourtie, a concrete baron, left the park grounds to his hometown. It's unique enough to definitely write home about!

Jackson

DAHLEM ENVIRONMENTAL EDUCATION CENTER

Jackson - 7117 South Jackson Road (I-94 to exit 138 - south) 49201. Phone: (517) 782-3453. www.dahlemcenter.org. Hours: Tuesday-Friday 9:00am - 5:00pm, Saturday 10:00am-5:00pm & Sunday Noon-5:00pm. Trails open Daily 8:00am - sunset. Admission: FREE to roam the grounds. $3.00-$5.00 fee for programs. Note: Gift shop. Cross-country skiing in winter. New and exciting seasonal programs including "Silent Salamanders", "Night of the Amphibians", "Creatures of the Pond", "Celebrating Loons Fest" and more.

Over 5 miles of hiking trails allow you to explore the fields, marshes, ponds, and forest of this "piece of nature" just a short drive from the city. All, regardless of age and physical abilities, can explore on the special needs (1/2 mile) trail. (All-terrain wheelchairs are available on request). Call or visit website for details on upcoming nature programs.

CASCADES

Jackson - 1992 Warren Avenue (I-94 exit 138, south on West Avenue) 49203. Phone: (517) 788-4320. www.co.jackson.mi.us/departments/Parks/parks_description/ cascade_falls_park.asp. Hours: Park open 11:00am-11:00pm. Cascades illuminated dusk -11:00pm in the Summer. Admission: General $3.00-$4.00 (ages 6+). Note: Snack Bar. Gift store and restrooms. Paddleboats, mini-golf.

It began in 1932 and you can still view the colorful and musical waterfalls and fountains. Sound response programs were developed so that the Cascades lights and fountains change patterns in direct response to pre-recorded or live music. Use seating provided or climb to the top and be refreshed by spraying water. Continuously changing patterns keep it lively. The Cascades Falls history museum is within the park.

HOT AIR JUBILEE

Jackson -   Jackson County Airport. www.facebook.com/hotairjubilee. Launches mornings & evenings, flight demo teams, stunt kites, Kids Kingdom, aircraft displays & carnival. www.hotairjubilee.com. Admission. (second or third weekend in July)

NITE LITES

Jackson - 200 West Ganson Street, Jackson County Fairgrounds, (I-94 exit 139). www.nitelitesshow.com or (800) 245-5282. A one-mile drive with 100,000 lights of "Candyland" (a candy cane treat is included with admission). They even have a drive up animated manger scene. Admission per vehicle ~ $5.00. (Wednesday - Sunday weekly beginning the week of Thanksgiving through Christmas)

Laingsburg

SLEEPY HOLLOW STATE PARK

Laingsburg - 7835 Price Road (off US 27 east on Price Road) 48848. Phone: (517) 651-6217. www.michigan.gov/sleepyhollow Admission: $8.00 per vehicle.

A river winds its way through the woods and fields of the park and Lake Ovid is nestled in the middle of it all. Lake Ovid is a 410 acre man-made lake which was developed by making a dam on the Little Maple River. A "no wake" lake environment is great for fishing and rough camping. More than 228 species of birds have been recorded in Sleepy Hollow, from the common Blue Jay to the Eastern Bluebird. During migration, look for waterfowl in Lake Ovid. The rarely recorded Bonaparte's Gull or Bald Eagle also have been sighted. Other features include a beach with snack bar, boating, hiking and bike trails, and winter sports

Lake Orion

BALD MOUNTAIN RECREATION AREA

Lake Orion - 1330 Greenshield (I-75 exit SR 24 north approximately 7 miles) 48360. Phone: (248) 693-6767. www.michigan.gov/baldmountain. Admission: $8.00 per vehicle.

Bald Mountain Recreation Area consists of 4,637 rolling acres. The picturesque park area has some of the steepest hills and most rugged terrain in southeastern Michigan. Two universally accessible piers makes fishing available to everyone. One pier is located East Graham and one at Lower Trout Lake. Beginning with a great kiddie beach at Lower Trout Lake, the park also features hiking trails, fishing, boating, horseback riding, winter sports, and cabins for camping.

Lansing

MICHIGAN HISTORICAL MUSEUM

Lansing - 702 West Kalamazoo Street (I-496 exit ML King, exit north follow signs to Capital Loop) 48909. Phone: (517) 373-3559. www.michigan.gov/museum. Hours: Monday-Friday 9:00am-4:30pm, Saturday 10:00am-4:00pm, Sunday 1:00-5:00pm. Closed state holidays. Admission: $6 adult, $4 senior (65+), $2 youth (6-17). Note: Museum store. Snack Shop open weekdays. Educators: Online lesson plans: www.michigan.gov/dnr/0,4570,7-153-54463_19268---,00.html.

A great way to understand Michigan society, land, and industry - and all in one building. If your travel plans around Michigan are limited, this would be a history time-saver. We really enjoy museum layouts with untraditional "real life" settings and odd turns and corners. We've found this keeps children's curiosity peaked! Follow the Paleo Indians of the past to industry of the present (Detroit Cars). Play teacher in a one-room schoolhouse. Explore the impact of deer hunting on Michigan's culture and identity. See tools used by prehistoric hunters, Ted Nugent's loincloth and other hunting artifacts. Museum "Don't Misses" include: the look and touch 3840 pound Float Copper that spans 4 feet by 8 feet and is hollow-sounding; entering rooms like the Mine Shaft or Lumber Barons parlor or old-time theater; and learning words you may not know like Riverhog.. As you enter the center, you'll find the three-story relief map of Michigan - it's wonderful to gaze at from many angles.

FENNER NATURE CENTER

Lansing - 2020 East Mount Hope Avenue 48910. Phone: (517) 483-4224. .www. mynaturecenter.org. Hours: Tuesday-Friday 10:00am-4:00pm. Sundays Noon-4:00pm (year-round).

Fenner Nature Center features 130 acres of mixed habitat with approximately 4 miles of self-guided hiking trails through maple groves, pine forests, swamp forests, old fields, and 3 different ponds. Cross country skiing is permitted on trails. A visitor's center and gift shop is on location. Call or visit website for special seasonal children's programs. Free admission.

APPLE BUTTER FESTIVAL

Lansing - Fenner Nature Center. www.mynaturecenter.org. Tempt your taste buds with fresh cider and apple butter being made right before your eyes. Nature walks. (second or third weekend in October)

LANSING LUGNUTS

Lansing - 505 East Michigan Avenue (Oldsmobile Park, downtown) 48912. Phone: (517) 485-4500. www.lansinglugnuts.com. Tickets: $8-$11.

The Lansing Lugnuts are a Class A minor league baseball team, affiliated with the Toronto Blue Jays, that plays in the Midwest League. Cooley Stadium seats over 11,000 fans and is one of the largest Class A Minor League baseball parks in the United States. Best for kids: Fireworks/Kids Days. Play area for kids.

POTTER PARK ZOO

Lansing - 1301 South Pennsylvania Avenue (entrance is just south of the I-496 Freeway, along Red Cedar River) 48912. www.potterparkzoo.org. Phone: (517) 483-4222. Hours: Daily 9:00am-6:00pm (April-October). Daily 10:00am- 4:00pm (winter). Varying hours in September, October and May. Admission: $10.00 adult, $3.00 senior (60+), $2.00 child (3-16). Parking fee. Lansing residents receive discount. Note: Pony or camel rides and petting zoo, too.

More than 400 animals (get a virtual visit on the website) await your family at this great educational and family friendly zoo. Snow Leopards, Black Rhinos, Siberian Tigers, Reindeer, Lemurs, Penguins, and Red Pandas are just a few of the exhibits featured. Welcome the River Otters and Arctic Fox exhibits and new babies here and there. Free flight birds. Farmyard Edventures. Wolves, ducks and a coral reef too. Don't you love the antics of the Primates? Cotton-Tops are the little monkeys that are black and white and look like they have snazzy mohawk hairdos. You can spot the babies clinging to their parents' backs.

WONDERLAND OF LIGHTS

Lansing - Potter Park Zoo. www.potterparkzoo.org. (517) 702-4730. Thousands of lights create a "Wildlife Wonderland" of unique zoo animal displays. Evenings beginning at dark. Admission. (late November through December)

WOLDUMAR NATURE CENTER

Lansing - 5739 Old Lansing Road (2 miles west of Waverly Rd.) 48917. Phone: (517) 322-0030. www.woldumar.org. Hours: Center open Monday-Saturday 10:00am-5:00pm. Park open dawn to dusk. Trail fee: $1.00.

Woldumar Nature Center is situated on 188 acres of diverse wildlife habitat along the banks of the Grand River. Over 5 miles of hiking and cross-country skiing trails take visitors through fields, wetlands, pine and maple-beech forests, old apple orchards and a prairie. Hike or ski anytime between dawn and dusk. The Visitors Center is a great place to start with interpretive and live creature displays. Nature Center facilities and grounds provide programs year round. Tours of Moon Log Cabin during special events.

AMERICAN HERITAGE FESTIVAL

Lansing - Woldumar Nature Center. www.woldumar.org. Pioneers and Native Americans, Farmers Market, pioneer toys, Apple cider pressing, spinning, live animals, blacksmithing, historic farm tool display, spinning, lace making, good old time music, Grand River pontoon boat rides, good food, WolduMarket and much more. Admission (age 13+). (last weekend in September)

IMPRESSION 5 SCIENCE CENTER

Lansing - 200 Museum Drive (Banks of Grand River, off Michigan Avenue, downtown) 48933. Phone: (517) 485-8116.   www.impression5.org.   Hours: Tuesday-Saturday 10:00am-5:00pm. Sunday 1:00pm - 5:00pm. Closed the first week of September (annually) and major holidays. Admission: $5.00 adult, $4.50 senior (62+) Note: Impressions to Go Café. Great Science gift shop, too. The center hosts a variety of educational programs and demonstrations, including those that teach kids how to make chromatography butterflies, sand art tubes, egg-drop vehicles, and flying oddities.

150 displays challenge all five senses (i.e. the reason for Impression 5 name). Although it's smaller than many science centers, it's well worth the lower admission cost. Highlights include:

THROWING THINGS - using different principles of physics, kids play with different forms of projectiles and balls...even giant slingshots. We've never seen this before - so many different ways to throw things! GIANT EYE - walk into this 7-foot tall model of a human eye to learn how this incredible organ transforms light into images. WATER - Build a water tower, navigate a ship thru locks, assemble a plumbing system and splash. BUBBLES - create bubble walls, circles. LIGHT AND COLOR experiments and COMPUTER LAB AND REAL CHEMISTRY LAB - where techs help you make your own experiment - slime! $2.00 extra to make slime and you get to take home your experiment! Outside the lab are "Roundtables" - simple experiments you do as a family.

Slime is made under the direction of a certified Slime professional who will tell you all about the ingredients used and reactions that take place to create the Slime.

MICHIGAN STATE CAPITOL

Lansing - Capital & Michigan Avenues (I-496 exit M.L. King Street. Follow Capital Loop) 48933. Phone: (517) 373-2353. http://council.legislature.mi.gov/lcfa/x1.htm. Tours: Monday-Friday 9:00am-4:00pm. Tours leave every half hour. Admission: FREE.

The House and Senate Galleries are situated inside a building that looks like the US Capital. Recently restored, the building was originally designed by foremost architect, Elijah E. Myers during the Gilded Age. You'll start out under the dome which is a view upward over 160 feet. This gets the kids' attention. Next, you take a peek in the Governor's Office. It's a very stately, very large office that was cleaned during the restoration with cotton swabs (at least, the ceiling was). The kids try to imagine doing their cleaning chores with only cleaning solution and cotton swabs - sounds impossible! Another highlight of this tour is the Senate Room. Magnificent to view (from the public access balcony), it has so much detail, the kids are mesmerized. There are illustrated seating charts, designed to help you locate your legislator's desk on the chamber floor outside each of the chambers. If the legislature is in session, you can pick up a session calendar from the House and Senate Sergeants here. They'll also learn about contemporary legislative processes and how citizens get involved. By looking around the corridors, try to determine who was the youngest and oldest governor. Outside, look for the Freedom Tree and the "mystery stone."

PLANET WALK

Lansing - River Trail along Grand & Red Cedar River (Outside Science Center - 200 Museum Drive) 48933. Phone: (517) 371-6730. www.friendsofaatrails.org/ planet_walk.htm.

AROUND THE SOLAR SYSTEM IN FORTY-FIVE MINUTES - sound unbelievable? It's a version of a walk through space that never leaves the ground. The Lansing Planet Walk is an exact scale model of the entire solar system, constructed along Lansing's River Trail, that can be traversed on foot in about forty-five minutes. Travel 93 million miles from the Earth to the Sun, almost another 4 billion miles to the farthest planet, Pluto. Want to walk it? Begin at the scaled down version of the sun (it's about the size of a giant play ball). Each step further out covers 1 million scale miles. Pass earth, the size of a pea, and Jupiter, the size of an orange. The total walking distance from the Sun to Pluto is 2 miles.

R.E. OLDS TRANSPORTATION MUSEUM

Lansing - 240 Museum Drive (Downtown off Michigan Avenue, next to Impression 5) 48933. Phone: (517) 372-0529 or (888) ASK-OLDS. www.reoldsmuseum.org. Hours: Tuesday-Saturday 10:00am-5:00pm, Sunday Noon-5:00pm. Closed major holidays. (Closed Sundays November - March) Admission: $4.00-$6.00 (over age 5). Family $12.00.

The museum is a reflection of R.E. Olds life and contribution to the transport industry from 1883 to the present. See the first Oldsmobile (1897), Toronado (first 1966), Stars, Durants and Olds car advertising. The final Oldsmobile, a dark cherry metallic "Final 500 Collector's Edition" (#500 of 500) Alero sedan, was donated to the museum on April 29, 2004. See autographed and experimental motors plus an REO Speedwagon or Cloud. This museum also houses a nearly-complete collection of Michigan license plates, early traffic signs and a working 1950's-era traffic signal. So many "old" cars to look at up close...be sure to look for the Spartan car, and the legendary "Hurst Hairy Oldsmobile" (a twin-engine, 4-tire burning, pavement melting) drag race car.

MICHIGAN WEEK

Lansing - Downtown.. (517) 323-2000. Celebrates events and people from Michigan's rich traditions in agriculture, industry, recreation, education, athletics and government. Parade Saturday. FREE. (third week in May)

SILVER BELLS IN THE CITY

Lansing - Downtown. (517) 372-4636. www.silverbellsinthecity.org FREE family entertainment featuring an electric light parade, musical entertainment, ice sculptures, horse-drawn wagon rides, performances, admission to downtown cultural institutions and the lighting of Michigan's official holiday tree with fireworks. (third Friday in November)

CLARA'S LANSING STATION RESTAURANT

Lansing - 637 E. Michigan Avenue. (517) 372-7120 or www.claras.com. Located in the historic Michigan Central Railroad Station, this place has the look and feel of a Victorian era station. Trains still pass by while you eat...and maybe you'll get lucky enough to eat on the platform for a great view. Daily lunch and dinner with moderate pricing. Children's Menu with basic American food fare priced between $3.00-$4.00. Nearby (Lugnuts) and Impression 5 Museum.

HOLIDAY INN WEST HOLIDOME

Lansing - 7501 W. Saginaw Hwy, 48917 (I-96 exit 93B). (517) 627-3211. Fun, clean Holidome for family fun. The pool temperature is just right and there are many "little tykes" playthings plus the arcade and ping pong games for older children. We liked having the TGIFridays restaurant right on the premises with their popular food and kids menu (even for breakfast).

MICHIGAN PRINCESS

Lansing (Grand Ledge) - Grand River Park 48837. www.michiganprincess.com. Phone: (517) 627-2154. Admission: $10.00-50.00 depending on the type of cruise. Children (3-12) are at 50% of adult rate.

This cruise line features a variety of cruising options. The "Michigan Princess" (which has three levels and luxurious woodwork and crystal) boat features fully air-conditioned and heated cabins that allow for year-round cruising. Be sure to ask about the "Celebration", luncheon or music cruise.

Marine City

ALGONAC STATE PARK

Marine City - 8732 River Road (2 miles north of the city on SR 29) 48039. Phone: (810) 765-5605. www.michigan.gov/algonac. Admission: $8.00 per vehicle.

On the St. Clair River, you can watch the large freighters pass by from this park. Algonac's lakeplain prairies and lakeplain oak savannas are considered globally significant. These special habitats include nineteen species that are on the state list of endangered, threatened, and special concern species. Other features include winter sports, hiking trails along a prairie area, fishing (walleye), rough camping, and boating.

Milan

CLEAN WATER BEACH

Milan - 16339 Cone Road (US 23 to exit 22 - follow signs) 48160. Phone: (734) 439-1818. www.cleanwaterbeach.com. Hours: Daily 10:30am-7:30pm (Memorial Day Weekend-Labor Day Weekend). Admission: $6.00 (weekends), $5.00 (weekdays), $3.00 child (9-12), Under 8 FREE (all the time).

Some people see a hole in the ground (in this case caused by the construction of US-23)...others see opportunity. In 1962, area resident Charles Heath gained a 6-acre lake (in his former cow pasture) along the new construction.

For years they used this recreation area as a family swimming hole. With the persuading of friends, Charles decided to make some improvements and open it to the public.

MILAN DRAGWAY

Milan - 10860 Plank Road (US 23 to exit 25) 48160. Phone: (734) 439-7368. www. milandragway.com. Hours: Season is April-October. Auto races held in the day, Saturday & Sunday. Motorcycle races held Friday nights. Admission: ~Adults $15.00, Children $5.00 (7-12), FREE (ages 6 and under). During special events - rates can be higher (average $5.00-$30.00). Call or visit website for details. Note: Drag and bracket racing. Events include junior racing, nostalgia days, RAM chargers, Harlet drags and invitationals. There's even a new track for off-road truck races.

A race that lasts 6 seconds or less? Don't blink or you might just miss it! See Michigan (and nationally known) racers compete to see who can travel the fastest on the ¼ mile drag "strip". Special events feature "dragsters" that can reach speeds of over 300 MPH (in a little over 4 seconds!) Be sure to bring earplugs for the kids (& parents) since these "open header" vehicles can be extremely loud! Hey Moms and Dads... Wednesday and Friday allow you (for an entry fee) to see just how fast the family "dragster" can go! Kids can also compete in special miniature drag cars...wow!

Milford

KENSINGTON METROPARK

Milford - 2240 West Buno Road (I-96 - Next exit past Milford) 48380. Phone: (248) 685-1561 or (800) 477-3178. www.metroparks.com/parks/pk_kensington.php#. Hours: Daily 6:00am-10:00pm. Admission: $4.00 per vehicle, rides/waterpark extra $2.00-$4.00. Boat and Ski rentals. Note: Food bar at the Farm Center.

Spanning over 4,000 acres (including the 1200 acre Lake Kent), this park offers family fun year-round. Some of the educational attractions include the Farm Center and the Nature Center (with wildlife exhibits and nature trails). Walk down the farm lanes and get a feel of farm life. Meet the animals, including horses, cows, ducks, sheep and pigs, and tour the barns, including a 150-year old restored horse barn and a poultry house. Hayrides/sleighrides on weekends.

For a break from the action, step aboard the Island Queen paddlewheel boat for a scenic trip around the lake (summer afternoons). Speaking of Lake Kent, it offers great fishing (you can even bring your own boat or use rentals including sailboats which are available) and 2 beaches in the summertime. Golfing is also available on the 18-hole course of the south side of the lake. Winter brings sled riding, tobogganing, cross-country skiing, and sleigh rides (minimum snow base of 4-6 inches required) to the park.

SPLASH 'N' BLAST: offers two, 250-foot twisted waterslides, and a water spray area with cannons, palm trees and serpents that spray water to cool off on a hot day. Irrigated with pool-quality water, the Splash 'n' Blast requires waterslide riders to be 48" high, and is open from 11:00am-7:00pm daily through late summer.

PROUD LAKE RECREATION AREA

Milford (Commerce Twp.) - 3500 Wixom Road (I-96 exit Wixom Road north) 48382. Phone: (248) 685-2433.   www.michigan.gov/proudlake.   Admission: $8.00 per vehicle.

More than 20 miles of trails cover several diverse habitats. During the winter months, skiers can enjoy seeing the evergreens draped with snow. In the spring, wildflowers abound. Guided interpretive walks and other nature activities are offered. This park includes part of the upper Huron River, featuring hiking trails, beaches and swimming, boating and canoeing, camping, and winter sports. It is also a great place to be (beginning the last weekend of April) when the site releases large batches of trout for fishing.

Monroe

RIVER RAISIN BATTLEFIELD VISITOR'S CENTER

Monroe - 1403 East Elm Street (I-75, exit 14) 48161. Phone: (734) 243-7136 or (743) 243-7137. www.riverraisinbattlefield.org or www.nps.gov/rira   Hours: MOnday-Friday 10:00am-4:00pm (Memorial Day - Labor Day). Weekends 9:00-5:00pm (late April, May, September). Admission: FREE (donations accepted) FREEBIES: ask for the Battlefield Scavenger Hunt.

An important stop for interesting regional history, this visitor's center focuses on the battle (during the War of 1812) that was the worst defeat for the Americans. The British and Chief Tecumseh's Indians killed over 800 settlers during this battle. A 10 minute presentation summarizes the importance of who was in control of the Great Lakes. The display includes dioramas & full-size British & American soldiers, as well as a fiber-optic map presentation on the Battle of the River Raisin.

STERLING STATE PARK

Monroe - 2800 State Park Road (off I-75) 48161. www.michigan.gov/sterling. Phone: (734) 289-2715. Admission: $8.00 per vehicle.

Walleye are plentiful in Lake Erie. Shore fishing is possible at Sterling's three lagoons, three fishing piers and at its access to River Raisin. A total of seven miles of trails provide opportunities for hiking, biking and exploring. The 2.9-mile paved Marsh Trail circles one of the marsh lagoons in the park. A 0.6-mile hiking trail follows the Lake Erie shoreline. These trails include interpretive stations, an observation deck and a covered pavilion with spotting scopes. Camping, boating, and swimming. Boat Rentals Memorial Day - Labor Day. Row boats, canoes, paddle boats.

Mount Clemens

METRO BEACH METROPARK

Mount Clemens - Metropolitan Parkway 48043. Phone: (586) 463-4581 or (800) 477-3172. www.metroparks.com/blog.aspx?ID=7 Hours: Daily 6:00am-10:00pm (May-September); Daily 7:00am-8:00pm (October-April). Admission: $4.00 per vehicle. Some additional activity fees.

A lakeside summer beach retreat (with a boardwalk over a mile long) that has several unique attractions including: The Tot Lot (a place for kids as young as 3 can ride their bikes without running over someone), Educational Nature Programs, Spray Zone and a heated pool. Also: VOYAGEUR CANOE Passengers help paddle a 34-foot (20-passenger) Montreal Canoe that makes trips daily from the North Marina. Advance registration required for individuals and groups. TRACKLESS TRAIN Shuttle service to Huron Point picnic and shore fishing areas, weekends and holidays.

New Boston

APPLE CHARLIE'S ORCHARD AND MILL

New Boston - 38035 South Huron Road. www.applecharlies.com. (734) 753-9380. Open mid-August to January. Call for seasonal hours. Apples, cider press, petting farm, hayrides and a country store with farm gifts and freshly-made donuts. FREE admission and parking. (September / October)

☒

Northville

MAYBURY STATE PARK

Northville - 20145 Beck Road (I-96 to I-275 north, west on Eight Mile Road) 48167. Phone: (248) 349-8390.   www.michigan.gov/maybury.   Admission: $8.00 per vehicle.

Mostly forest, features include horseback riding, cross-country skiing, hiking trails, bike trails, fishing, winter sports, and a visitors center and living farm featuring a petting area for kids. The MAYBURY FARM represents a small family farm where general farming practices are demonstrated. The Maybury Farm was originally used to raise food for the William H. Maybury Sanatorium. The farm, and its classroom building, give visitors a chance to experience a working farm from the early 1900's. Maybury Farm is open all year Summer Hours: 10:00am-7:00pm, Winter Hours: 10:00am-5:00pm. Guided Tours by Reservation Phone: (248) 349-3858.

Onstead

LAKE HUDSON RECREATION AREA

Onstead - 1220 Wampler's Lake Road (M-156 SE) 49265. Phone: (517) 445-2265. www.michigan.gov/lakehudson.   Admission: $8.00 per vehicle.

Nearly 2,700 acres of recreational opportunities around Lake Hudson. The park, which lies in southeast Michigan, offers premier muskie fishing and hunting. A new beach area provides an excellent place for sunbathing and swimming. Dark Sky Preserve: Since 1993, Lake Hudson has been designated a dark sky preserve for learning more about the night time sky. Camping, hiking, boating, fishing, swimming and winter sports.

HAYES STATE PARK

Onstead (Irish Hills) - 1220 Wampler's Lake Road (US-12 west to M-124) 49265. Phone: (517) 467-7401.   www.michigan.gov/hayes.   Admission: $8.00 per vehicle.

W.J. Hayes State Park, in the heart of the Irish Hills, is bordered by a group of inland lakes frequented by anglers and boaters. Anglers can find bluegill, sunfish, crappie, pike, muskie, smallmouth bass and largemouth bass in Wampler's Lake. During the winter, ice fishing is the park's primary activity. Camping, swimming and winter sports are offered.

Ortonville

ORTONVILLE RECREATION AREA

Ortonville - 5779 Hadley Road 48462. www.michigan.gov/ortonville. Phone: (248) 627-3828.

Fishing is allowed throughout the recreation area with access sites located on Algoe, Davidson, Round and Today lakes. The lakes and streams may produce a wide variety of fish such as pike, bass, and perch. The equestrian trails offer 6.5 miles of designated trails wandering through Hadley Hills. The 6.5-mile Equestrian trail is also open for snowmobiling with sufficient snow. Camping, cabins, hiking trails, boating, swimming and winter sports.

Pinckney

LAKELANDS TRAIL STATE PARK

Pinckney - 8555 Silver Hill, Rt. 1 48169. www.michigan.gov/lakelandstrail. Phone: (734) 426-4913.

A 13-mile gravel trail connects Pinckney and Stockbridge. Along the way, you'll pass through rolling farmland and wooded areas that offer spectacular views. The Pinckney trailhead is a quarter mile north of M-36 on D-19 in Pinckney. The Stockbridge trailhead is on M-52 in Stockbridge.

PINCKNEY RECREATION AREA

Pinckney - 8555 Silver Hill (I-94 exit 159, North) 48169. Phone: (734) 426-4913. www.michigan.gov/pinckney.   Admission: $8.00 per vehicle.

A paradise for backpackers, mountain bikers, anglers and other recreation enthusiasts, this 11,000-acre park is known for its extensive trail system and chain of excellent fishing lakes. An extensive trail system is available to the hiker and mountain biker. The trails all begin at Silver Lake Beach. Camping, hiking (Lakelands trail is popular), boating, swimming, and winter sports.

Plymouth

PLYMOUTH HISTORICAL MUSEUM

Plymouth - 155 South Main Street (one block north of Kellogg Park) 48170. Phone: (734) 455-8940.   www.plymouthhistory.org. Hours: Wednesday, Friday, Saturday, Sunday 1:00-4:00 pm. Admission: $5.00 adult, $2.00 student (6-17), $10.00 family.

A kid-friendly museum with exhibits that include a scavenger hunt where "every child wins a prize". Experience the changes in this community from forests to fields to factories. In addition visitors can now see the newly expanded Daisy Air Rifle Exhibit complete with the original flooring from the factory, a complete collection of BB guns and toys made here in Plymouth and learn about the other BB gun companies located here which made Plymouth the Air Rifle Capital of the World! See the "Images of Abraham Lincoln" exhibit that features Lincoln in 10 phases of life (from boy to hero), wax figures of Abraham & Mary Todd Lincoln, and even displays a lock of Lincoln's actual hair!

PLYMOUTH ICE FESTIVAL

Plymouth - Downtown. (I-275 to Ann Arbor Road west to Main Street). (734) 459-6969. www.plymouthicefestival.org. Up to 500,000 people walk the streets of downtown Plymouth to gaze at hundreds of blocks of carved ice (each several hundred pounds). Probably more ice to see here than anywhere and they even have a section for kids' make-believe carvings of delightful characters. Cozy shops and restaurants line the streets, plus many food vendors are on hand. Admission. (mid-January week)

PLYMOUTH ORCHARDS AND CIDER MILL

Plymouth - 10865 Warren Road, (Ford Road west to Ridge Road, follow signs). www.plymouthorchards.com. (734) 455-2290. Petting farm, hayrides to orchards to pick apples, lots of fresh squeezed cider or cinnamon-sugar donuts or caramel apples available to eat there or take home. (September)

Ray Township

WOLCOTT MILL METROPARK

Ray Township - (M-53, take the 26 Mile Road exit east to Romeo Plank Road north to 29 Mile Road) 48096. www.metroparks.com/blog.aspx?ID=11 Phone: (586) 749-5997 or (800) 477-3175. Hours: Weekdays 9:00am - 5:00pm, Weekends 9:00am - 7:00pm (May - October). Restricted winter hours. (November - April) Admission: $4.00 per vehicle. Hayrides extra.

A gristmill is always a fun experience (really, explain it to the kids like it is a giant "mousetrap" game inside - full of large gears and rubber bands, etc.). See the mid-1800's era gristmill grind wheat into flour on the huge millstones. (It's interesting to note that in a hundred years, most mills would only wear out maybe one set of millstones). Also featured is the Farm Learning Center (on Wolcott Road) that teaches the methods and importance of farming today. See cow milking, sheep demonstrations, and experimental vegetable plots.

Saline

CELTIC FESTIVAL

Saline - Mill Pond Park. 48176. www.salineceltic.org. (734) 944-2810. A free shuttle to the park brings you Highland athletic competitions, children's activities, thematic reenactments, Celtic music and dancing and food. Admission. (second Saturday in July)

☒ _____

South Lyon

ERWIN ORCHARDS & CIDER MILL

South Lyon - (888) 824-3377. www.erwinorchards.com. Wagon rides go to the U-Pick apple orchard, fresh red and yellow raspberry patch, and pumpkin patch. Free hay maze for kids, Nigerian dwarf goats to pet and feed, children's play area, daytime haunted barn and black hole. (daily, daytime September thru early November)

☒ _____

Sumpter Township

CROSSWINDS MARSH WETLAND INTERPRETIVE PRESERVE

Sumpter Township - (I-94 to exit 8 - go west) 48111. Phone: (734) 261-1990. www. michigantrails.us/wayne-county-michigan/crosswinds-marsh-wetland-preserve. html. Free admission (small fee for programs). Open daylight hours.

The marsh offers year-round activities including trails for hiking, horseback riding and cross-country skiing; and areas for picnicking and fishing. Over 100 species of birds (binocular rentals available for $1.00) can be viewed at this 1000 acre artificially created wetland - one of the largest in the country. Learn more about the plants and wildlife that were moved to this area by taking a 2 mile canoe trip that has interpretive markers to describe what you are seeing. (Canoe rentals are available for $5.00 per hour)

Waterford

PONTIAC LAKE RECREATION AREA

Waterford - 7800 Gale Road (off M-59) 48327. www.michigan.gov/pontiaclake. Phone: (248) 666-1020. Admission: $6.00-$8.00 per vehicle.

Archery ranges and horse trails/rentals make this park unique. Designated trails meandering throughout the recreation area are available for horseback riding, hiking and mountain biking. The 11-mile mountain bike trail has been ranked as one of the "Top 100 Trails" in the United States. Two new universally accessible fishing piers are located at the Pontiac Lake Beach Area. Camping, boating, fishing, swimming, and winter sports.

DODGE NO. 4 STATE PARK

Waterford - 4250 Parkway Drive (off M-59 west to Cass Elizabeth Road) 48328. Phone: (248) 682-7323. www.michigan.gov/dodgeno4   Admission: $8.00 per vehicle.

A white sandy beach and a one-mile shoreline on Cass Lake makes Dodge #4 State Park an excellent location for summer and winter water activities. Dodge #4 has recently added a universally accessible fishing pier on Cass Lake. Camping, fishing, boating, swimming and winter sports.

FRIDGE, (THE)

Waterford - 1702 Scott Lake Road (I-75 to Dixie Highway Exit - South) 48328. www.oaklandfridge.com Phone: In season: (248) 975-4440. Off season: (248) 858-0906. Hours: Wednesday-Friday 4:00-9:30pm. Saturday 10:00am-10:00pm. Sunday Noon-6:00pm. (All times are weather permitting, mid-December to mid-March). Closed Christmas Eve and Day. Admission: $4.00-$10.00/person/day rate. Single Ride: $2.50/person. No riders under 30" tall permitted, and riders under age 10 must be accompanied by an adult. Discount and Scout coupons online.

Drop 55 feet (rather quickly) and then travel over 1000 feet as you and 3 close friends discover the thrill of tobogganing. The park has 2 runs, over 200 toboggans, and even a place to warm up with a fireplace and food. In the summer you'll find a tennis courts, a 5-story raft ride, wave pool, and BMX bicycle course.

DRAYTON PLAINS NATURE CENTER

Waterford - 2125 Denby Drive (near Dixie Hwy. & M-59. Turn onto Edmore off of Hatchery Road). 48329. Phone: (248) 674-2119. www.dpnaturecenter.org. Hours: Grounds open 8:00am-9:00pm (April -October). Only open until 6:00pm rest of year. Interpretive Center generally open Tuesday - Friday 11:00am - 2:00pm and Weekends Noon - 4:00pm. FREE Admission.

An old fish hatchery is now the Drayton Plains Nature Center. The grounds include woods, ponds, streams, a pioneer log cabin, and a prairie. 137 acres of trails along the Clinton River plus a nice Interpretive Center. In the center are displays of mounted animals in re-created scenes of their natural habitats.

White Lake

HIGHLAND RECREATION AREA

White Lake - 5200 East Highland Road (off M-59 East) 48363. Phone: (248) 889-3750. www.michigan.gov/highland.

Highland Recreation Area offers 5,900 acres of forest, marshes and lakes in the rolling hills of Southern Michigan. With trails to accommodate equestrian riders, mountain bikers, hikers and skiers, there's an activity for every season in this park. Three different day-use areas provide ample space for picnics, swimming, horseshoes or volleyball. Access sites are located on four lakes within the park for fishing and recreational boating. Camping, boating, fishing, swimming and winter sports. Three dog field trial areas (FTA) are available. Horse rentals and trails too.

ALPINE VALLEY SKI AREA

White Lake - 6775 East Highland Road (I-96 - Milford Road exit to M-59 West, 12 miles west of Pontiac) 48383. Phone: (248) 887-4183. www.skialpinevalley.com.

You'll have a real "Alpine" feeling since this resort offers 25 runs (some of which have many trees and are steep). Rental equipment: Skis (also shaped skis to learn easier) and snowboards. Imagine not having to worry about rope tows or chairlifts to learn how to ski or snowboard - simply stand on their Wonder Carpet and you will glide to the top of the beginner area with no hassles at all!

Ypsilanti

ROLLING HILLS COUNTY PARK

Ypsilanti - 7660 Stoney Creek Road 48197. Phone: (734) 482-3866.

Summers: Wave pool, water slide, zero-depth pool, waterfall, picnic area, sports fields, fishing pond, grassy sunbathing area, sandy beach, 9-hole Frisbee golf course, tube rentals. Winter: Dual toboggan chutes, ice skating, and cross-county skiing.

COUNTRY FAIR WEEKENDS

Ypsilanti - Wiard's Orchards, 5565 Merritt Road, (I-94 exit 183 south to Stony Creek south, follow signs. (734) 482-7744. http://wiards.com/. Apple orchards, cider mill, fire engine rides, pony rides, wagon rides out to the apple-picking or pumpkin patch areas, face-painting and live entertainment. (September / October)

SOUTHWEST CHAPTER AT A GLANCE...

Albion * Whitehouse Nature Ctr

Augusta

* Fort Custer Rec Area

* Kellogg Biological Station

Battle Creek

* Binder Park Zoo

* Full Blast

* Kingman

* Cereal Fest

* Battle Creek Field of Flight

* Holiday Balloon Fest

Benton Harbor

* Blossomtime

Berrien Springs *Christmas PIckle Fest

Bridgman *Cook Energy Ctr

Buchanan * Bear Cave

Charlotte

* MI Apple Fest

* MI Pumpkin Fest

Coloma

* Deer Forest

* Jollay Orchards

Eau Claire

* Internatl Cherry Pit Spit

Hastings

* Charleton Park Village

Hickory Corners

* Gilmore Car Museum

Kalamazoo

* Kwings Hockey

* Echo Valley

* Kalamazoo Nature Ctr

* Kalamazoo Symphony

* Kalamazoo Valley Museum

* Silver Leaf Renaissance

* Kalamazoo Scottish Fest

* Wolf Lake Fishery

* Kalamazoo Air Zoo

Marshall

* Cornwells Turkeyville

* Mayfaire

Middleville * Yankee Springs

Niles

* Hunter Ice Fest

* Four Flags Apple Fest

Ostego * Bittersweet Ski Area

Saugatuck

* Mt Baldhead & Oval Beach

* Saugatuck Boat Cruises

* Saugatuck Dune Rides

Sawyer

* Grand Mere St Pk

* Warren Dunes St Pk

South Haven

* Dr. Liberty Hyde Bailey Museum

* Kal-Haven Trail St Pk

* Michigan Maritime Museum

* Van Buren St Pk

* Natl Blueberry Fest

St Joseph

* Curiosity Kids Museum/Discovery

* Silver Beach

Stevenville

* Barbott Farms

Chapter 6
South West

A Quick Tour of our Hand-Picked Favorites Around...

South West Michigan

After sunning at the beach one day, plan your next day around learning. You can explore the past, from Native American history, early settlers, and maritime history to a famous horticulturist. Learn about the natural history, see the most complete mastodon skeleton in Michigan, a saber-tooth tiger, or get some hands-on experience at an air and space museum. A storybook **Deer Forest** is in Coloma.

The Battle Creek area boasts a bird sanctuary (look for prairie chickens), Dairy Center, Zoo and the **Kingman Museum of Natural History**. Three floors of actual dinosaur bones!

Take I-94 a little further west to Kalamazoo (isn't that fun to say?). First stop downtown, either the **Valley Museum** or the **Nature Center** nearby. When you enter, either walk over to the Tropical Rainforest that's home to parrots, iguanas, tropical plants and exotic fish or walk through Bugs in our Lives and Nature Up Close. Outside, trek through 1000 acres of dense forest and check out the Butterfly House or Pioneer Homestead. If you head towards the airport, you can't miss the new **Air Zoo** featuring aircraft exhibits, space vehicles, flight simulators and indoor amusement rides. It's a land of lions and tigers and bear (planes, that is) – it's an Air Zoo!

Take I-196 north paralleling Lake Michigan for some fun Great Lakes maritime history. First stop, the **Michigan Maritime Museum** – a showcase of stories of vessels that passed through these waters and the people who built them. A kids' favorite may well be outside in the Lifesaving and Coast Guard exhibit or the Boat Shed where actual boats are being constructed. The replica Friends Good Will, a 19th Century sloop that served both American and British Navies in the War of 1812, is used as a floating exhibit. Beware of the Jolly Roger flag hoisted as pirates may be taking over the ship during your visit!

Sites and attractions are listed in order by City, Zip Code, and Name. Symbols indicated represent:

 Festivals    Restaurants   Lodging

Albion

WHITEHOUSE NATURE CENTER

Albion - 1381 East Erie Street (one-quarter mile southeast of the Albion College campus off Hannah St., on the North Branch of the Kalamazoo River) 49224. Phone: (517) 629-0582. www.albion.edu/naturecenter Hours: Monday-Friday 9:30am-4:30pm. Weekends, 10:30am-4:30pm. Closed major and college holidays. Free Admission.

A 135 acre outdoor facility for education that features 6 nature trails and 168 species of birds. Most of the trails are less than one mile long and each features different opportunities. Includes an observation room with live exhibits.

Augusta

FORT CUSTER RECREATION AREA

Augusta - 5163 West Fort Custer Drive (M-96 West) 49012. Phone: (269) 731-4200. www.michigan.gov/fortcuster.   Admission: $8.00 per vehicle.

Area comprises 2,988 acres located between Battle Creek and Kalamazoo. The terrain is typical of southern Michigan farm country, with second growth forests and remnant areas of prairie. Prairie restoration is in progress. The area features three lakes, the Kalamazoo River, and an excellent trail system. Camping, hiking, boating, fishing, swimming, bicycle trails, winter sports.

KELLOGG BIOLOGICAL STATION

Augusta - (13 miles northwest on SR89, between 40th and E. Gull Lake Drive) 49012. www.kbs.msu.edu/.

KBS is Michigan State University's largest off-campus education complex and one of North America's premier inland field stations. The 4,065-acre station includes Kellogg Bird Sanctuary, Kellogg Farm, the Kellogg Biological Laboratories.

BIRD SANCTUARY: On East C Avenue. (269) 671-2510 or www.kbs.msu. edu/bird_sanctuary/index.htm. An MSU experimental facility of birds of prey, wild geese, ducks, swans, pheasants and peacocks. There are displays and observation decks. Several endangered species, like the genetically endangered red jungle fowl and Reeves' pheasant are on display, as well as the rare sharp-tailed grouse and greater prairie chicken (which is no longer found in Michigan). Hours: Daily 9:00am-7:00pm (May-October). Daily 9:00am-5:00pm (rest of year). Admission: $2.00-$4.00.

DAIRY CENTER: open to the public for self-guided tours every day of the year from 8:00 a.m. until sunset. Gather and watch in the Feed Center or Milking Parlor. 10461 North 40th Street, Hickory Corners. www.kbs.msu.edu/ research/pasture-dairy (269) 671-2507.

Battle Creek

BINDER PARK ZOO

Battle Creek - 7400 Division Drive (I-94 to exit 100 - go south) 49014. Phone: (269) 979-1351. www.binderparkzoo.org. Hours: Monday-Friday 9:00am-5:00pm, Saturday & Holidays 9:00am-6:00pm, Sunday 11:00am-6:00pm (mid-April to mid-October). Admission: ~$8.00-$10.00 (age 2+). Kids pricing for group rates is generous. Note: Gift shop with unique animal items.

Natural settings offer over 250 animals in 80 exhibits that you can see while strolling along elevated wooden boardwalks. See exhibits like a Chinese Red Panda, and a Mexican Grey Wolf, interact with insects, and have fun learning at the Conservation Stations (a hands-on exhibit). The hands-on playground at the children's zoo is said to have the world's largest and most accurate dinosaur replicas, a petting zoo, and miniature railroad. Get nose-to-nose with one of the largest giraffe herds in the country as you explore Wild Africa and hand feed a giraffe! Binder Park Zoo welcomes the Binda Conservation Carousel, a wooden carousel from the 1900s, ready to delight people of all ages with lights, music, and motion. Best of all, it is outfitted with two chariots and 36 different species of animals, all hand painted with bright and vibrant colors, giving each their very own uniqueness.

FULL BLAST

Battle Creek - 35 Hamblin Avenue (I-94 to I-194/M-66 - north) 49017. Phone: (269) 966-3667. www.fullblast.org. Hours: Varies by activity and season but basically 10:00am-7:00pm. Afternoons only school days. FLASH FLOOD INDOOR/ OUTDOOR WATER PARK AND FAMILY ENTERTAINMENT CENTER AT FULL BLAST ARE CLOSED FOR THE WINTER SEASON. Admission: $3.00-$9.00 per activity or day pass of around $12.00 to everything. Note: Gymnasium with three full-sized basketball courts. Indoor running track on second level.

A family fun attraction with something for everyone. Attractions include a skateboard park, indoor and outdoor waterparks (with 2 –100 ft. waterslides, a river float, bubble beach), 3 basketball courts, full-service health club, café and food court, and teen nightclub. Imagination Station (indoor)/Adventure Land (outdoor) - a playground with slides, climbing nets, and endless tunnels (Guest must be 54" or shorter to play in playgrounds).

KINGMAN MUSEUM OF NATURAL HISTORY / LEILA ARBORETUM

Battle Creek - 928 West Michigan Avenue (I-94 to M-66 North, left on Michigan Avenue, near 20th St) 49017. Phone: Museum (269) 965-5117, Arboretum (269) 969-0270. www.kingmanmuseum.org. Hours: Saturday 1:00-5:00pm. (Arboretum) Daily Dawn to Dusk. Admission: (Museum/Planetarium) $7.00 adult, $6.00 senior (65+), $5.00 student (3-18). The arboretum admission is usually Free. Educators: Enrichment kits can be rented to take home for several weeks.

The arboretum features a sunken garden, a visitor's center, a children's adventure garden, and large floral displays (depending on season). The Kingman Museum of Natural History (West Michigan at 20th) has 3 floors of exhibits including dinosaurs and a planetarium. Look for a mounted Polar Bear that at one time was the largest ever harvested. One exhibit shows the remnants of a sabre-toothed tiger. On the mezzanine level you'll see extinct birds such as the Passenger Pigeon and the Imperial Woodpecker, of which only 140 or so skins are known to exist. Visitors can see actual bones of the tiger and view other skeletons as well.

CEREAL FESTIVAL

Battle Creek - (I-94 exit 98B). (800) 397-2240. www.bcfestivals.com. Hours: Thursday parade @ 6:00pm. Children's activities Saturday 8:00am - Noon (games, FREE samples / literature). Farmers Market, Festival Park. The World's Longest Breakfast Table began in 1956 (celebration was set up for 7,000 people – 14,000 showed up!). They could see it was a hit and so competitors Kellogg's, Post, and Ralston Foods team up each year to serve over 60,000 people. Over 600 volunteers serve complimentary cereals, milk, Tang, Pop Tarts, donuts and Dole bananas on more than 300 tables lining one street. It's really a treat for the whole family and very well organized. We were pleasantly and promptly served within minutes and the variety of food choices was abundant. (second week of June)

BATTLE CREEK FIELD OF FLIGHT AIR SHOW & BALLOON FESTIVAL

Battle Creek - W.K. Kellogg Airport, (I-94 exit Helmer Road). www.bcballoons.com. (269) 962-0592. 200 plus balloons (some shaped like Tony the Tiger, flowers, bears or fruit) take off in competitions, a top-level air show, fireworks choreographed to music, and many ground displays of aircraft. Admission. (five days starting right before the 4th of July)

HOLIDAY BALLOON FEST

Battle Creek - Kellogg Community College. Come experience the Holiday Balloon Fest with two evening Glittering Balloon glows and four Frosty balloon flights. This is a free family event, dress warm and bring your friends. www.holidayballoonfest.com. (first weekend in December)

Benton Harbor/St. Joseph

BLOSSOMTIME

Benton Harbor/St. Joseph - www.blossomtimefestival.org. (269) 925-6301. 20 plus neighboring Southwest Michigan communities celebrate Michigan's fruit-growing country making pilgrimages into the countryside to see the orchards in bloom. Carnival, youth parade, and the finale Grand Floral Parade with its 100-plus flowered floats and their queens. (last Sunday in April for one week)

Berrien Springs

CHRISTMAS PICKLE FESTIVAL

Berrien Springs - Downtown, I-94 to US-31 south. (616) 471-3116. Do you know about a German tradition at Christmas? The first child to find a glass pickle hidden in the tree gets an extra present! This is the town's inspiration for a holiday parade, street lighting, and pickle tastings. Pickle and non-pickle foods and gifts. Admission. (first week of December)

Bridgman

COOK ENERGY INFO CENTER AND DUNES

Bridgman - 1 Cook Place (I-94 exit 16 or 23, follow signs - off Red Arrow Highway) 49106. Phone: (800) 548-2555. www.cookinfo.com. Admission: Free. ONLY OPEN TO SCHOOL GROUPS ON PRE-ARRANGED TOURS. Note: Picnic areas.

Technology and nature together - sounds impossible. Nuclear power, electricity and future energy sources are explained. From your arrival in the Energy Center lobby, your group will be whisked off to Theater 1 for a private screening of Dr. Nate's nuclear energy video. You'll learn the secrets of nuclear energy and how we use it to make electricity at the Cook Nuclear Plant. Next you're off to Theater 2 to watch a 26-foot 3-D rotating exhibit rise from the floor, rotate, and flash as the intricate working of a nuclear energy plant are displayed. Hike dune trails along Lake Michigan shoreline including forests and wetlands. There are also energy video games and hands-on displays. Schedule a fun "Power Trip" with Dr. Nate for your class or group and learn how nuclear energy is produced and used.

Buchanan

BEAR CAVE

Buchanan - 4085 Bearcave Road (US 12 to 4 miles North on Red Bud Trail) 49107. Phone: (269) 695-3050. www.thousandtrails.com/getaways/michigan/bearcave.asp Hours: Daily 10:00am-4:00pm (Memorial Day-Labor Day). Note: Clubhouse, pool, Jacuzzi, fishing, game room, horseshoes, shuffleboard, boat ramp, playground, boating and canoeing. Open May through September.

One of the few caves in Michigan that is accessible to the public, Bear Cave (150-feet long) is accessed by a narrow, winding stairway. The temperature is a constant 58 degrees F. so be sure to dress appropriately. A taped narration explains the sights of stalactites, flowstone, and petrified leaves. The cave was part of the underground railroad for slaves, and a movie location for the 1903 "Great Train robbery." A warning though...the cave does contain bats. However, if you don't bother them, they usually won't bother you!

Charlotte

MICHIGAN APPLE FESTIVAL

Charlotte - Country Mill. www.michiganapplefestival.com. The Michigan Apple Festival is full of the sights, smells, and flavors of everything apples. The Cloggers will dance to a variety of country music; Corn Maze open & Train Rides to the Orchard. Petting Zoo, Apple picking, & Pumpkin picking. FREE. (third weekend in September)

MICHIGAN PUMPKIN FEST

Charlotte - Country Mill's Pumpkin Patch. (517) 543-1019 or www.countrymill.com. Michigan's only Pumpkin Carrying Contest. Come see how many pumpkins you can carry and earn the title of Pumpkin King or Queen. Load up the contestant and watch them walk 10 feet with as many pumpkins as they can carry in their arms. Keep all the pumpkins you carry. Prizes for highest carrier of the day. While you shop for mid-Michigan farm products, pick a pumpkin or tour the Michigan apple orchards be sure to enjoy hot donuts and a refreshing glass of cider made right here in their cider mill from delicious Michigan apples. Admission for contest entry. (first Sunday in October or last Sunday in September)

Coloma

JOLLAY ORCHARDS

Coloma - 1850 Friday Road, (I-94 exit 39). (269) 468-3075 or www.jollayorchards. com. Hayrides through enchanted/ decorated orchards to u-pick apples. Make your own warm caramel apples and bakery with pies baked in a brown paper bag. (September/ October weekends)

DEER FOREST

Coloma - Paw Paw Lake Road, 6800 Indian Lane (I-94 exit 39 north, follow signs) 49038. Phone: (269) 468-4961. www.deerforest.com. Hours: Daily 10:00am-7:00pm (Memorial Weekend-Labor Day). Open weekends 10:00am-6:00pm (September/October). Admission: $8.00-$12.00 (age 3+). Pony rides extra. Note: Gift shop. Picnic areas. "Wild Child Play Habitat". Mini-golf. Gold panning. Kid's entertainment like magicians. Mostly in the woods and shaded.

Their slogan, "More fun than a zoo" is true, mostly because it's designed as an Animal and an Amusement Park. Fun and different animals to pet are baby zebras and mini-horses (the size of dogs)  o r sit between the humps of a camel. Most every animal here is tame enough to pet (making it different than a zoo). You can also ride ponies and camels, a treetop Ferris wheel, a carrousel or mini-train. Our favorite part had to be Storybook Lane, a large park within the park, where you meander around the lane. Each setting illustrates a different Nursery Rhyme scene like "3 Men in a Tub" (in a pond with real frogs and small fish) o r "Baa Baa Black Sheep" (with what else but, black sheep). Deer Forest's Storybook Lane has a wonderful history. Who can forget the magic of getting your first elephant key, and bringing it to the Storybook Lane, then keeping and treasuring it forever? Today still, your children's faces will light up as they turn the elephant key, and listen to the many fairy-tale stories and children's songs (extra $3 for key, great souvenir). To get your money's worth, be sure to spend several hours here and plan a picnic or buy at the snack bar. Also, lots of photo ops everywhere.

Eau Claire

INTERNATIONAL CHERRY PIT SPITTING CHAMPIONSHIP

Eau Claire - Tree-Mendus Fruit Farm, (East on M-140 on Eureka Road). (612) 782-7101 or http://treemendus-fruit.com. The world record is almost 73 feet! Can you compete or do you just want to watch? Playground and petting corral too! (weekend before / after July 4th)

Hastings

CHARLTON PARK VILLAGE & MUSEUM

Hastings - 2545 South Charlton Park Rd (2 miles South on SR 37 then 4 miles East on SR79 - follow signs) 49058. www.charltonpark.org. Phone: (989) 945-3775. Hours: Daily 9:00am-5:00pm. (Memorial Day-Labor Day), plus festivals. After Labor Day historic buildings are only open for prescheduled groups and special events. Admission: $2.00-$4.00 (age 5+) for programs and special events. Special events are the best time to visit (many re-enactors): Civil War Muster or Steam Engine Show (July) & Pow Wow (September) or Of Christmas Past (early Dec).

A very authentic recreation of an 1890's rural Michigan town, this village offers 25 buildings that include a schoolhouse, an 1880's doctor's home, an 1885 church, a print shop. They may visit the General Store, watch the village blacksmith fashion tools over the forge, or walk through the woods to find a rustic cabin or wigwam. Also find a beach, boat launch, and playground in the recreational part of the park complex.

Hickory Corners

GILMORE CAR MUSEUM

Why did this 1948 Tucker have a headlight in the middle?

Hickory Corners - 6865 Hickory Road (M43 at Hickory Road) 49060. Phone: (269) 671-5089. www.gilmorecarmuseum.org. Hours: Daily 9:00am-5:00pm (April-November). Admission: $8.00-$10.00 (age 7+)

Have you ever had a dream about finding that "priceless" antique car in someone's barn? See more than 130 unique and rare cars all displayed in antique barns. Here you will find exhibits ranging from a 1899 Locomobile, to the classic Duesenberg or the elusive Tucker '48, and from the Model T to the muscle cars of the 60s. A few other cars that you will see include Cadillacs, Packards, and even a steam powered car. Also, you'll find a reproduction of the Wright Brother's plane and a narrow gauge train. For the "tikes" they have antique pedal cars. You'll want to also allow extra time to visit the NEW Miniature's Museum and have a snack or lunch in the authentic 1941 Diner.

Kalamazoo

K-WINGS HOCKEY

Kalamazoo - 3600 Vanrick Drive (I-94 - Sprinkle Road exit - Wings Stadium) 49001. Phone: (269) 345-5101 tickets or (269) 345-9772 office. www.kwings.com.

You'll experience hard-hitting, fast-paced action, great music, humorous on-ice promotions, contests, and the antics of Slappy, the K-Wings zany mascot. An UHL affiliate team (October - April). $7.00-$17.50. Public skating and rentals at rink, too.

ECHO VALLEY

Kalamazoo - 8495 East H Ave. 49004. www.echovalleyfun.com. Phone: (269) 349-3291. Hours: Saturday 10:00am-10:00pm. Sunday Noon - 6:00pm. (mid-December to early March). Special Winter Break Hours. Admission: (Toboggans) $12.00. All day passes $18.00. (Inner Tubing) $12.00. (Ice Skating) $5.00 Note: Lodge and snack bar. Outdoor ice skating rink. Parents & Chaperones who prefer to observe all the fun rather than participate may enter Echo Valley at NO COST.

Aaah...the feeling of that sled racing down a fresh snow covered hill...and the air getting colder on my face...is a childhood memory that I will never forget. Relive those memories and introduce your kids to the fun of tubing and tobogganing that makes winter a blast. Old wood toboggans have been replaced with super-fast custom made sleds molded from a single piece of polyethylene. The toboggans are equipped with padded seats and Teflon runners. Eight icy and fast tracks await you as you fly down a hill of over 120 feet, at speeds of up to 60 miles per hour. The best part of all is that at this resort there is a tow rope to pull the toboggans back up the hill.

KALAMAZOO NATURE CENTER

Kalamazoo - 7000 North Westnedge Avenue (I-94 to US131exit 44 east) 49004. Phone: (269) 381-1574.   www.naturecenter.org. Hours: Monday-Saturday 9:00am-5:00pm, Sunday and most holidays 1:00-5:00pm. (Extended summer hours). Closed winter holidays. Admission: $7.00 adult, $6.00 senior (55+), $4.00 child (4-13). Note: 8 miles of Nature trails (one is wheelchair and stroller accessible). Gift shop.

When you enter, either walk over to the Tropical Rainforest (3 stories) environment that's home to parrots, iguanas, tropical plants and exotic fish or walk through Bugs in our Lives and Nature Up Close. You'll walk through giant tree trunks and discover nature 10 times the size of life. Imagine 8 foot tall flowers and watch out for that huge frog - it's like the movie Bugs Life! We especially liked the pollen exhibit where the kids can try to help bees pollinate flowers. It's a clever demo and we learned bees pollinate by accident. Explore a bughouse kitchen inside and out to find unwanted—and beneficial—bugs crawling around inside. The Expedition Station is outstanding with a collection of stuffed birds and real bones - all hands-on. Visit the Sun/Rain Room for a visual experience with the enchanting "Crystal Rain...Glass in Nature" exhibit. See glass as "crystal rain" glitters, reflects, and delights in its natural surrounding. Outside, walk through 1000 acres of dense hardwood forest and check out the Butterfly House, Hummingbird Garden or Delano Pioneer Homestead - early life in Michigan.

KALAMAZOO SYMPHONY ORCHESTRA

Kalamazoo - 126 East South Street (Miller Auditorium) 49007. Phone: (269) 349-7759. Tickets: (800) 228-9858. www.kalamazoosymphony.com.

The season includes family concerts and FREE summer outdoor concerts. Young subscribers, ages 4-12, can join "Barry's Buddies," and everyone is invited to visit the Instrument Petting Zoo before the concert. Look for the Family Discovery Concert and the Musical Storybooks Concerts. The youth symphony provides an orchestral experience of the highest quality for talented young musicians in southwest Michigan. Players are drawn from the Kalamazoo metropolitan area and surrounding communities.

KALAMAZOO VALLEY MUSEUM

Kalamazoo - 230 North Rose Street (I-94 Westnedge Ave. exit 76 north to M-43 east) 49007. Phone: (269) 373-7990. http://kvm.kvcc.edu/. Hours: Monday-Saturday 9:00am-5:00pm, Sunday & Holidays 1:00-5:00pm. Closed some major holidays. Admission: FREE. $3.00-$5.00 charge for Astronomy/Space related activities. Note: Digistar Planetarium. Challenger Mini-Mission (5th graders and up as a group actually simulate an astronaut mission using working equipment!). A Preschool Performance Series is featured – FREE – on the first Saturday of every month.

What an unexpected surprise! The Kalamazoo Valley should be proud. It's interesting to learn that funds for the museum were raised by the community with the museum artifacts found mostly by locals in their attics and basements. In an 1860's farm kitchen, make a seed wreath or search for the lost town of Singapore or test your spelling skills in a schoolhouse. Our favorite hands-on displays were: the create your own sand dunes or tornadoes - can you stop them?... and the Race Cars that show you it's easier to work together than alone. What impressed us was that most displays were actual hands-on, not just push buttons. It was also interesting to learn about all of the products manufactured in the area over the years. Every young kid loves the Children's Landscape Play Area. Oops, almost forgot - check out their 2500 year old woman (mummy) !

GOOD OLD DAYS & KNIGHTS AT THE SILVER LEAF RENAISSANCE FAIRE

Kalamazoo - River Oaks County Park (I-94 exit 85). www.silverleafrenfaire.org. Over 100 scheduled events each day, transporting you back to a medieval village, populated by ladies and their knights in shining armor, artisans, sword battles, Celtic tunes, live theatre, peasants, fairies, dragons, merchants, storytellers and peasant-powered rides. Admission. (last three weekends in July thru early August)

KALAMAZOO SCOTTISH FESTIVAL

Kalamazoo - County Fairgrounds. Ceud Mile Failte – "A Hundred Thousand Welcomes". Ceilidh contests, Celtic fold entertainment all afternoon, a history tent, expanded activities for younger Scots, and an informal pipe band competition. Admission. www. kalamazooscottishfestival.org. (last Saturday in August)

WOLF LAKE FISHERY INTERPRETIVE CENTER

Kalamazoo (Mattawan) - 34270 County Road 652 (US 131 exit 38, 6 miles west of Kalamazoo on M43) 49071. Phone: (269) 668-2876. www.michigan.org/ property/wolf-lake-fish-hatchery-visitor-center-and-interpretive-center/ Hours: Wednesday-Saturday 10:00am-5:00pm, Sunday Noon-5:00pm. (Call for Winter hours) Admission: Free Note: Picnic Area. Trails.

If you've never been to a "fish farm" it's worth a trip. This one has a museum center with a stuffed sturgeon - it's big - the largest fish caught in the state - 87 inches long and 193 pounds! Learn about fish life cycles and habitats, as well as why they even have fisheries. There's a slide show of hatchery operations and occasional hatchery tours (several times, especially Saturdays in the spring and summer). The hatchery looks like a giant scientific engineering lab with all the pipes, basins and valves. Outside, there are display ponds with steelhead, grayling, sturgeon and Chinook salmon - you can feed the fish and watch them jump for food. Kids will love the fishing derbies (June-August). If you want them to have a positive fishing experience, they're almost guaranteed to catch here.

KALAMAZOO AIR ZOO

Kalamazoo (Portage) - 3101 East Milham Road (I-94 exit 78 to airport, corner of East Milham Avenue and Portage Road) 49002. www.airzoo.org. Phone: (269) 382-6555. Hours: Monday-Saturday 9:00am-5:00pm, Sunday Noon-5:00pm. Admission: $8.00 general. Addon fees include beyond basic rides, theaters, simulators and admission to both the Air Zoo, the Michigan Space Science Center and the East Campus. Educators: Bring home History in a Box to your students. Very interesting topics. Each multi-disciplinary program focuses on a different aspect of aviation, space, science or history, letting students explore the subject through fun, fascinating hands-on activities. Home School Discovery Days are held September to May. Lesson Plans: www.airzoo.org/page.php?page_id=121

The new 106,000-square-foot Air Zoo features aircraft exhibits, flight simulators and indoor amusement rides. "It's a land of lions and tigers and bears" – it's an Air Zoo! Enter the world of imaginative and colorful aircraft with names like Tin Goose... Gooney Bird... Flying Tiger and the "cats", Wildcat... Hellcat... Bearcat... Tigercat...and Tomcat. What a great way to intrigue those little guys who don't find aircraft museums amusing...until now. Let your kids try to count the number of different "species" represented. "Would-be aviators" can try a virtual reality ride as a family in a flight simulator (tilt, turns, even engine and wind noise) or cockpit cutaways where you can press, pull and push levers and buttons. Look for Snoopy as the World War I Flying Ace. Some productions are in a 4-D theatre. Kids Korner is designed for the littlest aviator, this play area is suitable for children from one to five years of age. This area features four arcade-style rides along with various aviation-related toddler toys. Gift shop. Theater (old war movies)

Marshall

CORNWELL'S TURKEYVILLE USA

Marshall - 18935 15 1/2 Mile Road (I-94 to I-69 exit 42) 49068. Phone: (269) 781-4293 or (800) 28-4315. www.turkeyville.com. Hours: Daily 11:00am-8:00pm. (April-October) 11:00am-7:00pm (November-March).

You're invited to the County Fair by Grandma and Grandpa Cornwell where tradition starts with farm-raised, preservative-free turkey. Choose from fun menu items (all contain turkey!) like "Sloppy Tom" barbecue sandwich or "Buttered Tom" cold sandwich. Also Ice Cream Parlour, Game Room, General Store and Country Junction bakery for dessert. Dinner Theatre with productions like "South Pacific" and "Christmas Memories". Call or visit website for schedule. If your kids need to use restrooms, make sure they know the difference between "Toms" and "Hens".

MAYFAIRE

Marshall - Wilder Creek Conservation Club. (269) 382-6120 or www.mayfaireren.com. Mayfaire comes complete with its own stone castle. Mayfaire takes place when the weather is similar to that experienced in Olde England. When there was a need for petticoats and all of the lavish garb that lends a truly magical feeling to an event such as this. Laurie's Fault provides excellent music and song and is touted as the "funniest and most amazing show in the past 500 years." Watch as Otto the Sword Swallower makes good on his name. There will also be a Royal Tourney, with one task held each day of the faire. Admission. (last two weekends in May)

Middleville

YANKEE SPRINGS RECREATION AREA

Middleville - 2104 Gun Lake Road (US-131, exit 61. East on A-42) 49333. Phone: (269) 795-9081. www.michigan.gov/yankeesprings. Admission: $6.00-$8.00 per vehicle.

Yankee Springs Recreation Area was once the hunting grounds of the Algonquin Indians and the famous Chieftain, Chief Noonday. The site of Yankee Springs was established in 1835 and the village was made famous by Yankee Bill Lewis who owned and operated a hotel along the stagecoach run from Kalamazoo to Grand Rapids. A modern campground is located on the shores of beautiful Gun Lake while rustic camping is available at Deep Lake. Nine lakes are located within the park boundaries providing excellent fishing and water sports of all kinds. As a year-round park, cross-county skiing on its more than 10 acres of Nordic ski trails, snowmobiling, snowshoeing and ice fishing are all popular winter activities. Three special points of interest in the park are: Devil's Soupbowl, a glacially carved kettle formation, Graves Hill Overlook and The Pines, accessible from the extensive trail systems. Favorite fair weather activities include 30 miles of hiking trails, 12 miles of challenging mountain bike trails, 9 miles of horseback trails, as well as two public beaches, picnic shelters, and two universally accessible fishing piers one at Gun Lake and one at Deep Lake.

Niles

HUNTER ICE FESTIVAL

Niles - (269) 687-4332. www.huntericefestival.org. The country's best carvers slide into town to cut 400+ lb. ice blocks into cool sculptures. Face-painting and carnival games, too. FREE. (mid-January weekend)

FOUR FLAGS AREA APPLE FESTIVAL

Niles - (269) 683-8870. www.fourflagsapplefestival.org. Southern Michigan's apple-growing region showcases its harvest with apple-peeling and apple-baking contests. Lots of apple pie, dumplings and doughnuts. Parade, carnival, fireworks and entertainment. (last weekend of September)

Otsego

BITTERSWEET SKI AREA

Otsego - 600 River Road 49078. Phone: (269) 694-2032. www.skibittersweet.com
Hours: Daily (December-March)

16 runs. Night skiing, lessons, rentals. Food service available.

Saugatuck

MOUNT BALDHEAD & OVAL BEACH RECREATION AREA

Saugatuck - (by the river near Oval Beach, Park Street) 49453. Phone: (269) 857-1701. www.saugatuck.com/beaches.asp

Rated among the 25 best shorelines in the world by Conde Nast's Traveler, Oval Beach has the right combination of sand dunes, seclusion and services. Discover it best by riding across the Kalamazoo River on a hand-pulled chain ferry from the town of Saugatuck, climbing 282 steps to Mount Baldhead. At the top, you'll be rewarded with a great view this huge dune and Lake Michigan. The hike to the beach is short but does involve a stairway of 282 steps, a climb that leaves most people, parents and kids alike, puffing at the top. Benches have been built into the sides of the stairs, allowing you to take as much time and as many breaks as necessary to scale the "mountain." Lifeguards, concession stand.

SAUGATUCK BOAT CRUISES

Saugatuck - 716 Water Street (off I-196) 49453. www.saugatuckboatcruises.com. Phone: (269) 857-4261. Hours: Leaves daily, several times, beginning at 11:00am or 1:00pm. Last trip departs at 8:00pm. (May-September). Weekends in October. Admission: $5.00-$18.00 (age 3+).

A 90 minute scenic cruise on the Kalamazoo River. Sit back and relax – listen to the water running off the paddlewheels as you gently glide down the Kalamazoo River. See Saugatuck from the water, a totally different view from what you see on land, and take in the majesty of Lake Michigan. One of the many sights you'll see is "Singapore", the lumbering ghost town buried under the dunes. A narration points out local landmarks and points of interest, as well as, providing local and maritime history of the area. The 67 foot paddlewheeler offers 2 decks, live narration, and can seat 150+ passengers per trip. Onboard facilities include restrooms and snack areas.

SAUGATUCK DUNE RIDES

Saugatuck - Blue Star Highway (A2) (I-196 exit 41southwest) 49453. Phone: (269) 857-2253. www.saugatuckduneride.com. Hours: Monday-Saturday 10:00am-5:30pm, Sunday Noon-5:30pm (May-September). Open until 7:30 (July & August). Weekends only (October) Admission: $17.00 adult, $10.00 child (3-10).

A calm, relaxing dune ride - NOT! An amusement thrill ride is more like it! The scenic ride on 20-passenger dune schooners (with airplane tires for "flying")

goes over dunes between Lake Michigan and Goshorn Lake. On a clear day, you'll get a view of the coastline from a tall peak, speed through woodlands and maybe get a view of the lost city of Singapore - an old lumber town left as a ghost town. The trip is well worth the money and very entertaining. Our driver was hilarious and there were dozens of comical signs along the way like "Bridge Out" or "Men Working". Meet the family of beech trees and the tree shaped just like the number four. Ladies, be prepared for a new hairdo by the end of your trip. They only go 35 mph but it's enough to give you butterflies every now and then. It may frighten small pre-school children - unless they love kiddie roller coasters.

Sawyer

GRAND MERE STATE PARK

Sawyer - 12032 Red Arrow Highway (I-94, exit 22 west) 49125. Phone: (269) 426-4013. www.michigan.gov/grandmere.   Admission: $8.00 per vehicle.

Great sand dunes and over a mile of shoreline on Lake Michigan. Natural area behind dunes with 3 lakes. No camping. Warren Dunes State Park is also here (see separate listing).

WARREN DUNES STATE PARK

Sawyer - 12032 Red Arrow Highway (I-94 exit 16 south) 49125. Phone: (269) 426-4013. www.michigan.gov/warrendunes   Admission:-$8.00 per vehicle. Note: The Warren Dunes Concession offers food, soft drinks, ice cream, clothing and souvenirs from May through September. Call 269-426-8368 for more information. The highlight is obvious - over 2 miles of Lake Michigan shoreline complete

For updates & travel games visit: **www.KidsLoveTravel.com**

with sandy/grassy dunes. The rugged dune formation rises 260 feet above the lake and offers spectacular views and excellent for hang gliding. The dunes are always changing, so each visitor is greeted by a different formation on each visit. If it's a windy day, you can almost hear the sand sing (or some say, squeak). The park has 2½ miles of shoreline, 6 miles of hiking trails and is open year-round. Also featured are hundreds of modern campsites, cabins, swimming and winter sports. Grand Mere State Park is also here and administered by Warren Dunes.

South Haven

DR. LIBERTY HYDE BAILEY MUSEUM

South Haven - 903 Bailey Avenue (off Blue Star Hwy. & Aylworth Avenue on Bailey Avenue) 49090. http://lhbm.south-haven.com/ Phone: (269) 637-3251 or (269) 637-3141. Hours: Thursday-Monday 1:00-5:00pm. Weekends only (January & February). Donations accepted.

The Museum marks the birthplace of world-famous botanist and horticulturist, Liberty Hyde Bailey. Mr. Bailey, was born on a fruit farm in South Haven, Michigan on March 15, 1858. He graduated from Michigan State Agricultural College. Later he studied at Harvard. Following graduation, he worked at Cornell University, where he was a professor and later dean of the College of Agriculture. During his life time he brought botanists, geneticists, and plant pathologists together to form the field of horticulture. He designed the first horticultural laboratory building at Michigan Agricultural College (now Michigan State). You'll find lots of Bailey family artifacts.

KAL-HAVEN TRAIL STATE PARK

South Haven - 23960 Ruggles Road (I-96, exit 22 west) 49090. Phone: (269) 637-2788. www.michigan.gov/kalhaventrail Admission: Annual passes are available through the Van Buren County Road Commission, by mail or in person, at its Lawrence office, 319 W. James St. The cost is $15 for one person and $35.00 for a family.

Journey onto the 34-mile crushed limestone path connecting South Haven and Kalamazoo. The trail wanders past farm lands, through wooded areas, and over streams and rivers. Along the way, see a camelback and covered bridge.

MICHIGAN MARITIME MUSEUM / PIRATE TOURS

South Haven - 260 Dyckman Avenue (I-196 exit 20 west on the banks of the Black River) 49090. www.michiganmaritimemuseum.org. Phone: (269) 637-8078 or (800) 747-3810. Hours: Monday-Saturday 10:00am-5:00pm. Sunday Noon-5:00 pm. Closed Tuesday Labor Day-Memorial Day. Closed Christmas and Easter. Admission: $6.00 adult, $5.00 senior, $4.50 child (5-12), $22.00 family. Includes Museum and Tall Ship boarding. Note: Boardwalk, museum shop.

This Great Lakes maritime history showcase tells stories of vessels that passed through these waters and the people who built them. They have displays featuring lumber ships, luxury steamboats, Native Americans, fur traders, and settlers. A kids' favorite is the US Lifesaving Service and Coast Guard Exhibit. See actual full-size rescue boats and stations.

"Are YOU Brave Enough To Be A Sailor In 1812?" is designed for kids to experience life onboard a ship through interactive activities and educational panels, kids will learn about everyday chores, food, hobbies, illness, sail training, lookout duties, sleeping and storage areas, and weather patterns.

The Boat Shed allows visitors to see and ask questions about actual boats being constructed. The replica of Friends Good Will, a 19th Century sloop that served both American and British Navies in the War of 1812, is used as a floating classroom and tourist attraction. The ship was built in Detroit in 1811 as a merchant vessel, but later commandeered to haul military supplies in the War of 1812. It was later captured by the Royal British Navy and recaptured by the Americans. The 56-foot replica sloop is licensed to carry 28 passengers and a crew of four.

PIRATE TOUR: A lusty ban of feisty young pirates under the command of the scroundrel Capt. Tom "One-eyed" Kastle seize the tall ship Friends Good Will from its mooring at the Michigan Maritime Museum. The ship's colors came down and the Jolly Roger was raised as the vessel took to the Black River in search of treasure and adventure. Each of the young pirates will receive their own pirate kit. While on board the pirates will be treated to more goodies from a special pirate chest and participate in planned pirate adventures. The ship will sail to the end of the pier and back and will not be venturing into the lake for this special cruise. Special prices for the shore events and cruise are $35.00 per pirate

If you thought you saw a Pirate Ship on the Black River in South Haven your eyes weren't deceiving you.

VAN BUREN STATE PARK

South Haven - 23960 Ruggels Road (south of town on Blue Star Highway to entrance) 49090. Phone: (269) 637-2788. www.michigan.gov/vanburen Admission: $8.00 per vehicle.

Their main attraction is the large, duned beach and swimming. A couple hundred campsites and hiking trails, too.

NATIONAL BLUEBERRY FESTIVAL

South Haven - Lake Michigan shores. (616) 637-5171 or www.blueberryfestival.com. Visit the "World's Highbush Blueberry Capital" with every blueberry food concoction, sand-sculpting contests and beach volleyball. (second long weekend in August)

☒

St. Joseph

CURIOSITY KIDS' MUSEUM/DISCOVERY ZONE

St. Joseph - 415 Lake Blvd. (I-94 exit 27 north, downtown) 49085. Phone: (269) 983-CKID. www.curiouskidsmuseum.org. Hours: Wednesday-Saturday 10:00am-5:00pm, Sunday Noon-5:00pm. (Extended summer hours - open Mondays and Tuesday also). Closed major holidays and two weeks in September. Admission: $6.00 general (age 1+). additional $6 for Discovery Zone.

This fun place has hands-on learning and curiosity building exhibits. From Geo Kids & the Global Child to the Toddle Farm, a TV studio or Bubbles...each exhibit has costumes to wear that match the type of activity. Serve customers in a diner or pick apples from trees, then process them and sell apple products at the market. A really cool room-the Rainforest Discovery Room, includes live animals! This exhibit includes bug terrariums with live insects naturally found in the Rain Forest such as hissing cockroaches and giant millipedes. The exhibit also includes a Gorilla Research Hut, an animatronics system with animals on the wall, Rain Forest puppets, a giant tree with artificial insects, discovery boxes, and a microscope center with rain forest items to examine. The "Ship" exhibit lets kids try their hand at navigating Great Lakes waters as a captain or pirate. Use coast guard signal flags, machines to load gear, and even build your own fish computer game. What fun!

DISCOVERY ZONE - climbing, splashing, sand castle-ing, mixing, creating.

SILVER BEACH COUNTY PARK

St. Joseph - 410 Vine Street & Lake Street (St. Joseph Train Station below the bluff) 49085. www.berriencounty.org/parks/. Phone: (269) 985-9000 restaurant or (269) 982.0533 beach.

The perfect beach for Sand, Sun, & Fun!

Silver Beach is below the bluff in downtown St. Joseph on Lake Street. It has a large parking lot, men's and women's bathhouses, park office and visitors' center, concessions, bike racks, playground equipment, volleyball nets and 1600-foot beach for swimmers (lifeguard on duty during the summer). Vehicle fee is $6.00-$8.00. Park opens at 5:00am. One of the cleanest family beaches you'll visit.

SILVER BEACH PIZZA: outside dining, smoke-free inside dining. 410 Vine Street, St. Joseph (269) 983-4743. www.silverbeachpizza.com. Daily, Lunch and Dinner. Moderate pricing. Very casual. Located in the train depot 200 yards from Silver Beach. In a historic, and still used, railroad station. Kids love waving at the conductors as they toot their whistles when the trains go by.

BARBOTT FARMS CORN MAZE

Stevensville - (269) 422-2378 or www.barbott.com. Come and enjoy the ultimate Corn Maze with animals, hayrides and pumpkin patches along with the corn maze that will delight everyone. Pumpkinville - There you can climb the hay fort, walk the stone labyrinth, take a pit stop at the picnic tables, and pick a pumpkin. Admission. (mid-September – first week of November)

For updates & travel games visit: **www.KidsLoveTravel.com**

Chapter 7
Upper East

A Quick Tour of our Hand-Picked Favorites Around...

Upper East Michigan

Once you head over the Mackinac Bridge, you'll want to stop at the first city St. Ignace. The **Museum of Ojibwa Culture** is downtown along State Street. Housed in Father Marquette's French Jesuit Mission Church, the focus is on the first inhabitants of this area – the Ojibwa Indians. A "kid-sized" longhouse and activity areas surround lifelike dioramas of an Ojibwa family network. Outside, you can't miss the giant longhouse or the realistic teepee with weaved bark mats. **Castle Rock** is just a few minutes away. See and climb the 189 steps of the limestone "sea stack" – nearly 200 feet tall – that Native Americans once used as a lookout.

From Castle Rock it's an easy drive on I-75 north to the **Soo Locks** in Sault Ste. Marie – where huge freighters make the "21-foot leap" from Lake Superior to Lake Huron. Check out an indoor working model of a lock (and, try your hand at operating it). Then, go outside to the observation platform to view the real locks in action. It's unbelievable how actual freight ships move precisely into concrete locks and then are lowered or raised. Although watching the ships go through the locks and enjoying the park is fun, it's much more thrilling to actually go through the locks on a **Boat Tour**!

Leaving Sault Ste. Marie, travel M-28 west to M-123 north until you can't go any further. You're at Whitefish Point, home of the **Great Lakes Shipwreck Museum** – the most 'moving' shipwreck museum we've ever found. The ballad, "The Wreck of the Edmund Fitzgerald," plays as you view and hear the actual pictures, voices, stories and artifacts recovered from shipwrecks on the Great Lakes. The working lighthouse and restored keeper's quarters are part of the campus tour.

Parts of the Upper Peninsula's 150 waterfalls are here. This is the land of Longfellow's Hiawatha – ("by the rushing Tahquamenaw" Hiawatha built his canoe) - **Taquamanon Falls**. The short walk out to the Upper Falls reveals one of the largest waterfalls east of the Mississippi. Nearly 50 feet tall and more than 200 feet across, its amber color is a pleasing site.

Get back on M-123 and head south to M-28, heading further west to the harbor town of Munising. The stunning multi-colored sandstone cliffs of **Pictured Rocks** resemble familiar shapes like ships or castle turrets. A picturesque cruise boat tour takes you as close to the rocks as you can safely get (you can almost touch them). The next day, board Michigan's only glass-bottomed boat to tour Grand Island's Shipwrecks below.

A QUICK GLANCE AT THE UPPER EAST CHAPTER

Escanaba

* Delta Cty Hist Mus & LIghthouse

* Hiawatha Natl Forest

* Upper Peninsula St Fair

Garden * Fayette St Historic Pk

Manistique

* Indian Lake St Pk

* Palms Brook St Pk

Munising

* Grand Island Shipwreck Tours

* Pictured Rocks Cruises

* Pictured Rocks Natl Lakeshore

Naubinway * Garlyn Zoo

Newberry

* Muskallonge Lake St Pk

* Oswalds Bear Ranch

Paradise

* Great Lakes Shipwreck Mus

* TAhquamenon Falls St Pk

Sault Ste Marie

* Museum Ship Valley Camp

* River of History Museum

* Tower of History

* Soo Locks Boat Tours

* Soo Locks Park

Seney Natl Wildlife Refuge

Soo Junction * Toonerville Trolley & Riverboat Ride

Sites and attractions are listed in order by City, Zip Code, and Name. Symbols indicated represent:

☒ Festivals   Restaurants   🛏 Lodging

Escanaba

DELTA COUNTY HISTORICAL MUSEUM AND LIGHTHOUSE

Escanaba - (Ludington Park, the east end of Ludington Street) 49829. Phone: (906) 786-3428 or (906) 786-3763. http://deltahistorical.org/ Hours: Daily 11:00am-7:00pm (June-Labor Day). Admission: $1.00-$3.00 per person (includes museum and lighthouse)

Chronicles the development of the Upper Peninsula and Delta County, especially logging, railroads and shipping industries. An unusual display of a 1905 motor launch powered by only a one-cylinder engine is there also. Most folks make a point to go nearby to the restored 1867 Sandpoint Lighthouse. The keeper's house is furnished in period with winding stairs leading to the lighthouse tower's observation deck.

HIAWATHA NATIONAL FOREST

Escanaba - 2727 North Lincoln Road (shorelines on lakes Huron, Michigan and Superior) 49829. Phone: (906) 786-4062. www.fs.fed.us/r9/hiawatha. Hours: Daily, open 24 hours. Miscellaneous: Point Iroquois Lighthouse & Maritime Museum, Sault Ste. Marie (906-437-5272).

The forest manages two uninhabited islands, Round and Government Islands which are accessible by boat. Boating and other outdoor activities are allowed on Government Island. On the northern tip of the forest is the Grand Island National Recreation Area and Pictured Rocks National Lakeshore. Fishing for bass, pike, trout and walleye are good. Cross-country skiing and snowmobiling, camping, canoeing, hiking or bicycling trails, and swimming are available. There is a visitor's center (Munising, open business hours, daily) and cabin rentals too. Near Munising are the Bay Furnace ruins, the remains of an 1870's iron furnace.

UPPER PENINSULA STATE FAIR

Escanaba - (Fairground - east side of Escanaba – US-2), 49829. (906) 786-4011. www.upstatefair.org All the usual fun is here from tractor pulls, motorcycle racing, live entertainment, great food, and rides for the whole family. Can't you just smell the barbecue? Admission. (mid-August for six days)

Garden

FAYETTE STATE HISTORIC PARK (GHOST TOWN)

Garden - 13700 13.25 Lane (US-2 to M-183 south) 49835. Phone: (906) 644-2603. www.michigan.gov/fayette Hours: Daily 9:00am-5:00pm (mid-May to mid-October). Longer evening hours in the summer. Admission: $8.00 per vehicle.

Travel back in time over 100 years as you walk around a preserved industrial community. It once was a bustling industrial community which manufactured charcoal pig iron for economical shipping to the Great Lakes steel companies. The Visitor's Center has a scale model of the city when it was buzzing and info on hiking trails around the complex. See docks where schooners tramped and mostly reconstructed iron furnaces and kilns along with support buildings for the then, booming, industry. Best to visit for guided tours in the summertime. Fayette offers plenty of fishing opportunities whether from shore, the Snail Shell Harbor, or on the open waters from your own boat. Five miles of hiking trails wind through beech and maple hardwood forests and throughout the historic townsite. Visitors will enjoy scenic views from the overlook trail. Rustic Camping, swimming, and winter sports are also available.

Manistique

INDIAN LAKE STATE PARK

Manistique - CR-442 West 49854. www.michigan.gov/indianlake. Phone: (906) 341-2355. Admission: $8.00 per vehicle.

Located on Indian Lake, the 4th largest inland lake in the Upper Peninsula is 6 miles long and 3 miles wide. The lake was once called M'O'Nistique Lake. According to surveyor records dated 1850, Native Americans lived in log cabins near the outlet of the Lake. The clean sandy beaches and shallow water make swimming a fun way to spend the day. Indian Lake has a maximum depth of 18 feet with about 90 percent of the lake with less than 15 feet deep. It is best suited for smaller boats. Camping/cabins, hiking, fishing, bicycle trails, and winter sports.

PALMS BROOK STATE PARK (BIG SPRING)

Manistique - (US 2 to M-149) 49854. Phone: (906) 341-2355. www.michigan. gov/palmsbrookAdmission: $8.00 per vehicle. Miscellaneous: The Palms Book Trading Post is open daily from mid-May to mid-October. Souvenirs, T-shirts, sweatshirts, books, ice cream treats and beverages are for sale. Call 906-387-2635 for more information.

Here can be seen one of Michigan's alluring natural attractions -- Kitch-iti-kipi, The Big Spring. The American Indians call this area "kitch-iti-kipi" or "Mirror of Heaven". Two hundred feet across, the 40-foot deep Kitch-iti-kipi is Michigan's largest freshwater spring. Over 10,000 gallons a minute gush from fissures in the underlying limestone. By means of a self-operated observation raft, visitors are guided to vantage points overlooking fascinating underwater features and fantasies. Ancient tree trunks, lime-encrusted branches and fat trout appear suspended in nothingness. Beaching and boating are the only activities offered (no fishing or camping) but most come to board rafts and float across the wide spring. In the middle of the spring, look below at the huge trout being swished around by the hot springs flowing out from below - and yet the water is kept at 45 degrees constantly.

Munising

GRAND ISLAND SHIPWRECK TOURS

Munising - 1204 Commercial Street (M-28 west of town - watch for signs) 49862. Phone: (906) 387-4477. www.shipwrecktours.com. Admission: $32.00 adult, $12.00 child (6-12). Tours: Memorial Day wkend thru middle of October. Daily Tours- Fully narrated two hour tour viewing three shipwrecks, rock cliffs & East Channel Light House.

When you realize that there are over 5000 shipwrecks on the bottom of the Great Lakes...it makes you probably wonder...why are you about to get on a boat? Don't worry, today you can safely voyage (and see) the underwater world of Lake Superior. Board Michigan's only glass-bottomed boat for your chance to see 3 of these wrecks. The clarity of the water is amazing and you will actually see an intact 136', 1860's cargo ship...right under your boat! It's a great idea to visit their website for the complete story (and photographs) of each boat that you will see. This is the only place in the United States that you can see real shipwrecks aboard a Glass Bottom Boat! Also pass by the South Lighthouse and an original settlement on Grand Island. Most of the island remains as it was during the fur-trading days of the Hudson Bay Company, which was established in 1670..

PICTURED ROCKS CRUISES

Munising - (Boats depart from Munising's harbor - downtown) 49862. Phone: (906) 387-2379. www.picturedrocks.com. Admission: $35.00 adult, $10.00 child (6-12). Tours: The Regular Cruise lasts approximately two hours and forty minutes makes runs from mid-morning throughout the afternoon. The Spray Falls tour extends beyond the regular cruise and includes the majestic Spray Falls. This cruise lasts roughly two hours and fifty-five minutes and takes place in the late afternoon. The last tour of every day is the Sunset Cruise which follows the same route as the regular cruise, but leaves port at a time which allows guests to view Pictured Rocks as the sun sets over Lake Superior.

Note: If you like to hike you will enjoy the nine mile Chapel Loop trail. This Trail offers views from the highest points of the cliffs. If you do plan to hike atop the cliffs use caution. The Cliffs are soft sandstone some reaching heights of 200' which pose as a danger especially if the cliffs are undercut by erosion, so Stay Back From The Cliff Edge.

The world famous Pictured Rocks sandstone cliffs are colored by minerals in the water, shaped by wind, ice, and waves. As the heavy ice formations and tremendous waves crash into the cliffs, the rocks are changed. The name "Pictured Rocks" is due to the pictures that seem to appear on the rocks from the multicolored sandstone and mineral stains on the rock surface. A picturesque 37-mile (3-hour) tour takes you as close to the rocks as you can safely get (you can almost touch them). See colorful and majestic formations along Lake Superior's shore, some are sharp pointed and rise over 200 ft. high. The cruise passes points such as Lovers Leap, Grand Portal, Miner's Castle and Indian Head.

To get the best view of the rocks from land you should visit the overlooks at Miner's Castle, the east end of Miners Beach, and the Lakeshore Trail that runs the length of the park.

These rock sculptures are described with legend and lore by your captain.

PICTURED ROCKS NATIONAL LAKESHORE

Munising - M-28 and CR-H58 49862. Phone: (906) 387-3700. www.nps.gov/piro Hours: (Visitor Center) Monday-Saturday, 9:00am-4:30pm. (year-round). Daily with longer hours (mid-May through October) Admission: No fees are charged for day use. Note: Camping, hiking trails, boating, fishing, swimming, winter sports. Michigan Great Outdoor Culture Tour mini-dramas and special talks/tours (summer). Pictured Rocks National Lakeshore has six traveling educational "trunks" available for free loan. Each truck is written for students in grades 3-6. Educators: www.nps.gov/piro/forteachers/wildlifemgtguide.htm

Sculpted by wind and water and painted by mineral-rich seepage, the towering sandstone cliffs of Pictured Rocks National Lakeshore in the Upper Peninsula are among Michigan's most spectacular natural wonders. The rocks are also multi-colored from the minerals that seep into the soil. The orange-red walls meet the blue-green water of Lake Superior for about 12 of the 42-mile stretch of shoreline. Tens of thousands of acres of wilderness along over 40 miles of Lake Superior where ice-carved rocks resemble familiar shapes. Look for parts of ships or castle turrets. There are several awe-inspiring platform stops (some 200 foot cliffs) like Miners' Castle or Grand Sable Dunes. Rough camping and rugged backpack hiking is popular for those accustomed to it. There's also a Maritime Museum and Au Sable Light Station in the area.

Naubinway

GARLYN ZOO

Naubinway - W9104 US US 2 (40 minutes west of the Big Mac bridge) 49762. Phone: (906) 477-1085. www.exploringthenorth.com/garlyn/garlyn.html Hours: Daily 11:00am-6:00pm (April-September). Friday, Saturday & Sunday Only 11:00am-5:00pm (November & March). Daily 10:00am-5:00pm (October). Admission: $8.00 adult, $7.00 child (3-16), $28.00 family. Note: Gift shop. Online links to animal educational sites.

The UP's biggest collection of animals (25+ species) that includes - black bears, white-tail deer, camels, wallabies, reindeer, llamas, cougar and coyote. For the most part the zoo has been built by hand and most of the trees and the terrain have been left as nature intended. The zoo is built in a natural park-like setting with cedar mulched trails to walk on as you pass under mature pine trees towering 60 to 80 feet above you. Grain can be purchased to hand feed many of the animals.

Newberry

MUSKALLONGE LAKE STATE PARK

Newberry - (From the Mackinac Bridge, continue north on I-75 to M 123 north. CR-407) 49868. Phone: (906) 658-3338.   www.michigan.gov/muskallongelake Admission: $8.00 per vehicle.

The 217-acre park is situated between the shores of Lake Superior and Muskallonge Lake and the area is well known for its forests, lakes, and streams. The park is traversed by the North County Trail, with short feeder trails linking the park campground to this national scenic trail hiking route from North Dakota to New York which includes more than 1,500 miles in Michigan. Camping, boating, fishing and swimming.

OSWALDS BEAR RANCH

Newberry - Highway 37 (four miles north on M- 123 to Deer Park Road (H-37) 49868. Phone: (906) 293-3147. www.superiorsights.com/oswaldsbearranch/. Hours: Daily 10:00am-5:00pm (Memorial Day weekend-September). Admission: $20.00 per carload or $10 per person.

Like any proud father, Newberry resident Dean Oswald enjoys sharing the accomplishments of his 23 grown North American Black Bears with visitors. The bears roam freely within their three well maintained natural habitats. Sleeping areas, or "dens", are provided for the animals, as well as plenty of climbable trees and swimming pools. Visitors are able to walk around the entire perimeter of the habitat to view the bears in all areas. While strolling the grounds, Oswald will point to each and list their different personalities, names and even their weight. This is not a drive-thru, it's a walkabout. However, a trolley is offered for senior and bus tour groups. This is the largest Bear Only ranch in the U.S

.

Paradise

GREAT LAKES SHIPWRECK MUSEUM

Paradise - 110 Whitefish Point Road (M-123 north to Whitefish Pt. Rd. for 11 miles) 49768. Phone: (906) 492-3747 or (877) SHIPWRECK. www.shipwreckmuseum.com. Hours: Daily 10:00am-6:00pm (May-October). Admission: $13.00 adult, $9.00

child (12 & under), $35.00 family. Overnight Accommodations: Relax in comfort in the adaptively restored 1923 Coast Guard Lifeboat Station Crews Quarters offering five themed rooms with queen size beds, a private bath, TV/VCR, and data ports with satellite technology, yet retain all the historic charm of a by-gone era. $125-$150 per room (2 persons to a room).

The working lighthouse and restored keeper's quarters are the oldest on Lake Superior since 1849 and a crucial point on the Lake. Gordon Lightfoot's ballad, "The Wreck of the Edmund Fitzgerald", plays as you view the actual bell recovered from the ship! Displays of ships claimed by Lake Superior's storms include the Invincible 1816, the Independence (story of sailor "The Man Who Never Smiled Again" survivor), and the Edmund Fitzgerald in the 1970's (29 sailors aboard, all perished). See the short film on the history of the Edmund Fitzgerald and the raising of the bell honoring a request by surviving family members to establish a permanent memorial. Also, take the time to tour the Lighthouse Keeper's home to discover how a family survived with little contact with the nearby community. To add to what is already an extremely emotional visit, take a reflective walk out on to the boardwalk and beach of Whitefish Point - the "Graveyard of the Great Lakes" as you watch large freighters fight the turbulent waters. Please make the trip to Whitefish Point to see this...we were very "moved" by this visit!

TAHQUAMENON FALLS STATE PARK

Paradise - 41382 West M-123 (Off SR 123 heading north, then west 5-12 miles. Watch for entrance signs) 49768. www.michigan.gov/tahquamenonfalls. Phone: (906) 492-3415 or (800) 44-PARKS. Hours: Daily, Dawn to Dusk. Admission: $8.00 per vehicle. Note: Modern camping near falls or on river. . Hiking trails. Fishing. Snowmobiling, snowshoeing, cross-country skiing. Snack bar (lower falls) & Camp 33 Gift Shop and Pub at Upper Falls.

This is the land of Longfellow's Hiawatha - "by the rushing Tahquamenaw" Hiawatha built his canoe. On the hiking trails, moose, balk eagles, black bear, coyotes, otter, deer, fox, porcupine, beaver and mink may be occasionally spotted. The short 4/10 of a mile walk out to the Upper Falls reveals one of the largest waterfalls east of the Mississippi. A maximum flow of more than 50,000 gallons of water per second has been

To us, the falls look like a smaller version of Niagara Falls...but still have the beauty of a very natural surrounding...

recorded cascading over these falls. Nearly 50 feet tall and more than 200 feet across, its amber color is a pleasing site. The amber color of the water is not from mud or rust - discover what causes it. The Lower Falls are four miles downstream. They are a series of five smaller falls and rapids cascading around an island. For the best photo-ops, we suggest a wide angle lens equipped camera (or purchase great postcards at the gift shop). The Tahquamenon River offers 17 miles of canoeing from the Lower Falls to the Rivermouth area. Put-ins are available both at the Lower Falls (rentals here, too) and at Rivermouth.

May we suggest a stop for a bite to eat at <u>TAHQUAMENON PUB</u> (a restaurant on the premises with a cozy wood beam décor). Lumberjacks, who harvested the tall timber, were among the first permanent white settlers in the area. The replica 1950 logging camp dining hall has two focal points - the beautifully displayed animal skins and the warm fireplace. This is a great place to try UP specialties like whitefish or pasties (pronounced "pass-tees" - so you'll sound like a local!).

Sault Ste. Marie

MUSEUM SHIP VALLEY CAMP

Sault Ste. Marie - 501 East Water Street (east of the locks - waterfront) 49783. Phone: (906) 632-3658 or (888) 744-7867. www.saulthistoricsites.com/museum-ship-valley-camp-3/ Hours: Daily 10:00am-5:00pm (mid-May to mid-October). Extended hours July -September. Admission: $12.00 adult, $6.00 child (5-12).

Walk-in tours are offered of the 1917 steam powered freighter containing the world's largest Great Lakes maritime museum. Many come to see the Edmund Fitzgerald Exhibit - two lifeboats from the actual boat along with multimedia shows of the tragic event. Several mechanical (dormant) parts of the ship are touchable. A long aquarium is along one wall with marine life found in the area. After seeing the large freighters and their crew go through the locks, kids will love to see an actual ship's pilot house, dining rooms and crew's quarters.

RIVER OF HISTORY MUSEUM

Sault Ste. Marie - 531 Ashmun Street, across from the Soo Theatre Arts Resource Studios (S.T.A.R.S.). 49783. www.thevalleycamp.com/river-of-history-museum-6/. Phone: (906) 632-1999.   Hours: Monday-Saturday 10:00am-5:00pm. Sunday Noon-5:00pm (mid-May to mid-October). Admission: $3.50-$7.00 (age 6+).

Learn St. Mary's River history through exhibit galleries of sight and sound. Join the River as she tells her story of the events she has witnessed, people she has met, and changes wrought along her shores and waters. Follow Chippewa Indians to French fur traders to modern industry. Kids can step into a French fur trader's cabin and try on clothes and other hands-on items. Trip motion sensors activate spoken stories as visitors enter each room. The sound of locks and canals being built is one of the audio enhanced exhibits.

SOO LOCKS BOAT TOURS

Sault Ste. Marie - Dock #1: 1157 E. Portage Ave; Dock #2: 515 E. Portage Ave. 49783. Phone: (906) 632-6301 or (800) 432-6301. www.soolocks.com. Hours: Daily 9:00am-4:30pm (mid-May to early-October). Later hours on summer weekends. Admission: $23.00 adult, $11 child (5-12).

Although watching the ships go through the locks and enjoying the park is fun, it's much more thrilling to actually go THROUGH the locks on a ship. On the Soo Locks Tour, you'll be in for a two-hour live narrated excursion that will actually take you through the Locks, right alongside the big freighters. Your tour boat will ride the water as it is raised twenty-one feet, straight up, to the level of Lake Superior. You will then cruise under the International Bridge and railroad bridge before crossing into Canadian waters where you'll see one of Canada's largest steel plants in operation. You will return to the lower harbor

See HUGE freighters...up close!

through the historic "newly restored" Canadian Lock and cruise past the St. Mary's Rapids.

SOO LOCKS PARK

Sault Ste. Marie - Downtown. 312 W Portage Avenue (Within view of International Bridge. Follow signs off I-75) 49783. Phone: (906) 632-2394. www.saultstemarie.com/index.php?catid=3&member_id=1   Hours: Daily 7:00am-11:00pm (mid-May to November 1). Admission: FREE Note: Run by the US Army Corp of Engineers. Theater showing film on history of operations.

The highlights at Soo Locks Park are:

OBSERVATION PLATFORM - 2nd level or Riverside view of the locks. It's unbelievable how actual freight ships move precisely into concrete locks and then are lowered or raised to the level of the next part of the lake. How do they do it? (Learn how...and they do not use pumps). Now the longest in the world, they are still the largest waterway traffic system on earth. A public address system lets

> To view live pictures of the Soo Locks, visit their website.

visitors know which vessels are coming through the locks and what their size, cargo, nationality and destination are. You would have to sign on-board as a crew member to get any closer than this. A beautiful, multi-colored lighted fountain, surrounded by park benches is found here as well. The fountain and lights dance in time to background music providing a pleasant backdrop to this gorgeous park. Dress appropriately for weather outside because you'll want to watch the large freighters rise up in the water before your eyes!

<u>WORKING MODEL OF A LOCK</u> (with real water moving a model boat) is inside the museum building and best to watch before outdoor viewing.

TOWER OF HISTORY

Sault Ste. Marie - 326 East Portage Avenue (east of the locks) 49783. Phone: (906) 632-3658 or (888) 744-7867. www.thevalleycamp.com/tower-of-history-4/. Hours: Daily 10:00am-6:00pm. Admission: $7.00 adult, $3.50 child (6-16).

A 21-story tower offering a panoramic view of the Soo Locks, the St. Mary's River Rapids, and many historical homes. The tower museum has Native American artifacts and a video show depicting the history of the Great Lakes and Sault Ste. Marie. The Lower Level features museum exhibits as well as a video presentation, the Upper Level, in addition to the view, features descriptions of the surrounding area. You ride to the top by elevator.

INTERNATIONAL 500 SNOWMOBILE RACE

Sault Ste. Marie - (906) 635-1500 or www.i-500.com. Admission. (first weekend in February)

Seney

SENEY NATIONAL WILDLIFE REFUGE

Seney - (M-77, 5 miles south of Seney) 49883. Phone: (906) 586-9851. www. exploringthenorth.com/seney/seney.html. Hours: Daily 9:00am-5:00pm (mid-May - mid-October). Admission: FREE

Take the family on a driving journey (7 miles, self-guided, starts at Visitor's Center parking lot) that allows the chance to see wildlife such as: nesting loons, cranes, swans, Canadian geese, bald eagles, deer, and others. An orientation slide show is shown every half hour. This show introduces viewers to the variety of wildlife found on the Refuge, as well as management techniques. The center is complete with a natural history book store and children's touch table. Over 70 miles of trails are also available for your hiking adventures.

Soo Junction

TOONERVILLE TROLLEY & RIVERBOAT RIDE

Soo Junction - Soo Junction Road (North off M-28 - Watch for signs to CR-38) 49868. Phone: (906) 876-2311 or (888) 778-7246. www.superiorsights.com/toonerville. Hours: Times vary - call ahead for schedule (mid-June - early October). Train only excursions Tuesday-Saturday (mid-June- August only) Admission: Train & Riverboat - 6 1/2 hours (depart at 10:30am): $45.00 adult, $29.00 youth (9-15), $20.00 child (4-8). Train only - 1 3/4 hours, departs at 12:30: $15.00 adult, $9.00 youth (9-15), $7.00 child (4-8). Kids 3 and under are FREE. Note: Food, Beverages and Restrooms available on the boat.

Nearly a day (a 6½ hour tour) awaits you as you journey to see Michigan's largest falls (50' high), The Tahquamenon Falls (see separate listing). Start with a 5 mile, 35 minute narrow gauge rail trip, and then connect with a narrated 21-mile riverboat cruise with lots of chances to see area wildlife. Throughout the river cruise enjoy the captain's educational narration on points of interest, history, Native Americans, animals, birds, fauna and flora. Once the boat docks, take a short walking trip to see the falls. What's really neat is that the falls are undisturbed and really do look like Niagara Falls might have looked to early settlers (smaller, but still very coool!). The train only tour does not go to the Falls.

St. Ignace

CASTLE ROCK

St. Ignace - N2690 Castle Rock Road (I-75 to exit 348) 49781. Phone: (906) 643-8268. www.castlerockmi.com Hours: Daily 9:00am-9:00pm. (early May to mid-October) Admission: 50 cents to climb the rock trails.

See and climb (189 steps) the legendary Castle Rock (a limestone "sea stack" - nearly 200 feet tall) that Native Americans once used as a lookout. Be sure to check out Paul Bunyan and Babe! A great piece of history and what a view for a half dollar! There are lots of Native American gifts in the shop below. This is a difficult climb, aerobically, so take your time  and don't plan on carrying the kids up...everyone will have to climb the stairs on their own (you'll feel like "Rocky" when you reach the top)! Don't worry, the walk down is much easier.

DEER RANCH

St. Ignace - W 1549 US Highway 2 West (US 2, 4 miles west of Big Mac Bridge) 49781. Phone: (906) 643-7760. www.deerranch.com. Admission: $4.50 (age 4+)

Gift Shop featuring Deer skin products including many sizes of moccasins. They have a nature trail where you can feed and photograph native Michigan Whitetail Deer and fawns. (May-November)

MUSEUM OF OJIBWA CULTURE

St. Ignace - 500-566 North State Street (at the north end of the boardwalk, downtown, across from waterfront) 49781. www.stignace.com/business/view/98. Phone: (906) 643-9161. Hours: Daily 11:00am-5:00pm (Memorial weekend - late June and Labor Day-early October). Daily 10:00am-8:00pm, except Sunday open at Noon (Late June-Labor Day). Admission: $1.00-$2.00 general, $5.00 family. Note: Native American Museum Store. Marquette Mission Park adjacent is supposed site of grave of missionary Father Marquette and also site of archeological discoveries.

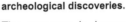

The museum is housed in Father Marquette's French Jesuit Mission Church and dedicated to his focus on Ojibwa Indians, the first inhabitants of this region. Learn traditions of the peoples through an 8-minute video presentation that relates the importance of the Ojibwa family, dioramas of an Ojibwa family network, and frequent demonstrations by Native American interpreters (esp. outside in the giant longhouse or the realistic teepee with weaved bark mats). There is a "kid-sized" longhouse indoors where kids can play, then walk diagonally over to the Interactive Kids Area: felt play, dark boxes, color drawings of Ojibwa symbols or make a paper canoe or scroll stories. The easy to understand descriptions with every display or activity really help you understand their way of life...they often relate it to our modern way of life.

MYSTERY SPOT

St. Ignace - 150 Martin Lake Road (US-2 West, 5 miles west of Mackinac Bridge) 49781. Phone: (906) 643-8322. www.mysteryspotstignace.com. Hours: Daily 8:00am-9:00pm (mid June - Labor Day). Daily 9:00am-7:00pm (after Labor Day - late October & mid-May to mid-June) Admission: $5.00-$7.00 per activity (age

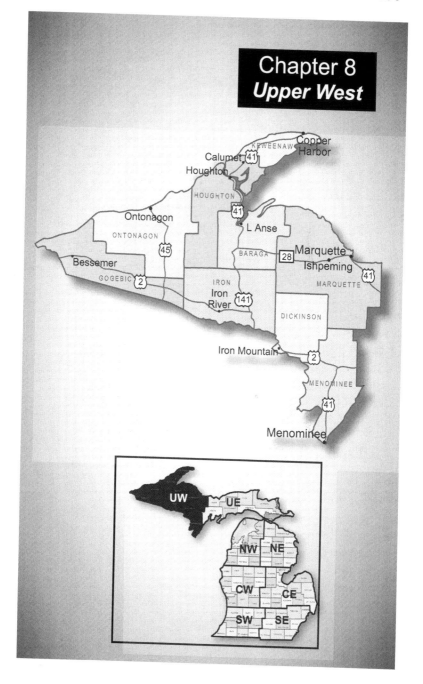

Chapter 8
Upper West

Copper Harbor

Calumet 41

Houghton

KEWEENAW

HOUGHTON

Ontonagon 41

ONTONAGON

L Anse

BARAGA 28 Marquette

Bessemer

US 45

GOGEBIC 2

IRON

Iron River 141

MARQUETTE 41

Ishpeming

DICKINSON

Iron Mountain

2

MENOMINEE

41

Menominee

UW UE

NW NE

CW CE

SW SE

5+). Add $2.50 for combo attractions package.

O.K. - Illusion or reality? Reality or illusion? That's up for you to decide, but one thing's for sure...you'll sure have fun doing it. See the laws of physics as we know them...and why they don't apply to the "Mystery Spot". The kids will love this science lesson. There's also mini-golf and a maze on the premises.

STRAITS STATE PARK

St. Ignace - 720 Church Street (I-75, exit onto US-2 East) 49781. Phone: (906) 643-8620. www.michigan.gov/straits. Season: (March-October). Admission: $8.00 per vehicle.

Great views from an observation platform of the Mackinac Bridge and the Straits of Mackinac. A hiking trail runs through the park. One end, has a viewing platform with an overlook of the Straits of Mackinac and Mackinac Bridge. The other end has a different view of the Mackinac Bridge. Camping/mini-cabins, picnicking, boating, fishing, swimming and winter sports. A visitor's center highlights Father Marquette exploration in the area.

The **FATHER MARQUETTE NATIONAL MEMORIAL** tells the story of that 17th-century missionary-explorer and the meeting of French and Native American cultures deep in the North American wilderness. Explore the National Memorial and an outdoor interpretive trail. (access to the Memorial is free, it is not necessary to pay the vehicle admission fee to view it)

TOTEM VILLAGE

St. Ignace - 1230 US Highway 2 West (US 2, 2 miles west of Big Mac Bridge) 49781. Phone: (906) 643-8888. Hours: Open daily, May-October. Admission: Small admission fee for museum.

They've set this place up for picture taking. For example, pose your family beside a teepee or next to a giant totem pole. The focus is on scientifically studied lifestyles of the Indian culture and significant contributions of Upper Peninsula people. There's a model of the first American Lake Superior sailing ship, a replica of Fort Fond du Lac, a Scale model of the first Soo Locks, a trading post, an old-time sugar camp and live bobcats, foxes & reindeer.

D

A Quick Tour of our Hand-Picked Favorites Around...

Upper West Michigan

Most of the favorite places to visit in this region are off of US 41 – beginning in the Marquette/Ishpeming area. This is the home of the **U.S. National Ski & Snowboard Hall of Fame and Museum**, founded in 1954 in the U.P. city of Ishpeming, the "birthplace of organized skiing." It is the home of Big Snow Country, which regularly measures over 200" average annual snowfall. Dogsled and snowmobile races are popular festivals held each winter. While in town, make a stop at **Da Yoopers Tourist Trap**. The UP life is "unique" to say the least. Not only can you learn how to really talk like a Yooper...but, where else will you ever see a snowmobile that was built for summer use, a chainsaw the size of an 18-wheeler or the world's largest firing rifle?

The Upper Peninsula, which is 90 percent forested, retains its own flare. Hundreds of islands also dot Great Lakes waters. **Isle Royale National Park**, off the coast of Houghton, is a remote wilderness retreat IN Lake Superior where moose and wolves roam free. Lakes, campgrounds, wildlife refuges and dozens of State Parks create a wide variety of outdoor recreation.

Stay a while in the UP's northernmost tip along US 41. Michigan's **Iron & Copper Mine** Industry began thousands of years ago when ancient miners chipped away at exposed veins of pure copper with huge hammerstones. Today, hard hat tours take you down a shaft of a real mine. Turn on the miner's light as you follow the path 300 feet underground. Later, you emerge from the depths of the mine onto an overlook bluff, mine ruins and rock piles along walking trails.

––––––––––––––––––––––––––

––––––––––––––––––––––––––

–––

Sites and attractions are listed in order by City, Zip Code, and Name. Symbols indicated represent:

⊠ Festivals   🍽️

Restaurants   🛏️ Lodging

UPPER WEST MICHIGAN AT A GLANCE

Brimley * State Park

Calumet

* Coppertown USA Museum

Caspian * Iron Cty Museum

Cedar River

* Laughing Whitefish Falls
* Wells State Park

Champion
* Craig Lake St Pk
* Van Riper St Pk

Copper Harbor
*Lighthouse Boat Tours
* Delaware Copper Mine Tour
* Fort Wilkins Hist St Pk

Crystal Falls * Bewabic St Pk

Grenland * Adventure Copper Mine

Hancock
* Mclain St Pk
* Quincy Mine Hoist

Houghton * Isle Royale Natl Pk

Iron Mountain
* Millie Mine Bat Cave
* Iron Mtn Iron Mine

Ironwood
* Black River Natl Forest
* Ottaawa Natl Forest

Ishpeming
* DA Yoopers Tourist Trap

* Tilden Open Pit Mine Tours
* US Natl Ski Hall of Fame

Lake Linden
* Houghton Cty Hist Mus

Marenisco
* Lake Gogebic St Pk

Marquette

* Marquette Cty Hist Museum

* Marquette Mtn Ski Area

* Marquette Maritime Museum

* Presque Isle Park

* Upper Peninsula Childrens Mus

* UP 200 Sled Dog

Negaunee

* MI Iron Industry Museum

Ontonagon

* Ontonagon Cty Hist Museum

* Porcupine Mtns Ski Area

* Porcupine Mtns Wilderness

Brimley

BRIMLEY STATE PARK

Brimley - 9200 West 6 Mile Road (I-75, take M-28 west to M-221) 49715. Phone: (906) 248-3422. www.michigan.gov/brimley. Admission: $8.00 per vehicle.

Brimley State Park provides recreational opportunities along the beautiful shore of Lake Superior's Keewenaw Bay. Brimley provides some of the warmest swimming areas on Lake Superior. Available for camping, boating, and fishing.

Calumet

COPPERTOWN USA MUSEUM

Calumet - 109 Red Jacket Road (2 blocks west of US-41) 49913. Phone: (906) 337-4354. www.uppermichigan.com/coppertown/main.html. Hours: Monday-Saturday 10:00am-5:00pm (mid-June to mid-October). Sunday 12:30-4:00pm (in July & August). Admission: $1.00-$3.00 per person.

Copper Rock

Michigan's Copper Industry began thousands of years ago when ancient miners chipped away at exposed veins of pure copper with huge hammerstones. Tools and techniques of mining advanced considerably in the centuries that followed and Coppertown's Mining Museum traces the evolution of miners. More than a copper museum, but rather a Visitor's Center (even includes a walk-in, simulated copper mine) for the Keweenaw Peninsula. See how copper mining has evolved from the early Native Americans who mined with stone hammers to the techniques used during the "Copper Rush". Exhibits include: Early Miners, Two Man Drill, Foundry - Casting Metal Products, The Hospital, Sheffield Pump Car and Loading Ore Cars.

Caspian

IRON COUNTY MUSEUM

Caspian - 100 Brady Avenue (off M-189 to CR-424) 49915. Phone: (906) 265-2617. www.ironcountyhistoricalmuseum.org. Hours: Monday-Saturday & Holidays 9:00am-5:00pm, Sunday 1:00-5:00pm (mid-May to October). Admission: $3-$8.00 (ages 5+).

A historic, educational site that has 20 buildings including pioneers' cabins, a logging camp, train depot, and schoolhouse. The community was built here because of the Caspian Mine (during its peak production, it was the area's largest producer of iron ore). The Headframe, or hoisting building, one of the earliest of its type, has been placed on The National Register of Historic Places. The very rare exhibit is the Monigal Miniature lumber camp, over 80 feet long and reputed to be the "largest in the world." The Mining Halls contain early mining tools and equipment, several glass dioramas showing underground ore bodies, tramming tunnels and mine levels, a memorial to the 562 miners killed, and the development of unions. One of the homes featured was the home of Carrie Jacobs-Bond who was a nationally known composer of the 19th Century. Composing over 200 songs, her hits included "I Love You

Truly" and "Perfect Day". This success allowed her to become the first female composer to earn a million dollars.

Cedar River

LAUGHING WHITEFISH FALLS SCENIC SITE

Cedar River - N7670 Highway, M-35 (2.8 miles north off M-94 at Sundell in Alger County (not far from Marquette) 49813. Phone: (906) 863-9747.   www.michigan.gov/ laughingwhitefish

One of the Upper Peninsula's many impressive waterfalls. Picnic area, foot trails, and 3 observation decks overlooking the falls. No camping or services.

WELLS STATE PARK

Cedar River - N7670 Highway M-35 (1 mile South of County Rd. G-12 and Cedar River) 49813. www.michigan.gov/wells. Phone: (906) 863-9747. Admission: $6.00-$8.00 per vehicle.

J.W. Wells State Park is located on Green Bay approximately 30 miles south of Escanaba, 25 miles north of Menominee or one mile south of Cedar River. Its 678 acres include a 3 mile shoreline with a beautiful sandy beach for swimming, a large picnic area, campground and rustic cabins that are available to rent year round. There are six miles of trails to hike in summer and cross-country ski in the winter. Also boating, fishing, and bicycle trails.

Champion

CRAIG LAKE STATE PARK

Champion - (8 miles West of Van Riper State Park - on US-41 / M-28) 49814. Phone: (906) 339-4461. www.michigan.gov/craiglake.   Admission: $8.00 per vehicle.

Craig Lake is a wilderness area (the most remote state park in the system) and access into the park is somewhat of an adventure. Only vehicles with high ground clearance are recommended due to the rocky conditions of the road. But if you're really into "getting away from it all" the park contains six lakes for fishing and a variety of wildlife such as black bear, deer, loons, beaver, and part of the Upper Peninsula moose herd.

VAN RIPER STATE PARK

Champion - SR 41 (west of town) 49814. Phone: (906) 339-4461. **Admission: $8.00 per vehicle. www.michigan.gov/vanriper**

This 1,200 acre park contains one-half mile of frontage on the east end of Lake Michigamme with a fine sand beach. The water temperature is generally moderate - a pleasant change from Lake Superior temperatures. There is also one and one-half miles of frontage on the Peshekee River. Lake Michigamme is one of the top walleye lakes in the Upper Peninsula and also produces fine catches of bass, perch, trout, northern pike and muskellunge. Improved woods roads also provide access to many streams, lakes and the great forest which lies to the north of the park. Camping, boating, and swimming are here but most come hiking to look for Canadian moose imported to this park by helicopters. Cabins and winter sports are also available.

Copper Harbor

COPPER HARBOR LIGHTHOUSE BOAT TOURS

Copper Harbor - (Copper Harbor Marina, 1/4 mile west of Copper Harbor on M-26) 49918. Phone: (906) 289-4966. www.copperharborlighthouse.com. **Admission: $17.00 adult, $12.00 child (12 and under). Children sitting on laps are FREE. Tours held Memorial DAy Wkend thru mid-October. Lighthouse Boat Tour and Sunset Tour. Sunset Tour includes full Lighthouse Tour and a scenic trip to the bell buoy at sunset.**

The only way to see the Copper Harbor Lighthouse (which is actually a part of the Fort Wilkins State Park) is by boat tour. Once ashore, short walking paths wind you among historic signposts and shipwreck artifacts. Such items include the keel of the first shipwreck on Lake Superior, the John Jacob Astor, which was blown onto the rocky shores of Copper harbor in the fall of 1844 while attempting to deliver supplies to those who would spend the winter here. You will then tour the original lightkeeper's dwelling, the oldest remaining lighthouse structure on Lake Superior, which preceded the 1866 building. Recently renovated and made into a lighthouse museum, the dwelling features maritime exhibits including a fourth order Fresnel lens. You can ask questions or listen to stories from the staff historian while enjoying interactive exhibits which tell of lighthouse construction on the Great Lakes. The daily lives of these keepers become real while walking among the period furnishings and hearing actual stories of the people who worked in the United

States Lighthouse Service. During this narrated tour, you'll have the chance to not only see the lighthouse, but also the first real attempts at creating a copper mine shaft (dates back to the 1840's).

DELAWARE COPPER MINE TOUR

Copper Harbor - (12 miles south on US 41) 49918. Phone: (906) 289-4688. www. copperharbor.org/site_files/del_mine/del_mine.html Tours: 10am-5pm (June-- October) Admission: ~$10.00 adult / Half Price child (age 6+).

This mid-1800's copper mine offers a 45 minute underground walking tour. The tour will take you down Shaft No. 1 to the first level (at a depth of 110 ft.) where you'll see pure veins of copper exposed. Above ground, take the walking trails to the mine ruins, sawmill, large antique engine display, and train collection featuring "G" scale and 7½" gauge. Stop by the zoo to visit the miniature deer or search the rock piles of souvenir copper. Dress for 45-50 degree F. temperatures.

FORT WILKINS HISTORIC STATE PARK

Copper Harbor - US-41 East 49918. Phone: (906) 289-4215. www.michigan.gov/ fortwilkins. Admission: $6.00-$8.00 per vehicle.

Fort Wilkins Historic State Park, in the northern Keweenaw Peninsula, offers camping and day use facilities and features a restored 1844 army military outpost and one of the first lighthouses on Lake Superior built in 1866. Fort Wilkins is a well-preserved example of mid-19th century army life on the northern frontier. Through Fort Wilkins' exhibits, audiovisual programs and living history interpretation, visitors may explore the daily routine of military service, experience with soldiers' families the hardships of frontier isolation

Running around the park, roughly parallel to the park boundary, is a two-mile bike/ hike/crosscountry ski trail that provides great views of Lake Fanny Hooe and Lake Superior.

and discover the life ways of another era. Attractions include 19 restored buildings, costumed interpreters, copper mining sites, evening slide programs, camping and picnicking. The fort was built to protect copper miners from local tribes - completely made from wood. The site also includes the Copper Harbor Lighthouse with a restored 1848 lightkeeper's dwelling, 1866 lighthouse, 1933 steel light tower and interpretive trails. The lighthouse is reached by boat (see separate listing).

Crystal Falls

BEWABIC STATE PARK

Crystal Falls - 1933 US-2 West 49920. www.michigan.gov/bewabic. Phone: (906) 875-3324.   Admission: $8.00 per vehicle.

A 137-site campground is situated in a shady, wooded site. Most of the sites have buffer strips between them to allow for privacy and most sites have electricity, a fire ring and a picnic table. Picnic areas, a hiking trail, two playgrounds, an excellent beach and a boat launch to Fortune Lake are among the additional amenities at this park. Bewabic State Park is site #9 of the Iron County Heritage Trail System. The park is also rich with Civilian Conservation Corps (CCC) History which is evident by several CCC structures still in use. Unique to Bewabic is the fact that it is the only state park in Michigan to offer tennis courts. Home to virgin woodlands and a wood bridge to the island.

Greenland

ADVENTURE COPPER MINE

Greenland - 200 Adventure Road (12 miles east of Ontonagon, off SR38) 49929. Phone: (906) 883-3371. www.adventureminetours.com.   Hours: Daily 9:00am-6:00pm (Memorial Day weekend - end of color season). Closed on Wednesdays after Labor Day. Admission: $12.50 adult, $7 child (6-12). Note: Gift Shop with copper crafts. Camping with hookups. Snowmobiling area and underground tours. A jacket and walking shoes are recommended.

In the early fall, look for hibernating bats!

Put on your hard hat for the beginning of your tour ride to the mine entrance. Turn on the miner's light as you follow the path 300 feet underground walking through passages worked by miners over 100 years ago. You'll see large clusters of pure copper with silver threads and quartz and calcite crystals. Look down into open mine shafts that run hundreds of feet into the earth. The second half of your tour, you emerge from the depths of the mine onto an overlook bluff for a great view of the distant hills and valleys.

Hancock

MCLAIN STATE PARK

Hancock - M-203 West (From US 41 in Hancock take Hwy M-203 9 miles north to park) 49930. Phone: (906) 482-0278.   www.michigan.gov/mclain.   Admission: $6.00-$8.00 per vehicle.

The sunsets at McLain State Park are spectacular and the view of the lighthouse is magnificent. McLain State Park is situated in the heart of the

Keweenaw Peninsula on beautiful Lake Superior. The park offers two miles of sand beach on Lake Superior. Visitors can also enjoy a variety of activities in the park: fishing, windsurfing, berry picking, beachcombing, rock hounding, Camping/cabins, hiking, boating, fishing, swimming and winter sports.

QUINCY MINE HOIST

Hancock - 201 Royce Road (along US-41 - part of Keweenaw Peninsula National Park) 49930. Phone: (906) 482-5569 or (906) 482-3101. www.quincymine.com. Hours: Daily 9:30am-5:00pm (mid-June through late October). Friday-Sunday only (late April through mid-June). Admission: (Surface & Underground Tour) $15.00 adult, $8.00 child (6-12). (Surface & Tram Ride) $12.00 adult, $5.00 child (6-12). Senior discounts. Note: Gift shop. As you can expect, this tour might not be suitable for younger children who don't like dark places, loud noises, etc.

The "hoist" is where all the ore was hauled to the surface, and what you will see is the world's largest. The shaft started in the mid-1800's and operated until the 1960's, eventually reaching a depth of over 10,000 feet! As you can imagine, at this depth it can get quite "hot" (with temperatures averaging over 90 degrees F.). On the outside, you can view the shafthouse which is over 150 feet tall and has hauled millions of pounds of copper to the surface. You can also travel over 2000 feet into the hill to view portions of the mine that were carved during the Civil War era.

Houghton

ISLE ROYALE NATIONAL PARK

Houghton - 800 East Lakeshore Drive (only accessible by boat or seaplane) 49931. Phone: (906) 482-0984. www.nps.gov/isro/ Hours: (mid-April to October) Admission: $4.00 per person per day. Note: Isle Royale Queen (906-289-4437) offers summertime boat trips (4 1/2 hours) from Copper Harbor and the Ranger III leaves Houghton summer times (6 1/2 hours). There's also a seaplane that floats over to the Isle.

The nation's only island national park is where roughed campers (no campfires permitted) or woodsy lodgers (only one on the entire island) gravitate. Backpacking hiking, canoeing, charter fishing trips or sightseeing trips are available. With 99 percent of the island still wilderness, many opt for marked trails like Greenstone, Minong, Mt. Franklin, Mt. Ojibwa, or the Rock Harbor Lighthouse. The trails are about 45 minutes in length along cliffs, paths of fir and wildflowers, and past many moose, wolves and beavers! Try to visit Siskiwit Lake's Ryan Island, the largest island on the largest freshwater lake in the world! For those of that would prefer to enjoy the beauty of Isle Royale in a more civilized manner, the Rock Harbor Lodge provides excellent accommodations. It is located along the picturesque shores of Lake Superior and has both American-plan rooms (meals and lodging inclusive) and charming light-housekeeping units. Other facilities and services available at the Rock Harbor Lodge include a dining-room, snack bar, gift shop, marina, rental boats, motors, and canoes, guided fishing, and sightseeing tours.

Iron Mountain

MILLIE MINE BAT CAVE

Iron Mountain - (Just off East A on Park) 49801. Phone: (906) 774-5480. www.michigandnr.com/publications/pdfs/wildlife/viewingguide/up/07Bat/index. htm.

Batcave...hummm...must be Batman's home right? Well, not really, but this IS the second largest (known in the North America) home for hibernating bats! The mine is 350 feet deep that has several rooms with a consistent temperature of 40 degrees...just perfect for the furry little creatures. You'll find a walking path, benches, and informational plaques. The bats come in for the winter in September and leave in April (if you're not scared...these are wonderful viewing times). The Millie Mine is a critical hibernating and breeding location for up to 50,000 bats—one of the largest known concentrations of bats in the Midwest. Big brown and little brown bats from all over the region come here to hibernate during the cold winter months. There is a "bat cage" preventing humans from entering the depths of the cave but still allowing bats the freedom to move in and out. FREE admission. Always open. Closed during snow months.

IRON MOUNTAIN IRON MINE

Iron Mountain (Vulcan) - (US-2 - 9 miles east of Iron Mountain - Look for "Big John!") 49852. Phone: (906) 563-8077. www.ironmountainironmine.com. Hours: Daily 9:00am-5:00pm (June - mid-October). Tours are 45 minutes long. Admission: $7.00+ per person (age 6+).

"But Mom and Dad, why do we need a raincoat...it's not raining outside?".

Well...you explain as you're buttoning up their raincoats... that it is probably raining INSIDE! Begin your journey by getting dressed properly for it with a raincoat and hardhat. Then you'll take a train ride through tunnels (over ½ mile long) into the mine on the same tracks that the miners used until 1945 (The mine actually produced over 22 million tons of iron ore). As you travel into the mine (over 400 feet deep), your kids will start to see the "rain" inside (the dripping water) and will be glad that they are dressed properly. Learn the drilling methods that were used like "Double Jack" or "Water Liner" and see demonstrations of both.

Ironwood

BLACK RIVER NATIONAL FOREST SCENIC BYWAY

Ironwood - County Road 513 (US 2/SR 28 to CR 513) 49938. Phone: (906) 667-0261. www.byways.org/browse/byways/10780/. Note: Ski flying is ski jumping's more extreme cousin, with standard runs sending the skier over 600 feet, or the length of two football fields. Only the best ski jumpers can participate in ski flying. The ramp at Copper Hill rises an astounding 26 stories from the top of an 800-foot hill, allowing jumps of over 450 feet. While you might not be up to ski flying, you can view most the surrounding country from the observation deck on the top of the ramp. For visitors seeking a more normal ski experience, Big Powderhorn Ski Area offers several downhill runs set in a charming Bavarian Village.

> The Copper Hill Ski area features the only ski flying ramp in the Western Hemisphere.

See the Black River with several beautiful waterfalls. Five waterfalls are 20 to 40 feet high and are named for their characteristics like Sandstone (red rock riverbed), Gorge, and Conglomerate (rock ledges). Paved sidewalks and a kid-friendly swinging bridge, and a pass by Ski Flying Hill (only one in the states) where you might see ski flying (jumping) events (especially late January).

OTTAWA NATIONAL FOREST

Ironwood - (Almost 1 million acres off US 2) 49938. Phone: (906) 932-1330 Visitor Center. www.fs.fed.us/r9/ottawa. Hours: Dawn to dusk.

More than 50,000 acres of the expanse are designated wilderness with barely untouched lakes and trees. With more than 35 waterfalls within the forest, many plan to take the marked trails to catch a view. The 500 lakes and 2000 miles of rivers provide good fishing for trout and salmon. When the ground freezes, many try snowmobiling, ice fishing and cross-country skiing. In Watersmeet there are two facilities - The J.W. Tourney Forest Nursery and Visitors Center (US-2 and US-45). Great Lakes tree seed and stock are supplied here, as well as, exhibits, audiovisual programs and naturalist-led group walks and talks. Camping, hiking, boating and swimming are also available. Lake Gogebic State Park is included as part of the forest.

Ishpeming

DA YOOPERS TOURIST TRAP

Ishpeming - 490 North Steel Street (US 41) 49849. www.dayoopers.com. Phone: (906) 485-5595.   Hours: Daily 9:00am-9:00pm (Memorial Day-September). Times vary rest of the year. Admission: FREE

The UP life is "unique" to say the least. When talking to locals, we often heard that one of the greatest things about living up here is that you have time for a

hobby (since you can only work 6 months a year). Well, "Da Yoopers" actually started as a singing group that promoted the "uniqueness" of this life around the state. They have fun "poking fun" and you'll see and hear it all at the "tourist trap". Not only can you learn how to really talk like a Yooper... but where else will you ever see a snowmobile that was built for "summer" use, a chainsaw the size of an 18-wheeler (in the Guinness Book...world's largest, really), or the world's largest firing rifle? We agree, be sure to pick up some "Da Yoopers" music before you leave to really get the most from your UP adventure.

TILDEN OPEN PIT MINE TOURS

Ishpeming - (depart from Ishpeming Chamber of Commerce) 49849. Phone: (906) 486-4841. www.miup.info/assets.asp?ait=av&aid=355 Admission: $9.00/person Tours: Tuesday-SAturday Noon-3pm (June -August)Note: For safety reasons no dresses, skirts, open-toed shoes, or children under age 10 are permitted on this tour.

One thing you'll know for sure after completing this tour is that the iron industry in Michigan is still very much a thriving business. We suggest to go to the

Michigan Iron Industry Museum (see separate listing) first to see how it WAS mined. Then, see this huge pit (that is over 500 feet deep!) where the iron ore is mined and refined by some of the largest mining equipment in the world. (We really think it would be fun if they painted "Tonka" on the sides of the equipment!)

US NATIONAL SKI HALL OF FAME AND MUSEUM

Ishpeming - (US 41 between Second and Third Streets) 49849. Phone: (906) 485-6323. www.skihall.com. Hours: Monday-Saturday 10:00am-5:00pm. Admission: Donations requested: $1.00-$3.00 (age 10+).

The museum is dedicated to the preservation and promotion of America's skiing heritage through the permanent recognition of nationally outstanding skiers, snowboarders and ski sport builders from the United States. Watch an 18 minute orientation tape, then explore the gallery of greats of American skiing. Within its walls discover the story of the ancient Birkebeiners, see Sun Valley's first snow groomer and learn about the historic 10th Mountain Division and its contribution both in wartime and peacetime to the development of skiing. Also study the development of the sport through trophies, photos, old grooming equipment and a cable car.

Lake Linden

HOUGHTON COUNTY HISTORICAL MUSEUM CAMPUS

Lake Linden - 53102 Hwy M26 (after crossing the Portage Lake Lift bridge, head north on M-26) 49945. Phone: (906) 296-4121. www.habitant.org/houghton. Hours: Monday and Friday 9:30am-Noon (June-September). Admission: $3.00-$4.00.

Eight historic buildings including themes of a Country Kitchen, Grandma's Room, Medicinal, Mining Room and Forestry Room. Kids will like trying to figure out what "bull ladle", "fanny", or "kibble" are. There's also a schoolhouse, log cabin, tool shop, church, railroad depot and Copperland sculptures. The train line is complete and runs short tours many summer Sundays.

Marenisco

LAKE GOGEBIC STATE PARK

Marenisco - N9995 State Highway M-64 (M-64 between US-2 and M-28) 49947.

Phone: (906) 842-3341. www.michigan.gov/lakegogebic. Admission: $8.00 per vehicle.

Lake Gogebic State Park covers 360 acres and nearly a mile of lake frontage on the west shore of the largest inland lake in the Upper Peninsula. Enjoy shaded, waterfront camping on the shore of Lake Gogebic, the largest inland lake in the Upper Peninsula. Two mile scenic nature trail that loops back to the campgrounds. Sandy beach, picnic area, boating, and fishing tournaments, too.

Marquette

MARQUETTE COUNTY HISTORICAL MUSEUM

Marquette - 213 North Front Street 49855. www.marquettecohistory.org. Phone: (906) 226-3571. Hours: Monday-Friday 10:00am-5:00pm. Summer Saturdays. Closed holidays. Admission: $1.00-$3.00 (over 12).

A pioneer focus on mining and lumbering with changing exhibits of artifacts. Some of the highlights include a Native American diorama, a fur trading post, an antique gun collection, and fully furnished dollhouses. William Austin Burt, inventor, legislator, land surveyor and millwright, patented the Solar Compass in 1836. This compass was used to set meridian (north-south) lines in federal land surveys - helping to build many mills in the UP. Anatomy of a Yooper is a special exhibit helps folks learn about Yooper's unique words and phrases, ethnic customs, coping with the weather, work ethic, unique foods and ways of preparing them, camps and camping, ingenuity with recycling items to make useful things such as Finnish rag rugs and snowshoes, coping with bug season and anything else that makes Yoopers stand apart from the rest. Loads of rooms are filled with colorful artifacts and stories that bring local history to life...with ease.

MARQUETTE MARITIME MUSEUM

Marquette - (East Ridge and Lakeshore Blvd.) 49855. Phone: (906) 226-2006. www.mqtmaritimemuseum.com. Hours: Daily 10:00am-5:00 pm (late May- mid October). Admission: General $3.00-$5.00 Museum Only or Lighthouse Only. Both $5.00-$9.00.

Marquette and Lake Superior maritime heritage with antique charts, boats and models. It preserves the unique romance, glamour, and history of the days when topsail schooners, Mackinac boats, fur trading canoes, work-a-day fish tugs, lumber hookers, and mighty steam barges plied the lakes. Children love the hands-on exhibits and recreated dockside offices of a commercial fishing and passenger freight companies. Ever seen a fishing shanty kids?

MARQUETTE MOUNTAIN SKI AREA

Marquette - 4501 County Road 553 49855. www.marquettemountain.com. Phone: (800) 944-SNOW.

8 runs, rental equipment, babysitting, and lessons are available. Great children's programs for all skill levels. Also now offering, Ski-by-the-hour rates as low as $4.00/hour (2-hour minimum), and Sunday Family Days.

PRESQUE ISLE PARK

Marquette - Lakeshore Blvd. 49855. Phone: (906) 228-0461 or (800) 544-4321. Hours: Daily 7:00am-11:00pm.

A beautiful 300+ acre park that is located on a rock peninsula on Lake Superior. Some interesting trivia…"Presque Isle" means "almost an island". As you can imagine, the views are incredible with many lookouts, nature trails along bogs (in winter they are cross-country skiing or snowshoeing trails), and picnic facilities. An outdoor pool and waterslide (160') are also available (FREE admission) in the summer.

UPPER PENINSULA CHILDREN'S MUSEUM

Marquette - 123 West Baraga Avenue 49855. www.upchildrensmuseum.com. Phone: (906) 226-3911. Hours: Monday-Wednesday & Saturday 10:00am-6:00pm. Thursday 10:00-7:30pm. Friday 10:00am-8:00pm. Sunday Noon-5:00pm. Admission: $5.00 (age 2 +)$25.00 family.

Marquette is home to the UP Children's Museum where kids can pilot an airplane and communicate with air traffic control as part of the Over the Air exhibit. There are displays on aviation, weather, health, science, and nature. There is also a creative performance workshop. Other exhibit halls include The World of Science and Nature, The Incredible Journey (walk thru giant-size parts of the body) and Micro Society. WONDER GROUND gives you a glimpse of the underground by digging. A very family friendly place that features exhibits that were suggested by local area kids.

UP 200 SLED-DOG CHAMPIONSHIP

Marquette to Escanaba - (finish in Mattson Park). (800) 544-4321. www.up200.org. Mushers race their teams across 200 miles of the Winter Upper Peninsula. Visitors can race through steaming stacks of pancakes and syrup served throughout the day. (mid-

Seasonal &
Special Events
Index

JANUARY / FEBRUARY

WINTER CARNIVALS

Things like polar bear dips, skating, snowmen building contests, ice bowling, broomball hockey, sleigh rides, cardboard tobogganing, sled dog races, snow mobile races and plenty of warm food and drink. (early February)

- **NE** – Mackinaw City. (888) 455-8100. Winterfest. (third weekend) www.mackinawinformation.com.

- **UE** – St. Ignace. (800) 666-0160. Mackinaw Mush Sled Dog Race, Mackinaw City 300 Snowmobile Race and Battle of the Straits Gumbo

MARCH / APRIL

MAPLE SUGARING WEEKENDS

- **CE** - Midland, Chippewa Nature Center. (989) 631-0830. With a naturalist along, tour the 1000 acre center, looking for maple sap. Learn how the sap is turned into syrup in the Sugar Shack. Donation admission. (weekends in March)

- **SE** - Jackson, Ella Sharp Museum. www.ellasharp.org. (517) 787-2320. Maple tree tapping at a turn-of-the-century farm. Watch sap being processed and help make maple sugar candy. Sheep-shearing demos. (fourth Saturday in March)

- **SE** – Lansing, Fenner Nature Center, 2020E Mount Hope. www. cityoflansingmi.com/parks/fenner. Walk into the woods and watch maple syrup being made. FREE. (mid-March weekend)

- **SW** - Kalamazoo, Nature Center. www.naturecenter.org. (269) 381-1574. Visit Maple Grove and old-time sugar house. Pancake brunch. Hike trails to visit pioneer sugar shack. (weekends in March)

- **SW** - Vermontville. (517) 726-0394. Michigan's oldest maple-syrup festival. Parade, petting zoo, carnival and maple-sugar treats sold. (last weekend in April)

COTTONTAIL EXPRESS

Bring the family for a fun-filled ride, including treats and children's activities. Admission. (near Easter weekend, usually April)

- **CW** – Coopersville. Coopersville and Marne Railroad. www.coopersvilleandmarne.org.

- **SE** – Walled Lake. www.michiganstarclipper.com. (248) 960-9440.

JUNE

FREE FISHING WEEKEND

STATEWIDE - Inland and Great Lakes Waters. (800) 548-2555. All weekend long, all fishing license fees will be waived for resident and nonresident anglers. All fishing regulations will still apply. (second weekend in June)

MICHIGAN LOG CABIN DAY

STATEWIDE - Example: **CE** - Log House at Port Huron Museum. (810) 982-0891, www.phmuseum.org. Celebrate with old-fashioned house party & square dance. FREE. (last Sunday in June)

4TH OF JULY CELEBRATIONS

Independence Day is celebrated with parades, carnivals, entertainment, food and fireworks.

- **CE** - Bay City. Bay City Fireworks Festival. 888-BAY-TOWN. Three days around the 4th.

- **CE** - Bridgeport. Valley of Flags, Junction Valley Railroad. (989) 777-3480. Rides through display of flags. Five days around the 4th. www.jvrailroad.com.

- **CE** - Flint. Crossroads Village and Huckleberry Railroad. (800) 648-PARK. Parade through park and American flags everywhere.

- **CW** - Grand Haven Area. (800) 250-WAVE.

- **NE** - Mackinaw City, A Frontier Fourth, Historic Mill Creek. (231) 436-4100. 1820's style Independence Day with games, music, sawmill demonstrations, patriotic speeches and reading of the Declaration of Independence.

- **NE** - Mackinac Island, A Star Spangled Fourth, Fort Mackinac. (231) 436-4100. 1880's celebrations include cannon firings. Admission to Fort.

4TH OF JULY CELEBRATIONS (cont.)

- **NE** - Mackinac Island, Old Fashioned Mackinac, Grand Hotel. (800) 33-GRAND.
- **NW** – Boyne City, Veterans Park. (231) 582-6222.
- **NW** – Cadillac. (800) 369-3836.
- **SE** – Lansing, Riverfront Park. (517) 483-4277.
- **SE** - Jackson, Cascade Falls Park. (517) 788-4320.
- **SW** – Hastings. Charlton Park. Old fashioned 4th of July. www. charletonpark.org.
- **SW** - Marshall, 4th of July Celebration. Cornwell's Turkeyville USA and downtown. (800) 877-5163.
- **SW** - Saint Joseph Pavilion. Patriotic Pops. (616) 934-7676.

FALL HARVEST FESTIVALS

Join the rural farm environments at these locations as you help perform the tasks of harvest and the celebration of bounty. Old-fashioned foods, living history dramas and music. Pumpkins and crafts.

- **CE** – Millington, Parker Orchard. (989) 871-3031 (first weekend in October)
- **NE** - Alpena, Jesse Besser Museum. (989) 356-2202. (first Saturday in October)
- **SE** - Dearborn, Henry Ford Museum & Greenfield Village, 20900 Oakwood Blvd. (313) 271-1620.
- **SE** - Jackson, Ella Sharp Museum, 3225 Fourth Street. (517) 787-2320. (first Sunday in October)
- **SW** – Middleville, Historic Bowen Mills/Pioneer Park. (269) 795-7530. Reenactments. (weekends in October)
- **SW** – St. Joseph, downtown. (269) 982-0032. Pumpkin patch, petting zoo, face paint, sawdust scramble and sing-alongs. (first or second Saturday in October)

CHRISTMAS OPEN HOUSES

Museum homes are decorated for the holidays, mostly with Victorian themes. Visits from old Saint Nick, cookies and milk, and teas are offered for kids and parents. A great way to see local history with the focus on old-fashioned toys and festivities instead of, sometimes boring to kids, old artifacts.

- **CE** – Midland, Dow Gardens. www.dowgardens.org. FREE. (first long weekend)
- **CW** – Grand Rapids, Frederik Meijer Gardens. (616) 957-1580.
- **CW** – Grand Rapids, Public Museum of Grand Rapids. (616) 456-3977. Teas and planetarium holiday lights shows. (most days in December)
- **SE** – Dearborn, Greenfield Village Holiday Nights. www.thehenryford.org. Carolers, bands, ice rink, bonfires, shops and fireworks finale. Admission. (first three weekends in December)
- **SE** – Dearborn, Henry Ford Estate. www.henryfordestate.org. Candles & Carols, Candlelight tours and Santa's workshop. Admission. (selected days in December)
- **SE** – Detroit (Grosse Pointe Shores). Edsel & Eleanor Ford House. (313) 884-4222 or www.fordhouse.org.
- **SE** – Detroit (Rochester), MeadowBrook Hall, 280 South Adams, Oakland University campus. (248) 370-3140. Admission for some activities. (all month-long)
- **SE** - Jackson, Ella Sharp Museum, 3225 Fourth Street. (517) 787-2320. Admission includes meal.
- **SE** – Okemos, Meridian Historical Village. www.meridian.mi.us. Christmas in the Village with German holiday traditions. FREE. (first Sunday in December)
- **SW** – Hastings, Charleton Village. (989) 945-3775. (second weekend in December)

SANTA EXPRESS TRAIN RIDES

Santa and his helpers ride along and play games and sing songs to get everyone in the holiday spirit. Admission.

- **CW** - Coopersville, Coopersville & Marne Railway. (616) 997-7000.

www.coopersvilleandmarne.org. (Saturday mornings, the first three weekends in December)

- **SE** – Walled Lake, www.michiganstarclipper.com. (248) 960-9440. (departures twice an afternoon on second and third Saturday of December)

Activity Index

PROUDLY

MADE IN THE USA

AMUSEMENTS

CE Bridgeport, *Junction Valley Railroad*, 7

CE Frankenmuth, *Bavarian Inn*, 12

CE Frankenmuth, *Bronner's Christmas Wonderland*, 13

CE Frankenmuth, *Riverplace*, 16

CE Frankenmuth, *Zehnder's Splash Village Hotel & Waterpark*, 16

CW Holland, *Dutch Village*, 45

CW Muskegon, *Michigan's Adventure Amusement Park & Wildwater Adventure*, 54

CW Rothbury, *Double JJ Resort*, 58

NE Mackinaw City, *Thunder Falls Family Waterpark*, 81

NE Ossineke, *Dinosaur Gardens Prehistoric Zoo*, 83

NW Traverse City, *Great Wolf Lodge*, 101

NW Traverse City, *Pirate's Cove Adventure Park*, 101

SE Detroit (Farmington Hills), *Marvin's Marvelous Mechanical Museum*, 132

SE Dundee, *Splash Universe Riverrun Indoor Water Park Resort*, 136

SW Battle Creek, *Full Blast*, 165

UE St. Ignace, *Mystery Spot*, 198

UW Ishpeming, *Da Yoopers Tourist Trap*, 212

ANIMALS & FARMS

CE Birch Run, *Wilderness Trails Animal Park*, 6

CE Frankenmuth, *Grandpa Tiny's Farm*, 15

CE Pinconning, *Deer Acres*, 20

CE Saginaw, *Saginaw Children's Zoo*, 26

CW Grand Rapids, *John Ball Park Zoo*, 39

CW Grand Rapids, *Robinettes Apple Haus*, 41

CW New Era, *Country Dairy*, 55

NE Grayling, *Grayling Fish Hatchery*, 68

NE Mackinac Island, *Original Butterfly House*, 74

NE Mackinac Island, *Wings Of Mackinac*, 74

SE Ann Arbor, *Domino's Farms*, 108

SE Carleton, *Calder Dairy Farm*, 112

SE Detroit (Royal Oak), *Detroit Zoo*, 131

SE Dexter, *Spring Valley Trout Farm*, 132

SE Hanover, *Buffalo Ranch*, 136

SW Battle Creek, *Binder Park Zoo*, 160

SW Coloma, *Deer Forest*, 165

SW Kalamazoo (Mattawan), *Wolf Lake Fishery Interpretive Center*, 170

UE Naubinway, *Garlyn Zoo*, 186

UE Newberry, *Oswalds Bear Ranch*, 187

UE St. Ignace, *Deer Ranch*, 193

HISTORY

CE Bad Axe, *Sanilac Petroglyphs Historic State Park*, 4

CE Bay City, *Bay County Historical Museum*, 5

CE Durand, *Durand Union Station (Michigan Railroad History Museum)*, 8

CE Flint, *Crossroads Village & Huckleberry Railroad*, 10

CE Frankenmuth, *Frankenmuth Historical Museum*, 14

CE Port Huron, *Edison Depot Museum*, 22

CE Port Huron, *Ft. Gratiot Lighthouse*, 23

CE Port Huron, *Huron Lightship Museum*, 24

CE Port Sanilac, *Sanilac County Historical Museum & Village*, 25

CW Grand Rapids, *Public Museum Of Grand Rapids*, 39

CW Holland, *Holland Museum*, 44

CW Holland, *Windmill Island*, 44

CW Ludington, *White Pine Village*, 49

CW Muskegon, *Muskegon County Museums*, 52

CW Muskegon, *SS Milwaukee Clipper*, 53

CW Muskegon, *Great Lakes Naval Memorial & Museum (USS Silversides/USCGC Mclane)*, 54

OUTDOOR EXPLORING

Need more great ways to keep the kids busy?

www.KidsLoveTravel.com

Best-selling "Kids Love" Travel Guides now available for:

Florida, Georgia, Illinois, Indiana, Kentucky, Maryland, Michigan, North Carolina, Ohio Pennsylvania, Tennessee, and Virginia.

State Coloring Books:

Kids can color and learn new facts. Lots and fun and educational too. Includes State Characters, Places, Facts and Fun. Color your way around the state! All ages will enjoy these books. Various states.

State Big Activity Books:

Kids will learn about State History, Geography, People, Places, Nature, Animals, Holidays, Legend, Lore and much, much more by completing these enriching activities. Includes dot-to-dots, mazes, coloring, matching, word searches, riddles, crossword puzzles, word jumbles, writing, and many other creative activities. Each book is state specific fun! Reproducible. Grades 1-5. Correlates with State Academic Standards. Various states.

State Pocket Guides:

This handy easy-to-use guide is divided into 7 color coded sections (State Facts, Geography, History, People, Places, Nature, and more). Riddles, recipes, and surprising facts make this guide a delight. Various states.

Invisible Ink Book Sets:

(Includes special marker). Hours of "clean" fun for all. The special marker is clear so it doesn't make a mess. The invisible ink pen reveals invisibly printed pictures or answers to quizzes and games. What are you interested in? Sports ... Trivia ... History ... The Bible ... Fascinating Facts ... or just plain fun ...

(Just a sample of the many titles available below)

"Travel Mystery Books"

Kids Our kids love these books! A great way to engage the kids and learn about places they may visit. An EXCITING new series of mystery books for kids ages 7 to 14 featuring REAL KIDS in REAL PLACES! This series plunks real children in a current-day adventure mystery set in famous settings across America. Historical facts add powerful educational value! Students read about famous places like the Whitehouse, Biltmore House, Mighty Mississippi, the first flight of Orville and Wilbur Wright, Historic times of the Underground Railroad, Blackbeard the Pirate, New York City, and more.

Travel Games:

Travel Bingo, Magnetic Paper Dolls Travel Tins, Magnetic Games in a CD case, etc.

www.KidsLoveTravel.com